OLD SPARKY

OLD SPARKY

The Electric Chair and the History
of the Death Penalty

ANTHONY GALVIN

Skyhorse Publishing

Skyhorse Publishing books may be purchased in bulk at special discounts for sales promotion, corporate gifts, fund-raising, or educational purposes. Special editions can also be created to specifications. For details, contact the Special Sales Department, Skyhorse Publishing, 307 West 36th Street, 11th Floor, New York, NY 10018 or info@skyhorsepublishing.com.

Skyhorse® and Skyhorse Publishing® are registered trademarks of Skyhorse Publishing, Inc.®, a Delaware corporation.

Visit our website at www.skyhorsepublishing.com.

10 9 8 7 6 5 4 3 2 1

Library of Congress Cataloging-in-Publication Data is available on file.

Cover design by Rain Saukas

Print ISBN: 978-1-5107-1133-4
Ebook ISBN: 978-1-5107-1135-8

Printed in the United States of America

TABLE OF CONTENTS

INTRODUCTION

Robert Gleason had waited long for this moment, and he took a perverse pleasure in it. He grinned as he was led into the small cinder-block room at the Greensville Correctional Center in Jarrett, Virginia, and looked at the window behind which he knew the observers—including the mother of one of his victims—were watching. The blue curtain was drawn back and he could see them, as they could see him. To hell with them—this was his hour.

He winked at his spiritual adviser who was with the group behind the blue curtain. Tim "Bam Bam" Spradling was a former biker buddy turned preacher. He nodded grimly back at the convict.

The execution room was dominated by a plain oak chair, large and solid like a throne. The rich red wood had the patina of age; the chair was over a hundred years old. The fittings were of polished brass, but the black leather straps looked ominous.

Gleason, burly and heavily bearded but with his head shaven for the occasion, was led over to the chair and he sat down, giving a thumbs-up as he settled. He was wearing flip-flops and dark blue prison pants, with the right leg cut short to accommodate the electrode. The bare leg allowed onlookers to see briefly the tattoo of a pinup on his calf before he sat. Quickly the guards buckled the padded ankle straps—one of which contained a damp sponge and the electrode—then began moving up Gleason's body, securing the prisoner to the chair. There were straps at his arms and a big strap at his chest. As soon as he was strapped in, the guards adjusted the back of the chair, removing all slack and ensuring that the prisoner could not move.

Gleason looked up and smiled at the observers through the glass window, sitting uncomfortably on their industrial green and white plastic chairs. Then he winked and began to speak: "Well, I hope Percy ain't going to wet the sponge. Put me on the highway to Jackson, and call my Irish buddies. *Póg mo thóin*. God bless."

They were his last words. Percy was a character in the movie *The Green Mile* who botched an execution by not wetting the crucial sponge on the convict's head. *Póg mo thóin* is a Gaelic phrase, meaning "Kiss my ass."

Then one guard got the thick leather headpiece and pulled it over Gleason's face. The mask covered his face entirely, leaving only the neck exposed and a hole under the nose to allow him to breathe. Now the world was plunged into darkness for Gleason. He could make out a flash of light if he squinted down the nose hole, but he could not see.

The guard swiftly placed a metal helmet over Gleason's head and adjusted the nut at the top to tighten it snugly against the skull. Gleason could feel the wetness of the sponge between the helmet and his shaved scalp. The neck strap was tightened and now talking was no longer possible. There was a moment of silence. The moment that Gleason had waited for, wished for, over the past number of years was finally here. Aged forty-two, Robert Gleason was about to die.

The electric chair is a peculiarly American institution. No other country has followed the lead of the United States in adopting electricity as a method of execution. When it goes right, death is quick (not instant). When it goes wrong, it goes terribly wrong. Even when it goes right, smoke rises from the body of the convict and the small execution chamber reeks of charred flesh. Prison officers habitually soak their clothes overnight before washing them to get rid of the smell after an execution.

Virginia began using the electric chair in 1909. Since the reintroduction of the death penalty in 1976, the state has executed 110 convicts. Now those on death row are offered a choice of lethal injection or the chair. Since lethal injection was introduced in 1995, seventy-nine have opted for the needle and only seven for the chair. Robert Gleason was one of those seven. He chose the chair because he believed that lethal injection was far more painful than authorities let on and the chair was the more comfortable way of passing. But there was also an element of machismo in his decision; he did not want to take death lying down.

Gleason, a career criminal, was born in Lowell, Mass, in 1970. He was a lifelong hoodlum, heavily involved in the drug business in and around Boston. He had a string of convictions—but there was another side to him as well. He was a loving and good father to his various children by different mothers. And he could be a charming and funny man.

A talented artist, he also worked in the tattoo business, taking great pride in the adornments he put on fellow bikers and drunk coeds. He organized a charity motorcycle run to raise funds for a child dying of cancer. But in addition to his legitimate activities, he was a big player with the local gangs. He claimed that he killed up to a dozen people and took pride in the fact that they were all criminals.

"I ain't saying I'm a better person for killing criminals, but I've never killed innocent people," he boasted. "I killed people that's in the same lifestyle as me, and they know, hey, these things can happen."

Whether or not he killed the many men he claimed to have (there is no evidence to back up his claims), he certainly killed in 2007. That spring, Gleason was involved in a methamphetamine ring being eyed by Federal investigators, and the son of one of his associates began giving information to Boston police. Gleason struck out at the informer's father, Michael Kent Jamerson.

Gleason and Jamerson Sr. were driving through a wooded area in Amherst County, Virginia, on May 8, 2007, when suddenly Gleason pulled a gun from Jamerson's waistband and ordered him to stop the vehicle. When the other man got out, Gleason told him to get right with God, then opened fire. A turkey hunter found Jamerson's body the next day, and the gun was found about three miles from the scene several days later. Gleason was convicted of first-degree murder and sentenced to life without parole.

There was always a paranoid streak in the Boston gangster, and in prison his mental condition deteriorated. In May 2009 he shared a cell with sixty-three-year-old Harvey Gray Watson, another inmate doing life for murder, at Wallens Ridge State Prison. Watson was even more unstable than Gleason and annoyed the younger man by constantly singing nonsensical verse in the tiny cell. Gleason hog-tied him, then stuffed a sock in his mouth and pressed a urine-soaked cloth to his face, suffocating him.

Gleason, telling the authorities he would keep killing unless he was stopped, demanded the death penalty. To press his claim, he did kill again. In July 2010 he was put in solitary confinement at the maximum security Red Onion State Prison. For one hour a day he was allowed to exercise in a recreational pen. In the adjoining caged pen was another lifer, Aaron Cooper, twenty-six. The two men got talking and Gleason told Cooper that he had made a religious necklace. He passed the white necklace through the mesh and Cooper put it around his neck. Suddenly Gleason jerked both ends, pulling the other man against the cage. He kept the pressure up until Cooper's face went purple and he stopped struggling. Then Gleason eased the pressure, allowing the victim to revive a bit. When Cooper began to regain consciousness, Gleason applied the pressure once more, this time keeping it up until Cooper was dead.

At the trial, Gleason's legal team argued that he was mentally unstable, but Gleason was having none of it. He insisted on the death penalty and refused any of the appeals or other delaying tactics that could prolong the stay on death row by more than a decade. He even fired his legal team, telling the court he intended to keep killing unless he was given the death penalty. He was eager to face Old Sparky. He had promised a loved one that he would not kill again and this was the only way he saw of keeping his promise.

"Why prolong it? The end result is going to be the same," he said. "The death part don't bother me. This has been a long time coming. It's called karma."

Robert Gleason woke early on his final morning and enjoyed his last meal. It was not the standard prison fare of steak and eggs washed down with milk and juice, but he asked that reporters not be told what he had requested. Following his meal, he was joined by his biker buddy Tim Spradling, who doubled as his spiritual adviser for his final hours.

Spradling, who preached at the Richmond Outreach Center, said, "We talked about how my life went one way and his went in the opposite

direction. He cried for his victims and asked God for forgiveness."
After two hours of contemplation and reflection, wardens summoned
Gleason to his final reckoning.

He was led into the execution chamber at nine o'clock in the morning. It took three minutes for the guards to expertly tie him down and
place the electrodes in contact with his calf and skull. Thick wires led
from the chair to the control panel. One guard stood by the red phone
on the wall—a direct line to the governor. But nobody—least of all the
prisoner—expected the tinkle of the receiver and a reprieve. Another
guard stood with a key, ready to insert it in the wall and activate the
mechanism.

At 9:03 a.m., the chamber was silent. The prisoner had uttered his
last words and was muzzled by the sci-fi contraption around his head.
The guards were in position. The man with the key inserted it and
twisted. In an adjoining room, the executioner stood poised. He could
see through the small window into the chamber with the chair. He put his
finger on the small round button and pressed. The execution had begun.

Noiselessly, the first cycle of electricity began to course through
the convict's body, entering through the top of his head and exiting
through his right calf. His body spasmed against the leather restraints,
as 1,800 volts at 7.5 amps surged through him. Smoke began to waft
from the top of his head and the two guards in the chamber twitched as
the stench of burning flesh filled their noses. Both had smeared Vase-
line in their nostrils beforehand but that could not block out the smell
completely.

After thirty seconds the power was reduced to 250 volts at 1.5 amps
and this was maintained for the next minute. Then the power automatically cut off and the prisoner visibly relaxed, slumping in the chair. He
showed no signs of movement. He was already unconscious and possibly his heart had stopped.

After a five-second pause, the machine began its work again. The
cycle of 1,800 volts for thirty seconds, followed by 250 volts for a minute was repeated. At the end of the second cycle none of the onlookers
could have any doubt. Sometimes prisoners needed up to five cycles
before expiring. Some remained conscious after the first—or even the

second—cycle, screaming in agony as their flesh burned. But that day, it had gone smoothly.

The observers continued to watch through the blue-curtained window for another two minutes. Then the door of the execution chamber opened and a white-coated doctor stepped in, wrinkling his nose in distaste. He stepped up to the slumped prisoner and held a stethoscope to his chest for a few moments before looking up and pronouncing: "Time of death, nine minutes past eight."

The whole process, from turning on the juice to the official announcement, had taken five minutes. The curtain was pulled and the spectacle was over.

Robert Gleason was the first prisoner to be executed in the United States in 2013 and the first in three years to choose the electric chair. Virginia is one of ten states that gives death row inmates that choice.

Old Sparky had claimed another life.

1

A HISTORY OF THE DEATH PENALTY

Mankind has always understood that electricity carries danger. Long before we knew what it was, we knew to avoid it. Lightning bolts come from the sky and shatter trees or bring down chimneys and the steeples of churches. The power is immense. If the lightning hits loose, wet sand it often leaves a physical mark behind. The bolt heats the sand to over 3,000 degrees, melting the silica in the sand to create glass tubes called fulgurites or thunderbolts.

These hollow tubes can be several inches across and can penetrate several feet into the ground. The largest one known to be found was over sixteen feet long, in Florida, though there are reports of fulgurites twice this length. The thunderbolts are formed in about a second. The ancient world knew all about them and knew the power of the lightning that caused them. They attributed the power to the weapons of the gods.

Now we know that electricity is the force behind the bolt of lightning and the thunderous crack that accompanies it. We have harnessed that power. It is not surprising that the idea arose to use electricity to kill people. But there is a problem; it doesn't always kill. There are many stories of people being struck by lightning and walking away and of people being badly injured but making a full recovery. YouTube is full of dramatic footage of lightning strikes. In one a bolt spears the field during a game of soccer in South Africa and several players hit the ground as if they have been shot. But within a minute all are moving, although two had to be taken away by stretcher.

Because electricity doesn't always kill, the electric chair has become one of the most controversial forms of execution in the modern world. A botched execution can be a slow and painful process. Today we like our executions to be clinical and efficient but that wasn't always the case. Sometimes the point was to make the convict suffer. The history of capital punishment is littered with methods that make Old Sparky seem humane.

Most ancient and primitive societies practiced some form of the death penalty. The biblical injunction of "an eye for an eye" was almost universal and if you killed someone, you paid the ultimate price. Imprisonment, as we know it, was not common. If the crime was not serious, you paid compensation. For more serious incidents, you risked physical punishment such as being stoned in the stock, losing a hand or an eye, or having your tongue cut out. But for murder, rape, and treason, among other crimes, you would be put to death, both as a punishment and as a deterrent to others.

Methods were imaginative and gruesome. Criminals were boiled to death, flayed until all their skin peeled off, slowly sliced or disemboweled, or crushed by huge weights. In India, the weight was often supplied by an elephant slowly bringing its foot down on the criminal's head until it smashed apart like a coconut.

The Code of Hammurabi was one of the earliest recorded legal systems. It came from Babylon around 1772 BC and contains the earliest mention of "an eye for an eye." Law 196 states: "If a man destroys the eye of another man, they shall destroy his eye. If one breaks a man's bone, they shall break his bone." However, you could avoid these punishments by paying a fine.

But if you stole property or took the slave of another out of the city limits, you would be put to death. The execution method depended on the crime. If a mother and son were caught committing incest, both were burned to death. But if a scheming lover murdered his rival, he would be impaled, his body balanced on a sharp spike which would penetrate him to cause a slow and agonizing death.

The Torah, the law that governed ancient Israel, was laid out in the first five books of the Old Testament and set down the death penalty for murder, kidnapping, practicing magic, violating the Sabbath, blasphemy, and sexual crimes. Executions were rare, however.

The ancient Greeks set out their legal system about twenty-six hundred years ago, with the death penalty as punishment for a wide variety of crimes. The Romans also had a highly evolved legal system and made good use of capital punishment. One of their favorite methods was crucifixion, where the condemned were tied to a tree or a cross with their hands outstretched. As their body fell forward against the restraints, their own weight would gradually suffocate them, causing them to expire after a lengthy period.

In medieval Europe, the death penalty became one of the most common forms of punishment, particularly when applied to the lower or peasant classes. It was cheaper than detaining someone. Generally dungeons were only used to house rich captives who might be ransomed. Those convicted of crimes were put to death. The modern concept of imprisonment was unheard of. During the reign of England's Henry VIII, seventy-two thousand people are estimated to have been executed, including two of his own wives.

Some of the medieval methods of execution were torturous. Being hanged and then drawn and quartered was one of the more barbaric. The prisoner would be hung until nearly dead and then cut down and revived. Once consciousness had returned, a sharp knife was applied to the gut and the entrails pulled out and presented to the victim. His penis was also hacked off. Finally, the executioner would chop the prisoner's head off with an axe, bringing his suffering to a close. The body was then hacked into four quarters and put on public display as a deterrent.

Women were spared this—instead they were tied to a pole and a fire built around them. They were then burned to death. This was a common punishment for those accused of witchcraft. Between the fifteenth and eighteenth centuries up to three hundred thousand women across Europe were subjected to this savage execution.

Times were harsher and most people accepted the rightness of capital punishment. But even then there were voices crying out against the practice. In the twelfth century, a Jewish scholar, Moses Maimonides, wrote: "It is better and more satisfactory to acquit a thousand guilty persons than to put a single innocent man to death."

It was a minority view.

2

CAPITAL PUNISHMENT IN THE USA

At present, capital punishment—the death penalty—is a legal sentence in thirty-two of the fifty states. It is also legal in the Federal justice system and in the military. While it was once a widely used sentence for rape, murder, kidnapping, burglary, and other crimes, now it is limited by the Eighth Amendment to aggravated murders committed by mentally competent adults.

The history of the death penalty in the United States is long. During the years before independence, all parts of the country, which then operated under English common law, used it. Hanging was the most popular method, but firing squads and other methods were also tried.

Capital punishment came to America with the early British colonists. The first legal executions in the colonies occurred in Virginia. In 1608 George Kendall was put to death for spying. Kendall, born in England in 1570, had settled in Jamestown, Virginia. In 1607 he was appointed a member of the first council of the colony, but a few months later was removed from the council and imprisoned, for sowing discord between the council members and plotting mutiny. Shortly after, a row broke out between the president of the council, John Ratcliffe, and a local blacksmith, James Reed. Reed was sentenced to hang, but as he stood on the gallows he confided to Ratcliffe that Kendall had been involved in a conspiracy against the council.

For divulging this information Reed was pardoned but Kendall was sentenced to death. He was held for nearly a year and in the fall of 1608 he was executed by firing squad, becoming the first victim of capital punishment in modern America.

Kendall had been convicted of spying but the first proper criminal to be executed was Daniel Frank, which again occurred in Virginia. Together with George Clark, Frank stole a calf belonging to George Yeardley, a rich landowner and future governor of Virginia. Pushed by starvation, they butchered the animal but were caught and tried. The trial took place on August 5, 1662.

The evidence showed that Frank had led the way and Clarke was just an accomplice—but that he helped bring the carcass to Frank's house and shared in the subsequent meal. Both men were sentenced to hang. Frank was an indentured laborer—common as muck—but Clarke was a skilled gunsmith. He was valuable to the colony, so he was pardoned. But Frank was led from the courthouse and hanged from a nearby tree within minutes after the trial ended. He holds the distinction of being the first criminal to be executed in what was to become the United States.

Ten years later, Jane Champion became the first woman to be hanged in North America. Her offense is unknown. A year later, Margaret Hatch was hanged for murder. Both executions took place in Virginia.

Almost from the start, America had adopted hanging as the favored method of execution.

Worldwide, hanging is one of the most popular methods of execution. It has a number of advantages. One of these is that it involves little equipment—a high tree and a rope are often enough, though in traditional places of execution, such as Tyburn in London, a gallows was built. This was a wooden platform from which the rope could be suspended. With a big gallows, several people could be hanged at once. Hanging a convict involved far less work than drawing and quartering, burning, or even mustering a firing squad.

Another advantage is that the body could be left on display as a deterrent to others.

In extrajudicial executions such as lynchings, hanging was almost invariably used as it was so easy to arrange. The victim was placed on a horse or a cart, or even stood on a stool, and the rope placed around an overhanging branch. The stool was kicked away and the person slowly choked.

There are four common ways of hanging someone: suspension, short drop, standard drop, and long drop. Prior to the nineteenth century, only the first two methods were used. Suspension is when someone is just jerked off the ground by the noose around their neck and their own body weight strangles them against the noose. The short drop is similar in effect; the person is on a ladder or stool or similar platform, and when it is removed they drop a short distance and the noose tightens around them. Typically the noose cuts off the carotid artery, the main blood supply to the brain, and unconsciousness results within the first minute—though this is not always the case. The condemned does not struggle because of the soporific effect of the blood supply being cut off, and goes limp. It takes about ten to twenty minutes for death to occur.

This was the method of execution used in Virginia in the early days of the colony, before the United States became independent.

In modern times the standard drop and the long drop, both British innovations, have become popular. The standard drop involves a trapdoor on the gallows through which the condemned prisoner falls. The distance of the fall is normally between four and six feet and often results in the neck breaking, which speeds up death considerably as well as resulting in almost immediate unconsciousness. The long drop is a more scientific advance on the standard drop. The distance of the drop is calculated based on the height and weight of the prisoner, and the noose is placed around the neck with the knot to the front, which forces the head back as the convict drops, guaranteeing that the neck will snap.

But the drop has to be calculated precisely because too big a drop can result in decapitation, which is considered a "cruel and unusual punishment" and thus illegal under US legislation.

During colonial times, the death penalty was widely used. Britain influenced America's use of the death penalty more than any other country. Hangings were done in public so that they would not just serve as a punishment—they were also a good moral lesson for the community. Hundreds would show up to see the victim swing. Normally a condemned person would be displayed on the gallows while a minister delivered a sermon. Then a mask was pulled over the face, a noose placed around the neck, and the platform the prisoner was standing on would drop away, plunging the condemned to his or her death.

Over the years the crimes for which hanging was considered an appropriate punishment changed. At one time, adultery was punishable by death, but this was later changed to public humiliation whereby the condemned were forced to stand on the gallows with a noose around their necks for an hour while everyone jeered at them. Then, for the rest of their lives, they would have to wear a red "A" on their clothing to alert people to their past sins. This was the Scarlet Letter made famous by Nathaniel Hawthorne in his book of the same name.

The more cruel European methods of execution rarely made their way to America. Burning at the stake was the European punishment for witchcraft. But when there was an outbreak of supposed "sorcery" in Salem, Massachusetts, those convicted were hanged rather than burned. In fact, burning was only ever used against black defendants and then only following slave revolts.

The deterrent effect of the death penalty was important. When pirates were executed, their bodies were often hung in gibbets, or body-shaped cages, by the shore or along a waterway. The flesh would rot away until all that was left was the skull and bones. In 1723 the Admiralty Court in Newport, Rhode Island, sentenced twenty-six pirates to death. When they were hanged, it was the largest nonmilitary mass execution in American history.

Death penalty laws varied from colony to colony. Some were more draconian than others. In 1612 in Virginia, Governor Sir Thomas Dale introduced the Divine, Moral and Martial Laws. This statute allowed for the execution of those convicted of stealing fruit, killing chickens, or trading with the natives. Other colonies were more lenient, but from the start executions were a feature of life on the frontier. For instance, Massachusetts Bay Colony executed a man in 1630 even though the capital laws of New England were not drawn up for years to come. The New York Colony operated under a penal code that allowed execution for striking one's mother or father or denying the "one true God." The Salem Witch Trials saw twenty people hanged for purely imaginary crimes.

Some of the executions from this period were horrific. During the Slave Revolts in New York in 1712, twenty-one black slaves were executed in the most brutal fashion. Twenty of them were roasted alive over a fire, dying in agony. One was broken on the wheel, a medieval torture. The slave was tied to a cart wheel and his limbs were shattered by repeated blows of a heavy hammer until he died of blood loss, trauma, and shock. The executioner was careful not to hit his head or torso, which would have sped up the death.

With the exception of the treatment of slaves, the colonies continued to be influenced by events occurring in Britain and Europe. By the middle of the eighteenth century an abolitionist movement had sprung up in Europe, backed by the writings of philosophers such as Montesquieu, Voltaire, and Jeremy Bentham; and British Quakers like John Bellers and John Howard. Austria and Tuscany, states in what is now northern Italy, were the first to remove death penalty from their statute books. All this happened around the time the United States gained their independence from Britain.

Taking this lead, Thomas Jefferson introduced a bill to amend Virginia's death penalty laws. He proposed that execution should be reserved for the serious crimes of murder and treason, rather than being used for minor matters like theft. He came close to succeeding, losing by just one vote.

In 1792 Dr. Benjamin Rush, one of the signatories of the Declaration of Independence and a founder of the Pennsylvania Prison Society, began to push an abolitionist agenda. He felt strongly that public punishments were not a deterrent. At that time, it was common for those convicted of minor crimes to be locked in stocks for the day while the whole community jeered at them—and for those convicted of serious crimes to be executed in a very public manner. Rush felt this "brutalizing effect" dehumanized society, making crime more likely rather than less.

Instead he proposed imprisonment, which would allow convicts to reflect on what they had done and to allow God back into their lives. He wrote a treatise in 1792 in which he said: "The punishment of murder by death is contrary to reason, and to the order and happiness of society."

He gained the support of Benjamin Franklin and Philadelphia Attorney General William Bradford and pushed the Pennsylvania legislature to abolish the death penalty for all but first-degree murder.

But executions were still a regular occurrence. Up to the gaining of independence, nearly 1,500 convicts had been executed. Between 1800 and 1900 the number rose sharply, to 5,381. Ten percent were in Virginia, while Texas accounted for only a tiny fraction—a trend that would dramatically turn towards the end of the twentieth century.

In 1790, the Bill of Rights was written. One of its provisions was that punishments could not be "cruel or unusual," which made roasting slaves illegal.

The period between 1800 and 1900 accounted for some of the most savage executions that the United States has seen. One day in 1862, thirty-eight people were hanged simultaneously, the largest single execution in US history. The public executions came at the end of the Dakota Wars of that year. Following the suppression of the Indian tribe, 303 Sioux prisoners were convicted of murder and rape by a military tribunal. They were all sentenced to death.

Some of the trials lasted less than five minutes—hardly due process for a capital case. None of the Sioux were represented by counsel and the proceedings were not explained to them. Aware of the deficiencies of the legal process, President Abraham Lincoln personally reviewed the trial records to try and distinguish who were guilty of murdering civilians and who deserved clemency on the grounds that they were fighting a war. General John Pope and Minnesota Governor Alexander Ramsey cautioned against leniency, with Ramsey saying: "Unless all 303 Sioux are executed, private revenge would on all this border take the place of official judgment on those Indians."

Lincoln eventually decided to commute the death sentences of 265 of the tribe, but 38 of the executions would go ahead.

The day chosen for the mass hanging was December 26, 1862, the day after Christmas. The location was Mankato, Minnesota. A single scaffold was built with a square gallows, allowing men to be hanged on all four sides. There was a large platform to hold all thirty-eight men while the nooses were secured. The Indians sang a war song as they stood and one exposed himself to the crowd, much to their horror. Then there were three beats of the regimental drum, and the executioner stepped forward with an axe and swung it, cutting a rope which held the platform in place. As the platform fell away, all thirty-eight Indians fell. Thirty-seven nooses tightened and jerked, and thirty-seven men began to twitch in the air as they slowly died.

The thirty-eighth man, Rattling Runner, fell to the ground as his rope snapped. He did not move and appeared to be dead from a broken neck. But, to be sure, a new noose was tied around his neck and thrown over the scaffold. He was hoisted aloft. After hanging for about fifteen minutes, the thirty-eight bodies were cut down and then buried in a mass grave in a trench by the river bank.

One landmark during the nineteenth century was in 1834 when New York and Pennsylvania decided that executions should be conducted within the prison rather than in public. This marked a change in thinking on capital punishment. A division was beginning to appear between the northern states and the southern states. In the North, states were bringing in legislation to limit capital punishment, while the southern states still used it as a punishment for a wide range of crimes. One reason for the division was that the north was industrialized, whereas the south was agricultural, relying on an underclass of slaves and poor whites who needed to be "kept in check."

In 1838 Tennessee ended mandatory death sentences, allowing juries to decide if life imprisonment would be a more appropriate sentence. In 1846 Michigan abolished the death penalty for all crimes except treason. It was the first state in the union to abolish the death penalty. In 1853 Wisconsin followed suit, ending the death penalty for all crimes. Rhode Island did the same.

Most states did not follow that lead and retained the death penalty. But one by one they changed their legislation so that a judge or jury had discretion on when to impose the death penalty and when to commute it to life imprisonment. The old days when certain classes of crime carried a mandatory execution were passing. It took until 1963, but the mandatory death penalty was now no more.

While each state moved at its own speed, trends were emerging. One trend was that imprisonment was becoming more common, providing an alternative to the gallows. A second trend was that the death penalty began to be seen as a brutalizing spectacle for a society. By the end of the nineteenth century, prisoners were always executed behind prison walls. Public executions—aside from lynchings in southern states—were seen as a legacy of the bad old days.

A third trend was that reformers began to think of new ways of conducting executions. Certain methods were left firmly in the past. Breaking on the wheel—used only on one occasion in the United States—would have been unthinkable by the mid-nineteenth century, even against slaves or Native Americans. In Europe the guillotine and the garrote had been perfected to make executions swift and painless. England still retained hanging but had worked out ways of making it more humane. The changing world attitudes towards the death penalty—attitudes that were reflected in the United States—is best illustrated by looking at accounts of two executions carried out in Cork, Ireland, around the time reformers were looking at the ultimate sanction of the law.

The first execution took place on April 26, 1828. Owen Ryan had been convicted of rape and was hanged in front of the city prison in a big public spectacle. There was great excitement in the town because the hanging was a free show. And a new type of gallows was to be tested, which should have made death instant. Here is how the local paper, *The Cork Examiner*, described the entertainment:

There was an immense concourse of spectators attracted, we presume, to witness the first operation of the dread apparatus at the prison. About an hour before the execution we went into the gate where we observed becomingly solemn arrangements. A black flag waved on high and minute bells tolled.

At half past twelve, the convict moved from his cell through the passages and yards leading to the house of death, accompanied by the Sheriff, Governor, and High Constables. Uncovered, he walked with firm step, his countenance fixed and solemn.

A door in the gate of the prison opened and the executioner could be seen working out figures as Ryan stood behind him, his face masked.

After a few minutes he was moved forward on the board that was to throw him into eternity and the work of horror commenced. Upon this fatal spot he was delayed several minutes, the board the while now and again rising under him, and the rope pulling him up on tip-toe; and, at length, only a gentle throw off and scarcely two inches of a drop. He torturingly and tediously died.

Instead of being flung into eternity, the drop snapping his neck, Ryan had been gently pushed off the board and dropped two inches, slowly strangling in front of hundreds of cheering spectators. Afterward, the officials explained that they were worried that if they used a big drop, the prisoner would swing over and back and could be dashed against the prison wall. Better they let him die slowly than be hurt during the process!

Just forty years later there had been a complete change in public attitude. *The Cork Examiner*, in 1866, reported on the last public execution:

Mr. O'Connor told a meeting of Cork Corporation that 'the respectable residents of Sunday's Well [where the prison was located] find appalling the spectacle of common criminals

being publicly hanged in front of the jail.' They agreed to
await the results of a commission, now sitting in the USA,
before coming to a conclusion. Executions were later brought
inside the prison walls.

The worldwide change in attitude was reflected within the United
States. One of the results of evolving standards was the creation of the
electric chair.

3

THE ELECTRICAL DEATH COMMISSION

Two things drove the move to reform capital punishment. One was what the Supreme Court would eventually call "evolving standards" in society. People wanted to get away from the barbarism of the past. The second thing was botched executions. Every time a hanging was done wrong, leaving a prisoner jerking on the end of a rope for twenty agonizing minutes as the life was slowly squeezed out of him or her, it fueled calls for a new and more modern method of carrying out executions.

These botched executions led to regular calls for the abolition of the death penalty, which rarely got anywhere. In 1832 the New York Assembly appointed a committee to consider abolishing capital punishment entirely. This followed a hanging that led to a riot where a number of people were killed. The committee introduced a bill which was heavily defeated. But executions were moved from public spaces into prisons a few years later.

After the horrors of the Civil War, Americans became more sensitive to suffering and less tolerant of brutal executions. Doctors and scientists began to follow the European lead, trying to come up with humane execution methods.

France had replaced the savage breaking on a wheel with the quick and painless guillotine. Spain had perfected the garrote, resulting in a speedy death. Britain had turned hanging into a fine art. But the advances in hanging techniques only made their way to America slowly, and the job was still done badly as frequently as it was done well. Soon some scientists with a social conscience began to look at the problem.

On July 24, 1886, Dr. Wooster Beach published his thoughts in the *Medical Record*. He recounted his studies on the victims of hanging. Even with the long drop favored by the British, only one in twenty of the victims ended up with a broken neck and an instantaneous death. The rest suffered "exquisite torture till asphyxia produces insensibility." He suggested changing the method by which the noose was tied to make the punishment less painful.

Others were turning to more modern approaches. *Scientific American* carried an article in the March 1883 edition entitled "Killing Cattle by Electricity," which hinted at the power of the new technology. The article argued that electricity could be used to kill worn-out horses and donkeys and even cattle for food. Two years later, that hint of things to come became explicit when the July 1885 edition of the magazine carried a piece entitled "Electricity for Executing Criminals." It urged that the "hideous violence" of hanging should be replaced by "judicial lightning." Two years later, the magazine actually described a prototype electric chair.

Many were taking up the call. One of these was a Buffalo dentist, Dr. Alfred Porter Southwick. Southwick was a strong advocate of electrocution from the start. Born in 1826, he had trained as a steamboat engineer before becoming a highly respected dentist with a practice in Buffalo.

Buffalo was one of the first cities in America to be "electrified." In 1880 a hydroelectric power generator was installed at nearby Niagara Falls, and by 1885, George Westinghouse installed a big generator on the Falls, powering the nearby town. There were so many incandescent bulbs that Buffalo became known as the City of Lights. But with the light came the danger of electrocution. Insulation was less reliable than it is today and many people got painful shocks—some fatal—from the naked wires.

In 1881 Alfred Southwick saw a drunk man stumble near a generator. The man reached out to stop his fall and touched the metal. There was a quick flash of light and the man dropped to the ground. When Southwick got to him, the man was dead. The shock had killed him instantly. Southwick's initial reaction was one of horror, but he was also struck by something else. The man's death, reported the *Buffalo Evening News* on August 9, 1881, had been instant and—according to Southwick—painless. He thought that this would be a far more humane way of killing prisoners than hanging, which often went wrong, leaving the victim to slowly choke to death, their legs twitching in the air for several minutes. This was known as "dancing the Tyburn Jig," named after the gallows at Tyburn in London, England. As a Quaker and a believer in progress, he believed technology should be used to take the pain out of the death penalty.

For the next decade, Southwick pushed for electrocution to replace hanging. As a dentist he was used to operating on people in chairs, so naturally he thought of using a chair to carry out electrocutions. Thus, the idea of the electric chair was born.

Once Southwick conceived the idea of electrical executions, he was tireless in his efforts to make it a reality. First, he had to prove that the concept worked, and to do this he began electrocuting stray animals around Buffalo. The experiments worked; the animals all died instantly. So Southwick began lobbying politicians to get the matter before the New York Assembly. He was pushing an open door; newly appointed governor David Bennett Hill was facing a fall election, and he knew that the anti-hanging lobby would be important. So he wanted to throw them a carrot.

"The present mode of executing criminals by hanging has come down to us from the dark ages and it may well be questioned whether the science of the present day cannot provide a means for taking the life of such as are condemned to die in a less barbarous manner," he said in a speech on January 6, 1885. Within days, State Senator Daniel MacMillan had persuaded the Assembly to appoint a committee to study the matter. The governor got on board and a commission was set up. As a close friend of Senator MacMillan, Southwick was appointed to the commission. The chair was Edridge T. Gerry, grandson of one of the signatories of the Declaration of Independence. A skilled attorney, he was a founder of the Society for the Prevention of Cruelty to Children and also worked with the Society for the Prevention of Cruelty to Animals. The final member was attorney Matthew Hale, from another family steeped in the heroism of the Revolutionary War period.

The Gerry Commission, which also became known as the New York Electrical Death Commission, began by surveying jurists, judges, and medical experts on methods of execution. In total, 199 agreed to be involved in the survey, which returned mixed results. Eighty respondents wanted to keep hanging, while eighty-seven were in favor of electricity. That left eight opting for poison (which is now the preferred method in the United States), five were for the guillotine, four for the garrote, and the remainder either went for their own obscure solutions or did not express a preference. While it might seem that there was a narrow majority in favor of electrocution, the survey had been skewered. Many were in favor of electricity only if hanging was abolished. So the true picture was that people wanted to retain hanging but would consider electrocution as an alternative.

Some of the responses were illuminating. Most accepted that electricity would provide a swifter and more humane death, and one suggested reserving it for women, while the men would still hang. Another suggested hanging unless there were mitigating circumstances which warranted the mercy of electrocution.

A very mixed result, but it was enough for the commission to work with. But Southwick quickly realized that Gerry was more open-minded than he and less committed to switching to electrocution. So he wrote to the famous inventor Thomas Edison, to ask for his support. Edison's initial response was not helpful; as a liberal he was opposed to the death penalty. But he eventually conceded that if executions had to occur, then they should be done in the best possible manner. He wrote: "This, I believe, can be accomplished by the use of electricity, and the most suitable apparatus for the purpose is that class of dynamo-electric machinery which employs intermittent currents. The most effective of these are known as 'alternating machines' manufactured principally in this country by George Westinghouse. The passage of the current from these machines through the human body, even by the slightest contacts, produces instantaneous death."

This letter, sent in December 1887, seemed to be an endorsement of electrical execution, but in fact was not. It was a move in a commercial war. Thomas Edison had been losing ground to George Westinghouse in a battle on how to deliver electricity to American households. Edison favored direct current while Westinghouse championed alternating current. And Westinghouse was winning the commercial war. Edison hoped to damage the reputation of his rival if he could associate Westinghouse with the vileness of executing prisoners. The battle between the two industrialists was very influential in the eventual development of the electric chair and will be examined in more detail in the next chapter.

The Gerry Commission published its report on January 17, 1888. In the report, they considered a number of alternatives when it came to imposing the death penalty.

The commission listed thirty-four separate methods of execution from various parts of the world and various historic periods. Some were unbelievably vicious, some were insane, but others were sincere attempts to put a prisoner to death humanely. The report reeled the methods off in alphabetical order:

"Beating with clubs, beheading, blowing from a cannon, boiling, breaking on the wheel, burning, burying alive, crucifixion, defenestration, dichotomy, dismemberment, drowning, exposure to wild beasts, flaying alive, flogging, garrote, guillotine, hanging, hara-kiri, impalement, iron maiden, *peine forte et dure*, poisoning, pounding in mortar, precipitation, pressing to death, rack, running the gauntlet, shooting, stabbing, stoning, strangling, and suffocation."

Some of the terms need explanation to the modern reader. Defenestration comes from the Latin word fenestra, or window. It means tossing someone out through a window—hardly a practical method of execution. There are several instances of it in European history but always as a spur-of-the-moment method rather than a planned execution. Hara-kiri is a traditional method of suicide in Japan, involving people disemboweling themselves with a short sword—again, not a practical method of execution. Dichotomy means sawing someone in half—great for a magic show, less appealing as the ultimate sanction of the law. *Peine forte et dure* was a medieval European method which involved crushing the victim under an enormous weight. It was both a torture and a death and was quickly dismissed by the commission. Precipitation, like defenestration, involved throwing a prisoner from a height, but this time without the intervening window. Running the gauntlet involved a prisoner running through a double line of armed men, with each one taking a swing at him.

Several methods could be dismissed without further discussion, but that left half a dozen or more viable methods of execution which had to be properly considered. And to understand why America went for the electric chair, we must look at the alternatives, just as the commission did.

One of the first things the commission noted was that executions were traditionally less brutal in America than in the rest of the world. They also said that the purpose of execution was to kill the prisoner, not torture them in vengeance. So whatever method New York opted for would have to be as humane as possible.

The methods that were effective and/or widely used were beheading (with a guillotine or without), blowing from a cannon, burning, garrote, hanging, poisoning, shooting, and stoning. The commission had to consider a number of factors in relation to each method. The method had to be sure, it had to be practical, and (according to the constitution) could not be cruel or unusual. There was another consideration—there had to be no chance of resuscitation after an execution. Like the commission, I will be look at the methods in alphabetical order.

METHOD ONE: BEHEADING

Few things are more certain to cause death than losing one's head. Beheading is an instant (thus humane and painless) method of execution, refined by the invention of the guillotine to make it fast, efficient, and modern. The guillotine, the engine of death so overused during the

French Revolution, was one of the first attempts to introduce humanity into the execution process.

Beheading has an ancient history. In fact, the term capital punishment comes from the Latin word caput, meaning head. Losing one's head for serious offenses goes back millennia. In medieval Europe it was often used on noblemen to save them the indignity of hanging or of being drawn and quartered if their offense was treason. In some countries that beheaded as a matter of course, such as the Scandinavian nations, nobles were beheaded with a sword, while commoners got an axe.

The headsman, or executioner, would ensure that his axe was very sharp. The victim knelt down and placed his head on a wooden block. The headsman then stood over the prisoner and raised the axe. If his aim was true and the blade honed, death was instant. But if he was nervous or if the prisoner struggled, it could take multiple blows to sever the head. When Henry VIII ordered the execution of sixty-seven-year-old Margaret Pole for treason, the terrified old lady struggled so much the axe struck her across the shoulders. She jumped up from the block and ran into the crowd of onlookers, screaming, as the executioner chased her, raining blows on her back with his axe. She was eventually brought back to the block, but a total of ten blows were required before her head was severed.

In Saudi Arabia to this day beheadings are carried out with a sword. The sword is heavy, a two-handed weapon with a very sharp blade. The prisoner kneels and the sword is swung from behind. No block is used. Beheadings by axe continued in Europe until 1825 when Tahvo Putkonen was executed for murder in Finland. He had killed a neighbor the day after Christmas because he objected to the neighbor's table manners. He was also fined for disturbing the holiday peace, a fine that was extracted before his execution.

Beheadings moved into the modern age in France with the invention of the guillotine. There were precursors to this killing machine. The Halifax Gibbet was a wooden structure with two uprights which supported a heavy blade. It was used from 1280 until 1650 in Halifax, England. There were other beheading machines used in England, though rarely, in medieval and early modern times.

French doctor Antoine Louis, together with German engineer Tobias Schmidt, took the old idea and modernized it, replacing the straight blade of earlier models with a slanted blade, which made it far more efficient. He invented his beheading machine shortly before the start of the French Revolution. It followed an appeal in 1789 by Dr. Joseph-Ignace Guillotin to the National Assembly to adopt beheading as the universal method of execution and to come up with a machine to make it swift and humane. The new machine was to replace the breaking wheel, the traditional method of capital punishment in France. As previously described, victims of the breaking wheel were strapped to a cart wheel and their limbs broken by repeated hammer blows until they died. As the blows were to the arms and legs, rather than to torso and head, death was prolonged and painful.

The machine was ready within three years and was tested on highwayman Nicolas Jacques Pelletier on April 25, 1792. Death was instantaneous. Over the following few years the machine was well and truly tested, with often hundreds of aristocrats being decapitated before large crowds of Parisians during the gory years of the revolution. It proved to be very efficient at handling the large numbers.

One peculiarity of death by decapitation is that it takes a few seconds for the brain to die. There is some evidence that consciousness could last for up to eight seconds following the fatal blow. That means that when the executioner held the head aloft to the cheering crowd, the victim could see the faces swimming in front of him before the blood loss and oxygen starvation switched off the brain for good. However, there is no evidence that the brain could perceive pain after the spinal column is severed.

The guillotine remained in use in Germany until 1949 and in France until the abolition of the death penalty in 1981. Of all the methods of execution designed to increase the efficiency and humanity of the death penalty, it is perhaps the best. A prolonged and painful death was an impossibility. It was a simple mechanism that could not be botched. It should have been a natural alternative to the electric chair. But North America had no history of beheading. The territory of Utah had allowed it as an option for those condemned to die but no one had ever chosen it. And when Utah became the forty-fifth state of the Union in 1896, it was removed as an option.

The New York Commission failed to consider the most efficient and humane death machine of all. Their objection was that the "profuse effusion of blood" would be too shocking for witnesses and the guillotine was too much associated with the bloodshed of the French Revolution to be considered.

METHOD TWO: BLOWING FROM A CANNON

Blowing from a cannon sounds horrific but on closer examination it is actually quite a humane method of execution. Typically a prisoner is tied to the mouth of a cannon, which is then shot, tearing the prisoner's body apart and killing him instantly. It was widely used for nearly three hundred years, mainly in Asia. This description comes from George Carter Stent, a British official with the Chinese Maritime Customs in the 1870s: "The prisoner is generally tied to a gun with the upper part of the small of his back resting against the muzzle. When the gun is fired, his head is seen to go straight up into the air some forty or fifty feet; the arms fly off right and left, high up in the air and fall at, perhaps, a hundred yards distance; the legs drop to the ground beneath the muzzle of the gun; and the body is literally blown away altogether, not a vestige being seen."

The practice began among the Moguls in the Indian subcontinent in the early sixteenth century. When the British Raj was in control of India they needed a method of execution for natives guilty of mutiny or desertion from the army, and just like the New York Electrical Death Commission, they set up a committee to look at the alternatives. The normal method of execution at the time was flogging the prisoner to death. This was a slow and painful death, dragged out over several minutes. It was traumatic on both the victim and the executioner. The committee chose blowing from a cannon as a more humane alternative.

It also had the advantage of being a huge deterrent. The sight of a prisoner being literally blown apart would inspire fear in other potential mutineers and keep the natives in line.

The cannon was normally loaded with a blank charge—just powder and wadding. But still, things could go wrong. At a mass execution in Firozpur, Punjab, India, in 1857 someone accidentally loaded grapeshot into the cannons instead of the blank charge. Several of the spectators were hit with the grapeshot resulting in one death and two serious injuries. The two who were injured had to have limbs amputated as a result of the botched execution.

Another danger was flying body parts. Soldiers who did not get clear of the cannon in time risked injuries from whizzing pieces of flesh and bone, and there is one instance, again in Firozpur in 1862, of a soldier being concussed by a falling arm.

Most methods of execution fail on occasion, and that is true of blowing from a cannon. This account comes from the *Bombay Gazette*:

> After the explosion, the grouping of the men's remains in
> front of each gun was various and frightful. One man's head
> was perched upon his back, and he was staring round as if
> looking for his legs and arms. All you see at the time was a
> cloud like a dust storm composed of shreds of clothing, burn-
> ing muscle, and frizzing fat with lumps of coagulated blood.
> Here and there a stomach or a liver came falling down in a
> stinking shower. One wretched fellow slipped from the rope
> by which he was tied to the guns just before the explosion,
> and his arm was nearly set on fire. While hanging in his agony
> under the gun, a sergeant applied a pistol to his head. This was
> the most horrible sight of all. I have seen death in all its forms,
> but never anything to equal this man's end.

Then there were the birds of prey which circled overhead, swooping down to catch the flying flesh of the condemned—and the dogs that swarmed the field after every execution. Gruesome. Blowing from a cannon never spread beyond Asia, aside from a few instances in Portuguese colonies in Mozambique and Brazil. It was used up until 1930 in Afghanistan.

But it was too cruel for American sensibilities, and was never seriously considered by the commission.

METHOD THREE: BURNING

One of the most ancient and widespread methods of carrying out the death penalty is by burning. This was recorded from ancient times right up to the last century, and was used in Europe, Africa, Asia, and America. It even has biblical backing. It certainly fulfills the function of being a deterrent—no one would choose it as a method of dying. Spectators were horrified—and strangely fascinated—by the sight of victims being immolated in large public squares throughout Europe.

The most common method was that victims would be tied to a stake and a large fire built around them. Once the fire was ignited, they would burn. If the fire was large, death normally came by way of smoke inhalation and carbon monoxide poisoning long before the flames began to consume the body. This meant that while it looked barbaric, it was actually quite a gentle death. Aside, that is, from the panic that it would cause its victims.

But if the fire was small, the victim often died in agony of heatstroke, shock, or simply from their internal organs cooking.

Throughout medieval Europe this was a very common method of execution, often reserved for treason, witchcraft, and sexual and religious crimes. Estimates vary, but up to three hundred thousand women may have been put to the torch for the imaginary crime of witchcraft before the Enlightenment ended the practice. It was generally women that went to the stake but sometimes men suffered that fate. The religious nature of the execution was backed up by biblical references aplenty. It was a common practice in the Middle East in biblical times.

In Genesis 38, there is an account of Judah, the founder of one of the Tribes of Israel, condemning his widowed daughter-in-law to death because she became pregnant outside of marriage. But the sentence was set aside when he realized that he was the one who got her in that interesting condition.

Through Roman times and on into the Christian era, burning continued to be carried out. It became the favored method for certain classes of crime. For instance, in the Byzantine Empire burning replaced an older punishment for those convicted of killing a member of their family. The older method involved stuffing the convict in a sack with a rooster, a viper, a dog, and a monkey, then throwing the sack into the sea. A truly bizarre method that never caught on outside of that small corner of the world.

By the Middle Ages, burning was the execution method of choice for heretics and others who offended against the power of the Church. By the thirteenth century it was laid down in law as the principal execution method throughout the sphere of influence of the Roman church. There are many recorded instances of whole Jewish communities being burned at large public spectacles for the next few hundred years. In one day in the winter of 1349, two thousand Jews were burned on a large scaffold at the cemetery in Strasbourg—blamed for bringing the Black Death plague to Europe.

Equally heinous were the actions of the Inquisition, a religious tribunal which policed matters of faith in Spain and Portugal in particular, but also elsewhere in Europe. Established in 1478 in Spain to preserve Catholic orthodoxy, the Inquisition clamped down on heresy, Judaism, and witchcraft. In the first twelve years, two thousand victims burned. In its three hundred-year history, up to fifty thousand others may have met the same fate. A similar number were burned at the stake as witches throughout this period.

Burning also became the punishment of choice for sexual deviance, including homosexuality. But by the nineteenth century, burning had died out as a punishment. The last two instances of it occurred in Germany, in 1804 and 1813. Johannes Thomas was convicted of arson and sentenced to die on July 13, 1804. But he was placed several feet above the pyre—in a wooden chamber attached to a stake. Sulfuric smoke was piped into the chamber, suffocating him before the flames engulfed him. Twenty thousand people watched the execution. In 1813, lovers and arsonists Johann Horst and Friederike Delitz were sentenced to burn. But both were secretly strangled to death by the executioner as he secured them to the stakes, saving them a painful death.

Burning was a popular, though never legally sanctioned, method of execution in North America for centuries. Native Americans used it as a form of execution against members of rival tribes or against white settlers during the eighteenth and nineteenth centuries. Their method was slow and painful; the victim was roasted over a fire in a prolonged torture, unlike the quicker "burning at the stake" of the Europeans.

White settlers also occasionally used burning as an execution method. In Massachusetts there are two known cases. In 1681, a slave was burned for trying to kill her master by burning his house down, and in 1755, another slave was burned for killing his master, at Cambridge. In New York there were several cases, generally of slaves. Following the Slave Revolt of 1712, twenty rebels were burned to death, and one was slowly roasted, to act as a deterrent against further revolts. The roasting took ten agonizing hours. The slave was put on a lattice of rods and a smoldering fire lit beneath him—the fire kept hot enough to ensure that his screams rang out for hours.

Thirty years later, following another revolt, thirteen more slaves were put to the torch.

Following the end of slavery, burning continued to be a popular method of carrying out illegal executions on members of the black community, particularly in the southern states. Those lynchings, which continued to the 1960s, are one of the most shameful aspects of American history.

Variants on burning included pouring molten metal down the convict's throat, boiling the victim alive, and even frying them in oil. These painful methods never made an appearance in America. Though the United States had a history of burning black citizens, it was never used against whites and was not considered seriously by the commission. Although it could be managed to make death painless, and although it left no possibility of resuscitation and no body to martyr, burning was a horrific spectacle that the new nation did not want to consider.

METHOD FOUR: GARROTE

At its simplest, a garrote is a length of rope, wire, or similar ligature which is wrapped around the victim's neck and tightened, choking or strangling him or her to death. It is a common tool of the assassin and is also used by soldiers who want a quick and silent kill on clandestine missions. The garrote was also, for centuries, the favored method of execution in Spain and its colonies.

Done correctly, it mimics the effect of a short-drop hanging. The victim dies of strangulation. This has two immediate effects—the carotid artery in the brain is compressed, resulting in loss of consciousness and eventual death; and the windpipe is constricted, cutting off oxygen to the lungs. This causes death within minutes at the most. Unlike short-drop hanging, the pressure is applied from the rear, rather than from a rope above the prisoner's head. This means that far more pressure is applied directly on the neck, resulting in a faster death. As any wrestler or mixed martial artist will attest, a correctly applied choke hold results in unconsciousness in seconds, making a garrote a very efficient tool for executions.

The method came from the Moors and Arabs and was perfected in Spain several hundred years ago. It is named from "garrote," a small stick or club. Traditionally a garrote had two short sticks with the ligature between them. The executioner used the sticks for grip and to tighten the pressure. But the initial garrote executions involved prisoners being beaten to death with the short sticks; strangulation only gradually crept in. Eventually garroting became a precise science.

By the eighteenth century, the garrote consisted of a chair with a pole behind it. The prisoner sat in the chair and a chain or rope was wrapped around his neck strapping him to the pole. Then a screw was turned which rapidly tightened the noose, resulting in quick loss of consciousness. A further refinement was a bolt or spike that came out of the pole and pressed into the back of the neck as the screw tightened. This bolt would snap the spinal column, resulting in instant death from a broken neck. This way the garrote was slightly slower than a perfect hanging (though much quicker than a botched one), but absolutely guaranteed to end the life of the prisoner without undue suffering. Of man's many attempts to find a humane execution method, it is one of the methods that came closest.

As the electric chair is peculiarly American, the garrote was a Spanish specialty, being used in that country and its empire for centuries. It was the method of choice in the Philippines until the United States captured that colony in 1898. The new US authorities maintained the garrote for a few years until it was replaced, briefly, with the electric chair. United States military authorities also used the garrote in Puerto Rico. In a report to Congress, the American military governor Brigadier General George Davis said, "Execution by the garrote is far less inhumane and revolting than execution by hanging."

Despite this endorsement from a man who had overseen both sorts of execution, the garrote was soon replaced with the gallows. The last public garroting in Spain happened in Barcelona in May 1897. Like most countries in the developed world, executions moved inside to the confines of the prison. The last garroting occurred in March 1974. George Michael Welzel and Salvador Puig Antich were anarchists. During a shoot-out a young police officer was killed and both men were condemned to die. It was an unpopular decision by the Franco-led fascist government and the death penalty was abolished a few years later.

The last country to abandon the garrote was the tiny kingdom of Andorra, in the Pyrenees Mountains between France and Spain. They took the method off the books in 1990. But the removal was largely symbolic; there had been no garroting in the principality since the twelfth century.

Despite being considered one of the most humane and practical methods of execution, garroting was never a serious contender to replace hanging in New York. Perhaps it was a bit too hands-on for late-nineteenth century sensibilities. The commission noted its "celerity and certainty," but argued that the fact that it had not spread beyond Spain showed that it might not be the method to adopt.

METHOD FIVE: HANGING

There is a broad spectrum in executions from the barbaric, such as breaking on a wheel or stoning—to the swift and painless, such as a bullet to the back of the head, the guillotine, or the garrote. Hanging falls more on the humane side but retains an element of the barbaric. It is a gruesome sight to see the convict drop through the trap and dangle in the air, legs twitching. Normally, hanging results in a swift death, but it can go wrong. Too long a drop, and the head snaps off as the body plunges to the ground. Too short, and the convict dies a painful death from strangulation, taking up to ten minutes to die.

Worldwide, hanging is one of the most popular methods of execution. In the English-speaking world, it was almost universal for a while. It has a long history. Initially, hanging was a lot more brutal than it is today. A noose was placed around the convict's neck and thrown over a beam of some sort—perhaps a gallows or a branch of a tree. The prisoner was hoisted up and slowly strangled by the weight of his own body against the noose.

Because of the way the pressure was applied, death could be prolonged. In a garrote the pressure is applied directly from the back of the neck, whereas in a hanging the pressure is upwards, reducing its efficiency. That is why a garrote results in speedy loss of consciousness, whereas a hanging can leave the prisoner fully aware of all that his body is suffering. Because of this, the prisoner often twitches and kicks his legs for several minutes as he dies. This death dance became known as the Tyburn Jig. Tyburn was a place of public execution in London, England, for centuries. At Tyburn, there was a three-sided gallows which could hang up to twenty people at a time.

In 1866 an Irish doctor, Samuel Haughton, worked out a new way of hanging. If the noose was placed to the side of the head and the prisoner had a four to six foot drop from the gallows, the noose would snap the prisoner's neck. This would cause immediate paralysis and unconsciousness, making death come swifter and without pain. Within months, this new method was in use throughout the English-speaking world, where it was considered a vast improvement over the previous slow strangulation. In 1872 William Marwood introduced a refinement, calculating the length of the drop according to the height and weight of the prisoner. This refinement became the standard for executions by hanging.

Of course, a swift and painless death was not always the aim of an executioner. Other variants of hanging were created which prolonged the suffering of the victim. One of the worst was when victims were hung by the ribs. A small incision was made with a knife between two ribs and an iron hook was inserted. The prisoner was suspended by the hook. Normally they would survive for three days or more before succumbing to dehydration. It was used occasionally in Eastern Europe and by the Dutch in Suriname.

Another variant was to hang a convict by the feet. This was used in medieval Europe, often against Jews. The prisoner would take a week or more to die. To add to the public spectacle, the person was often hung between two rabid dogs who would bite and harry the condemned man.

Hanging had a long history in America, being the method of execution used by the early colonists. The largest mass execution in US history was the hanging of thirty-eight Sioux Indians in Minnesota in 1862. Hanging remained in use long after the introduction of the electric chair. In 1979, Billy Bailey shot and killed two elderly people in Delaware. On January 25, 1996, after a last meal of well-done steak and baked potato, he stepped through the trap and into history as the last man to be hanged in the United States.

The New York Commission (which introduced the electric chair) was set up to replace hanging as an execution method. It took ninety years to completely succeed. Their main objection to hanging was that it could go badly wrong. It also created a very grisly public spectacle, especially if the condemned was a woman or someone else who would excite public sympathy. This was a real concern. A few decades after the commission had done its work, there was an armed rebellion in Ireland against British rule. That happened in 1916 in the middle of World War I, and the rebels had virtually no public support. The leaders were executed by firing squad. But one of the leaders, James Connolly, had been injured in the fighting and was placed in a wheelchair for his execution. The reports of a badly injured man being executed in a wheelchair was enough to turn the tide of public opinion against the British authorities and cause the uprising to escalate into an all-out war.

A second concern was the possibility of resuscitation. If a person was cut down too early from a gallows, and the neck had not broken, there was a real possibility he would later wake up. This had happened on a number of occasions, both in the United States and abroad.

METHOD SIX: POISONING

Poisoning has ended up the execution method of choice throughout most of the United States, having replaced the electric chair many decades ago. Lethal injection and the gas chamber are two modern and high-tech systems of delivering poison, nothing more.

Poisoning has a long and sordid history but was used more often as a secret method of murder or assassination rather than as the ultimate sanction of the law. There are so many poisons; the choice is bewildering. There are poisons that kill in seconds (cyanide), that kill over weeks or months (arsenic), or that kill without leaving a trace (curare). People can choose how much pain they wanted their victim to suffer—an easy end or a hard one. But there is something sneaky about the poisoner, and lawmakers have historically been reluctant to make something so underhand a method of execution.

The exception was the ancient Athenians, who often sentenced a criminal to drink a potion containing hemlock. Hemlock is a relative of the carrot, but deadly poisonous. The death is a hard one, prolonged over several hours. Symptoms include vomiting, diarrhea, abdominal pains, headache, weakness, and tremors. The most famous victim was Socrates, the philosopher condemned to death for corrupting the youth of Athens. In 399 BC he took a cup of hemlock under the watchful eye of his executioner. His death was described by fellow philosopher, Plato: "He walked about until his legs began to fail and then he lay on his back and the man who gave him the poison now and then looked at his feet and legs; and after a while he pressed his foot hard and asked him if he could feel. And he said: 'No,' and then his leg, and so upwards and upwards, and showed us that he was cold and stiff. And he felt them himself . . . and said: 'When the poison reaches the heart, that will be the end.'"

It was almost peaceful, in Plato's account. The truth is that Socrates died in agony.

Poison was often administered to save an important person from the ignominy of a public execution. It was occasionally used to secretly execute someone. There are very strong suspicions that the British authorities used arsenic to poison Napoleon Bonaparte during his exile on the island of St. Helena in the mid-Atlantic. His death in 1821 was officially ruled as caused by stomach cancer, but later analysis showed very high levels of arsenic in his hair; prolonged arsenic poisoning mirrors the symptoms of some cancers.

Poisoning was seriously considered by the New York Commission, as the method of injecting anesthetic was just coming onstream. But the medical profession was against the use of the new hypodermic needles in executions. Needles were already scary, and the profession did not want them to be labeled as an instrument of death. And the commission felt that medical expertise would be needed to make the method work. Two poisons were considered—prussic acid and morphine. Prussic acid was considered too dangerous for non-doctors to handle, and morphine, ironically, was considered too gentle a method of execution. It would eliminate the "great dread of death" and take some element of punishment away from execution.

Poisoning eventually did replace the electric chair in most states. The two methods of poisoning in the United States are the gas chamber and lethal injection.

The gas chamber evokes horrible memories of the Nazi regime in Germany where millions of Jews were killed in the concentration camps and death camps. But smaller gas chambers are found in several prisons in the United States, including Alcatraz in San Francisco. Currently three states use a gas chamber. The first prisoner to go to the chamber was Gee Jon, a Chinese Triad member who killed a member of a rival gang. He was sentenced to die in 1924, and Nevada had just introduced a bill allowing gas to be used in executions. He was the guinea pig.

The execution was almost comical. The California Cyanide Company refused to deliver the poisonous gas to Nevada State Prison in Carson City, so a warden was dispatched to collect the deadly cargo. It was contained in a mobile fumigating unit, normally used for getting rid of pests in houses. When it arrived, the officials in charge of the execution tried to pump the gas under the door of Jon's cell as he slept, but it leaked back into the corridor and they had to rapidly retreat.

A makeshift gas chamber was hurriedly constructed in the butcher shop of the prison. To make sure it worked, one of the prison cats was locked in the chamber. The experiment was a success. The dead cat was removed and Jon was strapped into a chair in the small room. He was in tears and the warden brusquely told him to "Brace up." Four pounds of hydrocyanic acid were sprayed into the chamber, but it was a very cold day and the electric heater in the chamber failed to work. Instead of forming a gas, the acid condensed into a puddle on the floor. But enough of it got into the atmosphere and as Jon inhaled, the gas entered his lungs, and after about six seconds his head fell forward. Though he was unconscious, he continued to move for another five minutes. After ten minutes, there was panic in the witness room as some of the gas began to leak. Everyone ran while the warden tried to set up a fan to vent the gas from the chamber. But it was three hours before anyone dared enter the chamber to remove the body.

Eleven states eventually sanctioned the use of gas chambers. Currently six offer it as an option, generally alongside lethal injection. Its use dwindled over the years, and since the reinstatement of the death penalty in 1976, only eleven executions have been carried out in this manner. The problem is that it can be slow, taking up to ten minutes. And prisoners can often resist, breathing shallowly or trying to hold their breath. It is a painful experience for the witnesses.

Lethal injection is the method that has superseded the electric chair throughout most of the country. The condemned is injected with a fatal dose of three drugs—a barbiturate, a paralytic, and a potassium solution. The first causes unconsciousness, the second paralyzes the breathing, and the third stops the heart, in that order.

The method was first proposed as early as 1888 by New York doctor Julius Mount Bleyer. He felt it would be cheaper and easier than hanging, but New York was swinging towards electrocution, so the idea gained no traction.

In 1977, Oklahoma's state medical examiner, Jay Chapman, proposed a new and painless method of execution, stating that: "An intravenous saline drip shall be started in the prisoner's arm, into which shall be introduced a lethal injection consisting of an ultra short-acting barbiturate, in combination with a chemical paralytic." The state legislature agreed, approving the new method.

Texas was the first state to actually try lethal injection on Charles Brooks Jr., an African-American from a good middle-class background. Brooks and an accomplice had stolen a car from a dealership and had shot the salesman in the head. On December 7, 1982, after he had a last meal of T-bone steak and fries followed by peach cobbler and iced tea, he was strapped onto a gurney and wheeled into the death chamber at Huntsville Prison, Texas. The needle was fitted, and then he made a last statement. He had converted to Islam in prison and said a brief prayer to Allah. Then the mixture was pushed through his veins and he passed away peacefully.

Lethal injection proved very popular. It was clinical and efficient, and was adopted by thirty-six of the thirty-seven states that allowed the death penalty. Only Nebraska refused to switch, retaining the electric chair as their exclusive method of execution. Other countries also switched, including China (which leads the world in executions), Taiwan, Guatemala, the Philippines, Thailand, and Vietnam.

But in recent years the lethal cocktail of drugs, which is imported from Europe, has become difficult to get for many prisons as European Union countries are refusing to export those drugs to the US justice system. As a result, the electric chair may be about to make a comeback.

METHOD SEVEN: SHOOTING

Florida, Missouri, Wyoming, and Utah are seriously considering the use of firing squads if the drugs for lethal injections become difficult to get. Worldwide, shooting is the overwhelming favorite as a method of execution, having replaced the universal dominance of hanging. It is clean, efficient, and clinical. Death is instant.

There are two methods commonly used. A single shot to the head or back, or a firing squad. The single executioner administering the coup de grace was common throughout the Eastern Bloc of Europe under Soviet influence. The only European country that still has the death penalty, Belarus, still uses this method.

The condemned prisoners were marched from their cell through a maze of corridors towards the prison yard. When they got there, they were suddenly shot in the back of the head or neck, dying instantly. Similar methods were used throughout Asia. Until lethal injection became popular, shooting was the first choice in China. Typically, a prisoner was shot once in the back of the head by a rifle or else the executioner opened fire with an automatic rifle, strafing the prisoner's body with a volley of shots from behind. In neighboring Mongolia the method used is a bullet to the back of the neck from a revolver. This is very hands-on and could probably not work in America because it would be difficult to find willing executioners.

Taiwan has attempted to make shooting as humane and clinical as possible. The prisoner is given a strong anesthetic to render them completely senseless. Then a single shot is aimed at the heart. If the prisoner has volunteered to donate his organs, the shot is aimed at the back of the head instead, ripping through the brain stem. Thailand, until recently, also used a single executioner. The prisoner was shot in the back with a burst of fire from a mounted machine gun.

Other countries opted for the firing squad. A prisoner would stand against a wall or be tied to a stake, with a target pinned to his chest. A team of shooters, generally five or more, would face him and on a command they would all fire simultaneously. Death was normally instantaneous. Sometimes a blank round was mixed with the live rounds, so that the members of the firing squad would not know who had fired the fatal shot. This was done to reinforce the sense of diffusion of responsibility among the shooters. If the shooters felt that they were not personally responsible for the death of the prisoner, they were more likely to aim true. Firing squads were very popular for military courts and were used frequently in war situations.

The only problem is that a single executioner will make sure of the placement of his shot, whereas with a firing squad the marksmen are sometimes less precise.

I remember getting a taxi ride in Boston from a Ugandan driver. While stuck in traffic, he told me about a school tour he was taken on when he was aged twelve. The entire school was bussed to the football stadium in Kampala, where the dictator Idi Amin was staging a mass execution. He gleefully told me how a dozen prisoners were tied to stakes and shot, then replaced by another dozen. The bodies would fall on top of those executed a few minutes earlier. After one group of prisoners were shot and fell, one man staggered to his feet to great cheers from the full stadium. But the firing squad reloaded and all of them shot him again. He fell on top of the heap of bodies, then, unbelievably, he rose again. But after the third volley, he stayed down.

The taxi driver was laughing as he recalled the incident and described it as one of the highlights of his childhood.

This gruesome memory highlights one problem of public executions: they desensitize people to violence. This is one reason why all western countries now conduct executions behind prison walls.

The United States has used firing squads often during war but less often for civilian executions. Since 1608, only 142 men have been judicially shot in America or by the British colony that preceded it. One of the most remarkable executions happened in Nevada in May of 1913. Andriza Mircovich, a barely literate Serbian immigrant, was convicted of murder and offered the choice of death by hanging or firing squad. He opted for the bullet—but there was a problem. No one had ever faced a firing squad in Nevada and no one was willing to be part of the squad. So a shooting machine was created. The machine consisted of a rack of three guns which would be fired automatically when a string was cut. Despite the fact that there was no human shooter, the prison authorities loaded a blank charge in one of the guns. There were three strings and no one knew which ones were connected to the shooting machine. Three prison warders were chosen and given scissors; they cut the strings simultaneously.

The machine worked perfectly but was never used again. Nevada went back to hanging before switching to the electric chair, gas chamber, and lethal injection. Since the reinstatement of the death penalty in 1976, there have been only three executions by firing squad, all in Utah. The last was of Ronnie Lee Gardner, a double murderer. He was shot by a five-man squad on June 18, 2010. But that may change with the decline in support for lethal injection.

The commission's objections to the firing squad were, first of all, that it needed a number of trained marksmen rather than a single executioner—secondly, that it might make the public blasé about the use of firearms against people.

METHOD EIGHT: STONING

This is a horrific method of execution, still used in a dozen countries around the Middle East and Asia, from Pakistan to the Persian Gulf. The victim, often a woman, is buried in the ground with her head and torso (or her head only) protruding, and the crowd of onlookers all throw stones at her until she is reduced to a bloody pulp. It is a slow and torturous form of death, one of the few medieval and ancient barbaric methods to survive into modern times.

Stoning has a long history; it is mentioned several times in the Bible. A sentence of stoning could be for crimes such as cursing God, gathering wood on the Sabbath, and adultery. Today it is reserved for adultery and similar offenses against morality and is confined to Muslim countries, being a part of Sharia Law, the religious law based (very loosely, some would say) on the Koran and other traditional sources.

Depending on the local interpretation, stoning is the punishment for adultery or the punishment for married people committing adultery. In Afghanistan, Iran, Nigeria, and Saudi Arabia married adulterers get stoned, while unmarried adulterers get flogged 100 times. Other countries stone them all. What is truly horrific is that their definition of adultery is very loose. A thirteen-year-old girl gang-raped in Somalia in 2008 was stoned to death for adultery, despite her age and her complete lack of consent. In Pakistan, a woman was stoned for possessing a mobile phone. Often the sentences are imposed by ad hoc tribal courts in areas where Sharia law is accepted.

Many Muslims, including senior scholars and clerics, are unhappy with stoning as a punishment, claiming that it is not a legitimate part of Sharia law, as it was never mentioned in the Koran. But it has widespread public support. A survey by PEW Research in 2010 found that the majority of people in four out of seven Muslim countries surveyed supported stoning as a punishment for adultery. Turkey and Lebanon were sharply opposed to the punishment, but countries like Egypt, Jordan, and Pakistan overwhelmingly supported it. The survey did not include Saudi Arabia or the Gulf States, where support would likely be very high.

Beyond listing it as a method, the Gerry Commission did not consider stoning as appropriate for America.

A NEW METHOD: ELECTROCUTION

Having considered all the methods then in use, the commission turned to a possible new method, namely electricity. They argued that it was the duty of the justice system to impose death as quickly, painlessly, and efficiently as possible. As electricity travels so much faster than a nerve impulse, they maintained that death would occur before a pain signal could return to the brain and be registered there, making electrocution a truly painless method. If the current was kept on for a minute, the nervous system overload and heart failure caused by the electricity would be irreversible, making resuscitation impossible.

Their opinions were backed up by experts, including Professor Elihu Thomson. Professor Thomson, originally from Britain, was an inventor and academic with unparalleled experience in the new science of electricity. He was a founder of the Thomson-Houston Electric Light Company, which would eventually merge with Edison's company to form General Electric. The professor wrote to the commission saying that alternating current would provide the swiftest death and that an apparatus could be constructed cheaply. He suggested applying the current from the base of the spine to the top of the head. The commission report also included the letter from Edison, backing alternating current as the executioner's current.

But in addition to expert testimony, they had practical experiments to back up their findings. A Buffalo native, Dr. George E. Fell, had been experimenting with the lethal current and the commission had watched some of his experiments. Fell was a member of the Society for the Prevention of Cruelty to Animals and when the Buffalo society decided to rid the streets of the city of stray animals, he stepped forward to volunteer for the job. A friend of Southwick's, he was equally convinced that electrocution would prove a painless death. So he devised a method of electrocuting the stray animals.

The commission watched a demonstration in the police station of the city. He did not use a chair for his grisly work. Instead, he had a pine box lined with zinc, a good conductor. The box was half-filled with salty water, another good conductor. Each animal to be euthanized had a muzzle placed over its snout and a bare copper bit in its mouth. The animal then stood in the brine, and the switch was thrown on. The result, in trial after trial, was instant death. Dr. Fell told the commission that even a full-grown man would be killed instantly by the amount of power in an ordinary electric light circuit. This, as it turned out, was far from true. But the principal was proved. Electrocution did kill.

After studying all the facts, the commission suggested a special chair be constructed, with a headrest and a footrest for the electrodes. It would cost just fifty dollars to construct and would not be expensive to hook up to the local power supply. Alternatively, the prisons could purchase generators to allow far greater current to be used. The commission suggested three generators be purchased, one for each prison that would be carrying out executions. The chairs would run on the generators, but could use local power as a backup if the generators failed.

One of the controversial recommendations of the commission was that executions should be held in secret, with no press observers. The commission said that this was not to limit the freedom of the press, but rather to prevent the press feeding the "vicious and morbid appetite" of the public.

Early in 1888, Charles T. Saxton, the chair of the Assembly's Judiciary Committee, brought a bill before the assembly based on the findings of the Gerry Commission. Opposition was surprisingly strong, much of it coming from Catholic politicians. Their objection was not so much to the execution, but to a recommendation from the commission that the bodies of the executed should be buried anonymously in the prison rather than being returned to relatives for Christian burial. In the end, there was a compromise; relatives could ask for Christian burial in a spot of consecrated ground within the prison. After this, the opposition evaporated and the bill passed comfortably. Just eight opposed it when it came to a vote, with eighty-seven in favor. The bill got a rough ride in the Senate, but passed. On June 4, 1888, Governor Hill signed the Electrical Execution Bill into law. It would come into effect at the start of the following year.

The electric chair was now a reality. Everyone waited in anticipation of its first victim. But the details still had to be worked out. The chief detail was how the power would be delivered to the chair. Would the prison service use Edison's direct current, or the newer alternating current? It was a question that would embroil the nascent electric chair in a commercial war that had nothing to do with the administration of justice.

4

THE WAR OF THE CURRENTS

Two things drive America: power and money. Not power in the political sense—that follows the money. But power in an industrial sense. An industrial nation needs power to drive the wheels of commerce, and America relies on oil. This need drives foreign policy, tax regimes, and even environmental policy. But oil is not the only source of power. America has been dependent on electricity for nearly one and a half centuries.

Electricity has been vaguely known about for a millennium but only since 1600 has it been studied in any systematic way. Benjamin Franklin was one of the most important of the early scientists who tried to understand what the force was. Famously, he flew a dampened kite in 1752 with a key hanging from it and drew sparks from the key during a lightning storm, proving that lightning was electricity.

In 1800 the voltaic pile was created by Alessandro Volta in 1800. This was a primitive battery consisting of layers of zinc and copper in acid, and it provided a steady current that researchers could study. The understanding of electricity swiftly grew. In 1821 Michael Faraday, an English scientist, invented the first electric motor. Ten years later he invented a machine that would turn rotary motion into electricity—the world's first electric generator. If you spun the generator, power would come out. How much power depended on the speed at which you spun it, the strengths of the magnets used, the amount of copper in the coil, and other factors. It was a major advance, but it would be another forty years before the primitive dynamo was refined to such an extent as to be commercially viable.

By 1860, with the work of physicist James Clerk Maxwell, electricity was understood enough to be exploited. Inventors and electrical engineers such as Alexander Graham Bell, Thomas Edison, Ernst Werner von Siemens, Lord Kelvin, Nikola Tesla, and George Westinghouse began to explore ways of using electricity to power a range of inventions that would change the world. Electricity was no longer a scientific curiosity. It was swiftly becoming an essential tool for modern life. As steam (and thus coal) had been the driving force for the first industrial revolution from the middle of the eighteenth century, now electricity became the driving force for the second industrial revolution.

Faraday's dynamo was now coming into its own. If power could be provided to turn a generator, electricity could be produced. The power came from a number of sources. Oil or coal could be burned to turn a steam engine which would drive the generator, or a river could be dammed and the falling water used to turn a wheel attached to a generator. Two types of power were produced—direct current and alternating current.

To understand the difference is crucial to understanding the War of Currents that shaped the history of the electric chair. At its most basic, electric current is the flow of electrically charged subatomic particles (electrons) along a wire. Let's take the example of a light bulb, as perfected by Thomas Edison. The electrons, or electric current, flow into a bulb. The wire narrows to a thin filament of tungsten which the electricity flows through. But as it flows, it heats the filament until it glows white-hot, and this produces the light that illuminates our homes. The electricity can flow from one side of the filament to the other and out again, or it can move over and back across the filament. Imagine the filament is a tube containing a handful of marbles. In the first case, the marbles enter from one side, flow through the tube, and flow out the other side. In the second case, the marbles shake over and back across the filament, but never leave it. The first case is direct current or DC; the second is alternating current or AC. In direct current, the electricity moves from the generator, through the system of wires and appliances, and back to the generator, like water going from a reservoir through the pipes and out the other end at the faucet. In alternating current, the generator causes the electrons in the wire to vibrate over and back, but no electrons travel along the complete circuit of wires to arrive back at their starting point.

Both systems have their advantages and disadvantages. As with driving on the left- or the right-hand side of the road, it was fairly much a matter of choice at the start. Like Betamax and VHS in the early days of videotape the market would eventually decide which would prevail. Each side had its champions. The favorite of Thomas Edison was DC, while George Westinghouse preferred AC. The battle between both men for how America would have its electricity delivered is now known as The War of the Currents. It shaped so much of the modern world, including how we executed people, for more than a century.

Thomas Alva Edison was born on February 11, 1847, in Milan, Ohio, and grew up in Port Huron, Michigan. After three months of traditional schooling he was homeschooled by his mother and developed a love for natural philosophy (what we now call science). When he was old enough, he began earning a living selling snacks on trains that ran from Port Huron into Detroit, but he also maintained a small laboratory in the train where he conducted experiments and continued his education. From the start he had an entrepreneurial streak, setting up his own newspaper, the *Grand Trunk Herald*, for the trains. He was a talented young businessman with a passion for science.

Eventually he set up fourteen companies, including General Electric, which is still one of the largest publicly traded companies in the world. He moved to New Jersey in his early twenties and his career really took off. He set up a research facility at Menlo Park, a part of Raritan Township, Middlesex County, New Jersey (near Newark). His first invention was an improved telegraphic device, but when he patented the phonograph in 1877 he became a nationally known innovator.

It allowed, for the first time, the human voice to be recorded and became the basis of today's multibillion dollar music industry. He became widely known as the Wizard of Menlo Park.

At the research facility he had a large number of talented staff working for him. At one point his roster of employees included Nikola Tesla, the only man to rival him as the most prolific inventor and shaper of the modern world. The research facility took up two full blocks and was stocked with just about every device and material known to man, so that Edison would have whatever he needed instantly on hand.

Other notable inventions flowing from the wizard's lair included the motion picture camera and the light bulb. Contrary to popular myth, Edison did not actually invent the bulb, but he designed the first practical, mass-produced bulb that would not blow every second time it was used. In the case of the light bulb, he perfected the ideas of others. By the end of his career, he held 1,093 patents for new inventions. It would not be unfair to say he helped shape the future of the world. His innovations led to electric light and power, sound recording, motion pictures, and telecommunications. He produced a machine for counting votes, a battery for an electric car, new telegraph transmitters—the list goes on.

Edison founded the Edison Electric Illuminating Company of New York on December 17, 1880. He began by installing a central generating station on Pearl Street in Lower Manhattan. The "Jumbo" dynamos (the largest ever built and named after a popular circus elephant) each weighed twenty-seven tons and had an output of 100 kilowatts, enough to power more than 1,100 lights. There were six dynamos in all, powered by large steam engines. In the summer of 1881, Edison began laying underground cables to deliver the power.

On September 4, 1882, the switch was thrown and the power began to flow through the first power grid in the world. The new electric light could compete price-wise with gas light and was brighter. Within a month he had fifty-nine customers, and within a year, five hundred. This was the business of the future. But there were rival developers. The Brush Electric Light Company installed carbon arc lights along Broadway. The Brooklyn Bridge was lit by seventy arc lamps from the United States Illuminating Company. In 1887 H. H. Westinghouse (a younger brother of George) established the Safety Electric Light and Power Company to exploit the new alternating current in New York. Other companies were set up to power neighboring boroughs. By 1900 there were more than thirty companies generating and distributing power in New York alone.

And Edison had problems aside from his rivals; as a self-educated man, he had his blind spots. One was that his knowledge of science was extensive but patchy. He knew some areas backwards, but to the end of his life it is doubtful whether he ever fully understood AC. Many of his competitors did. One of those was George Westinghouse.

As an inventor, only the enigmatic and eccentric East European Nikola Tesla could rival Edison. But as a businessman, Westinghouse was the real competition.

George Westinghouse was born on October 6, 1848, in Central Bridge, New York. At the age of fifteen he enlisted during the Civil War. After the war he went to college but dropped out quickly. At nineteen he patented his first invention, the rotary steam engine. This technology eventually led to the internal combustion engine, the basis of the automobile industry. He followed up with a number of transport inventions. The most important was a train-braking system capable of stopping all the carriages simultaneously. It is still used to this day.

By 1870 Westinghouse was investing in gas distribution and telephone lines, which led logically to an interest in the new technology of electricity. He began by studying Edison's distribution system and decided that it was fine on a small scale but would prove difficult to scale up. Edison was using DC, at a low voltage. There were serious power losses during the transmission of the current. But if AC was used, the voltage could be stepped up with a transformer. This high voltage current could be transmitted over high-tension wires, then stepped down at the other end so that it could be used domestically. Far less power would be lost during transmission.

In 1885 Westinghouse imported a number of transformers from Europe, along with a Siemens AC generator, and set up his own network in Pittsburgh. He refined the system a year later in Great Barrington, Massachusetts. He set up a hydroelectric generator that produced 500 volts. A transformer stepped this up to 3,000 volts for distribution, and then a transformer at the other end dropped it down to 100 volts so that householders could power their lights. It was a far more efficient system than the direct current grid of Edison and allowed power to be delivered over far greater distances. The Current War was on in earnest.

Initially the advantage seemed to be with Edison. Not only was he an American institution, his DC had some advantages. It could be used in conjunction with batteries, which meant there was a backup in case of power outages (not possible with alternating current). It worked well with his new light bulb (the chief electrical device of the day) and it could power an electric motor. At that stage, an AC motor had not been invented.

More importantly, Edison had invented a meter which could measure how much current had been used, essential for billing purposes. He held the patents, so he was paid every time a rival company used his technology. He was going to make money not just off his own work, but off everyone else's. He was not prepared to lose that.

Alternating current technology was being steadily developed in Europe though, and slowly made inroads in America. Westinghouse was the first advocate of the new system and by 1888 he had backed Nikola Tesla who invented an engine that could work off the newer current. He then hired Tesla for a year. Tesla had worked previously with Edison but walked out after a short period when the Wizard of Menlo Park had refused to pay him a bonus agreed upon for vast improvements he had made in Edison's dynamos. The presence of an inventor every bit as clever and visionary as Edison—but a lot better versed in AC—was a decisive factor in the trade war.

Edison had banked on a large number of medium-sized generators, delivering power at a steady voltage of a little over 100 V through a series of heavy copper wires. The wires were expensive, but the low voltage meant that contact with an exposed wire was rarely fatal. Safety was a big consideration for Edison. One huge drawback, though, was that the power station could not be more than a mile from the end user or the power would not reach the whole way. That meant every small town needed its own generator, and every city would need several of them. A city like New York might need several hundred power stations.

Westinghouse's system, AC at high voltage, would allow power to be transmitted over far longer distances, and the higher the voltage, the longer the wires could stretch. Today voltages of up to 765,000 are common. With AC one could use fewer but bigger power stations. Because Westinghouse used transformers to drop the voltage back down, he could control what the customer got. Households could get 100 volts for their bulbs. Heavy industry could get 500 volts for their motors. For Edison to offer this service with DC, he needed to run a separate wire for each voltage level needed, an expensive and cumbersome undertaking. Although he liked to lay wires underground, Edison was often forced to string his heavy wires (heavier by far than Westinghouse's) on poles. During the Great Blizzard of 1888 several New Yorkers met their deaths when the wires came down under the weight of snow and electrocuted them.

Alternating current was even more dangerous. And this was the key to Edison's battle strategy.

His first step was a massive publicity campaign highlighting the dangers of alternating current. He had two targets—the general public and politicians. He urged several states to limit the voltage in transmission wires to 800 volts, which would have severely hampered the AC entrepreneurs. And he distributed thousands of pamphlets, purportedly from safety organizations, to the public outlining the dangers of high voltage AC. It was a smear campaign that would have done justice to the dirtiest political dogfight of the last century.

One of Edison's favorite ploys was to stage a press conference at which he would subject animals to electric shock in front of the assembled reporters. His team of technicians would scour the neighborhood for stray cats and dogs and would bring one of the unfortunate animals to the event. The animal would be placed upon a metal plate or in a shallow basin of water (a good conductor), and his team would begin by administering an electric shock.

The first shock would be DC and the animal would squeal, jump, and in other ways make plain its discomfort. Once the poor animal was calmed down, a second shock was administered, this one at a higher voltage of DC. Again the animal would suffer but survive the experience. Finally, the animal was secured in place, and the alternating current was sent coursing through its body. There were often sparks and occasionally the smell of burnt flesh. The animal would drop dead, proving conclusively that DC was dangerous but survivable while AC was a proven killer.

Edison even tried to popularize the phrase "westinghoused" for being electrocuted. But as one reporter pointed out after watching the execution of an animal in the name of commerce, the poor beast was so weakened by the two shocks of DC that he was only hanging on to life by the merest thread. A loud noise would have been sufficient to have finished him off at that point.

Cats and dogs were the most common victims of "westinghousing," and Edison's employees began going to animal shelters; but the ASPCA objected, so Edison's employees picked up strays from the streets. They even put a donkey and cow to death during these grisly demonstrations. Their message was clear: alternating current kills.

The first of these demonstrations was held in 1888 in New York. The circumstances were as follows: the New York legislature passed a bill on June 4, allowing electrocution to be used as a method of execution. The following day, self-taught engineer Harold Brown wrote a letter to the *New York Evening Post* outlining the dangers of alternating current and accusing George Westinghouse of placing greed ahead of public safety. Brown then teamed up with Edison.

Brown had been a salesman with the Western Electric Company and the Brush Electric Company, selling devices such as the Electric Pen, one of Edison's less successful inventions. It was a primitive duplication system, soon replaced by the typewriter. But Brown had ambitions to move out of sales. His opportunity came with the Current Wars, when his letter to the paper brought him to Edison's attention. He was taken on board for the campaign of disinformation but was paid in secret so that he could appear to be independent.

Engraved invitations were sent out to the members of the New York City Board of Electrical Control, leading figures in the new electric light industry, other interested parties, and the press, inviting them to a demonstration in the School of Mines, Columbia College.

During that demonstration, a large seventy-six-pound dog named Dash was produced. Brown first sent 1,000 volts of DC through the animal, which caused it considerable discomfort but did not kill it. Then he used 300 volts of AC and kept the current flowing until the animal stopped jerking and whimpering and was declared dead. Brown then told the audience that AC was only suitable for "the dog pound, the slaughterhouse, and the state prison."

There were a few things that the public did not realize about the electrocution of animals. The first is that the human body can withstand very high voltages if the current is low—Tasers frequently use very high voltages. What kills is not the voltage but the current. And Brown and Edison made sure to use very high current levels for the AC portion of their demonstration. Also, the animal had been weakened by the first shock and so was more likely to succumb to the second.

Following the lecture, Brown began paying local children twenty-five cents a dog to continue his demonstrations. During one of the executions, Edison employee Arthur Kennelly had been severely shocked himself while holding down a small dog.

The second demonstration, also in the School of Mines, involved the electrocution of three animals. A sixty-one pound mongrel and a ninety-one pound Newfoundland were quickly dispatched, the deaths taking only seconds. Then they came to the third animal, a fifty-three pound setter-Newfoundland cross. They ran the 300 volts AC through the dog for a full four minutes before it finally collapsed, tongue lolling out and a smell of burning flesh filling the hot and fetid room. Brown smiled afterward and said, "All of the physicians present expressed the opinion that a dog had a higher vitality than a man, and that therefore a current which killed a dog would be fatal to a man."

Brown was confident that his efforts would result in AC being limited to 300 volts, which would completely eliminate its advantage over DC when it came to power transmission. If this happened, Edison would win the War of the Currents.

Some time before the War of the Currents had begun, the New York Commission had started looking for alternatives to hanging and other methods of execution. Although he was personally opposed to the death penalty, Edison knew that the findings of the commission could make a powerful propaganda tool. Although he did not invent the electric chair or personally work on creating it, he backed those who did. Edison's key message—his only real message—was safety. On every other front, alternating current had him beaten. But if condemned prisoners were executed with alternating current, what greater statement of its dangers to human life would be needed? He made his equipment and research available to Brown, but it was his last desperate throw of the dice. Eventually economics dictated that AC was the most practical way of transmitting power over long distances. In 1890, the DC power station in Willamette Falls, Oregon, was destroyed by a flood and the company replaced their dynamos with AC ones from Westinghouse, paving the way for the first proper long-distance transmission of electricity. The same year, a station was built in Niagara Falls to supply New York with affordable AC power. The war was over; Edison had lost. In 1892 his company, General Electric, had to switch to AC.

One of the legacies of this turbulent era was Old Sparky.

5

THE DEVELOPMENT OF THE ELECTRIC CHAIR

The death penalty commission had reported back to the New York State Legislature, recommending electrocution as the most modern and humane method of executing prisoners. But how was it to be done? You could not ask convicts to urinate on live wires or to touch a non-insulated spot and hope for the best. Some mechanism was needed. The Legislature sought advice from the Medico-Legal Society of New York. The society's chair was Dr. Frederick Peterson, who had assisted Harold Brown in his dog-killing experiments. So from the start he leaned towards AC. He contacted Brown.

The two men retired to Edison's laboratory in West Orange and began to experiment in earnest on how to kill animals with AC. On November 15, 1888, they reported back to the society, and their report was honest. Either current would kill. But they said they would prefer to use AC. The society postponed a decision for a month.

Brown knew he had to pull off a spectacular stunt to ensure AC triumphed over DC and would become known as the killer current. So he decided to scale up his experiments, electrocuting, or "westinghousing," large animals closer to humans in size. On December 5, he conducted a public demonstration before doctors, reporters, and two members of the New York State Death Commission, including the Buffalo dentist Dr. Southwick, long a proponent of electrocution. This time, Edison himself attended, lending the macabre proceedings a veneer of respectability.

They began by leading a calf onto a sheet of tin. The calf was cut on the forehead and the upper spine, and wet sponges were applied. Wires from the sponges ran via an alternator back to the tin base. After thirty seconds of applying 700 volts, the calf fell heavily to the floor, dead. A second calf took just five seconds to collapse. But this was merely the appetizer; the entrée was yet to come.

A large horse weighing 1,230 pounds was led forward. Copper wires were tied around its forelocks, and everyone stood back. If this went wrong, no one wanted a broken shoulder from the flailing hooves. When everyone was well clear of the animal, the current was turned up. As it reached 700 volts, the horse slumped forward to its knees and keeled over, dead. The following morning the *New York Times* proclaimed: "The experiments proved the alternating current to be the most deadly force known to science, and that less than half the pressure used in this city for electric lighting by this system is sufficient to cause instant death. After January 1, the alternating current will undoubtedly drive the hangman out of business in this State."

A few days later the Medico-Legal Society gave their verdict: it was a thumbs up for AC. It recommended that prisoners be electrocuted in "a recumbent position, on a table covered with rubber, or the sitting position, in a chair especially constructed for the purpose."

Brown and Peterson got to work immediately. Dr. Southwick was a dentist and was used to dealing with patients in a chair, so that is what he wanted. They began working on a chair that would electrocute someone to death quickly and with the least possible drama.

George Westinghouse was furious; he did not want his transmission system associated with killing prisoners. He fired off a letter to the newspapers, pointing out that many people had received shocks of

1,000 volts or more from AC and had not only survived, but had been uninjured. He accused Harold Brown of carrying out misleading experiments for publicity.

Brown responded by challenging the industrialist to an electric duel! He suggested that he be wired to a DC generator while Westinghouse was attached to an AC generator. Both men would be given an initial shock of 100 volts. Then the voltage would be increased in steps of 50 volts until one or other passed out or admitted that their system was more dangerous. It was getting preposterous.

Westinghouse wisely ignored the challenge and the duel of the currents never happened. But Brown was employed by the New York State prison system as their first electrical expert. He was officially the man who would build the first electric chair. It was a solid oak affair, with sturdy legs and arms with straps, so that a prisoner could be held in place. Most importantly, it would be connected to one of Westinghouse's generators. It would be a spectacular PR coup. Criminality and AC linked in one very public death. Edison was delighted. Westinghouse was horrified.

Brown constructed and tested the apparatus until he was sure it would kill a human infallibly. Then he sold the chair and its accoutrements to the State of New York for $8,000. Old Sparky was ready for the first victim to be sacrificed to the progress of science.

Of course, it had not been a smooth development. For one thing, George Westinghouse refused to sell a generator to Brown. He might not have been able to prevent AC from being used, but he was under no obligation to help it. Eventually Brown had to turn to his benefactor Edison, writing in March 1889: "I have been trying for the past week to buy, borrow, or steal a Westinghouse dynamo, but have been unsuccessful. I am afraid therefore that we shall have to trespass again upon your good nature."

He proposed that Edison modify one of the Siemens AC dynamos in the laboratory so that it could produce a continuous stream of 1,000 volts AC. Edison agreed and experimentation continued. After watching the progress, the state finally agreed that they would purchase three AC generators for $7,000, but only if the first execution went smoothly. The generators were for Sing Sing, Auburn, and Dannemora prisons.

At this point, Brown got a break. A competitor of Westinghouse's, Charles Coffin of the Thomson-Houston Company, secretly agreed to acquire three second-hand generators and sell them to Brown. With the chair built and the generators secured, they were now ready for the first modern execution.

6

WILLIAM KEMMLER, THE POOR PEDDLER

William Francis Kemmler was an illiterate son of German immigrant parents, raised in near poverty in Philadelphia. He was one of only two children who survived out of a family of eleven. Born on May 9, 1860, he had finished with his education within the first decade of his life and was out on the street hustling for a living. For seven years, he shined shoes, sold newspapers, and helped out in his father's butcher shop. But at the age of seventeen, he got a job in a brickyard and began putting money aside. Within two years he had purchased a horse and cart, allowing him to set up as an independent trader, peddling fruit and vegetables.

Once he could afford to, he developed a taste for whiskey. He became a heavy drinker, and like many a drinker before him, he did not display his best judgment when under the influence of the bottle. After one spectacular bender he woke up to find that he had married Ida Forter in Camden, New Jersey. Two days later he came to his senses when he realized that she was already married and had not divorced her first husband. He left her and ran back to Philadelphia, where he immediately moved in with another married woman, Matilda (Tillie) Ziegler. She had left her husband because of his fondness for drink and lewd women—that could have described her new man, Kemmler, to a tee. She had a young daughter, Ella.

A little over a week after moving in with Ziegler, Kemmler sold his fruit and vegetable business and the little property he had; and the couple, with Ella, moved to Buffalo, where they lived together as husband and wife. He even used the name John Hort to further the deception, and he applied locally for a peddler's license. He began working with a partner, John de Bella.

But all was not rosy in the new household. Kemmler was regularly drunk and Ziegler was regularly unfaithful. A year and a half passed in constant bickering and Kemmler was convinced that his lover was cheating on him with his business partner. He was drinking more than ever but still managed to run and grow his business. That all came to an abrupt end on the morning of March 29, 1899. That morning, he entered the barn where he stored his horse and supplies, and he seemed sober and in control, according to his employees. But as he was giving them their instructions for the morning, Tillie came out of their apartment and asked him to fetch her some fresh eggs. She then turned and walked back into the building.

Instead of getting eggs, Kemmler picked up a hatchet and followed her into the kitchen. She was at the sink, clearing away the breakfast crockery. Ignoring four-year-old Ella, who stood by watching with horror, he walked up behind Tillie and struck viciously at her back with the hatchet. As she staggered and turned, he continued to rain blows down on her head and shoulders. He struck her twenty-six times in all, leaving her in a bleeding pulp on the floor. Tossing the hatchet aside, he turned and rushed from the room, leaving Ella still paralyzed with fear.

Kemmler made no effort to conceal what he had done. He walked straight to the front of the house, which was the part occupied by his landlady Mary Reid. His hands and arms covered in gore, he calmly told her, "I have killed her. I had to do it; there was no help for it. One of us had to die. I'll take the rope for it." A moment later, Ella rushed in, confirming the grisly news, saying, "Papa has killed mamma."

Kemmler calmly picked up his stepdaughter and placed her on a chair before cleaning his hands and arms and leaving the house. He was accosted by a neighbor who demanded that he fetch a doctor. Instead, he went in search of a public house. He banged on the counter and called for a drink, but the neighbor, who had followed him, told the barman not to serve him. While the two men quarreled, the first police officer, John O'Neill, arrived on the scene.

"Have you been licking your wife?" he asked.

"Yes—with a hatchet," said Kemmler.

They returned to the bloody kitchen where, unbelievably, Tillie Ziegler was still alive. Her arms were moving ineffectually and she was moaning in pain. She died a number of hours later in the hospital.

Kemmler was unrepentant, blaming the killing on his quick temper, and telling investigators that the sooner he was hanged the better.

Five weeks later, on May 6, the trial opened. The accused was subdued, and one newspaper described his appearance as that of "mild-eyed imbecility." He was accompanied by his brother Henry Hort. Henry's feelings must have been mixed. The two brothers had ended up with two sisters; Henry's wife was the sister of Kemmler's lover and victim. Henry's wife also attended the court, but she was definitely not on William Kemmler's side. She was there for her sister.

The prosecution painted a picture of a man who was a heavy drinker and prone to violent outbursts of temper. He was jealous of his business partner, whom he suspected of sleeping with his wife.

The defense case was simple. Kemmler was a habitual alcoholic and was incapable of premeditated murder. That required a clear and calculating mind. He had killed while his judgment was befuddled with drink. While he was not actually drunk at the time of the killing, habitual drinking had left his mind deeply affected.

Alcoholic insanity is a difficult case to prove. At best, Kemmler could hope to escape the rope. His defense knew there could not be an acquittal for a man who had hacked his partner to death in front of her daughter.

Defense witnesses established that Kemmler had been drunk every day for two months prior to the killing. He often spent four or five dollars a day (the equivalent of over a hundred dollars today) on drink and was frequently incoherent. Several medical experts testified that continued abuse of alcohol rendered a man less capable of rational decisions

The jury took over two hours to reach a decision, long for those days. But at 11:18 a.m. on May 10—just one day after Kemmler's twenty-ninth birthday—they returned a verdict of guilty.

The *Buffalo Courier* reported that as Kemmler rose to receive the verdict, "There was a sharp clap of thunder. Rain dashed against the windows, and as Kemmler turned to face the jury there was a flash of lightning typical of his coming fate . . . The moment was decidedly prophetic."

Sentencing was put back to May 14, and the courtroom was packed. Everyone was wondering if Kemmler would be the first person sentenced under the new Electrical Execution Act. The peddler, who had remained calm and sullen throughout the trial, was suddenly looking nervous.

Judge Henry Childs turned to the prisoner and pronounced the dreaded sentence: "Within the week commencing Monday, June 24, 1889, within the walls of Auburn State Prison or within the yard or enclosure thereof, that you suffer the death punishment by being executed by electricity, as provided by the code of criminal procedure of the State of New York, and that you be removed to and kept in confinement in Auburn State Prison until that time. May God have mercy on your soul."

Kemmler went pale and sank to a chair before being escorted from the courthouse.

Though the execution was scheduled for six weeks later, it would be more than a year before the appeals procedure had been exhausted. William Bourke Cockran, a young Irishman who had moved to America at the age of seventeen, took up the cudgel for Kemmler. He was a rising star of the Democrat Party, a noted orator, and a highly skilled lawyer. There is some suspicion that his hefty fees, which were beyond the purse of Kemmler, were paid by Westinghouse. Legend has it that the mercenary Cockran was paid $100,000—though this figure is certainly exaggerated. What is certain is that Westinghouse was prepared to spend freely to ensure that his dynamos were not associated with the electric chair.

Cockran appealed against electrocution as being "cruel and unusual," and thus unconstitutional. There is no doubt that it was unusual at that point, but its supporters thought it was anything but cruel—though nobody would know for sure until after the first execution. It was known that if the voltage was too high there could be burning of the flesh at the point of contact with the electricity, but if the person was killed or rendered unconscious instantly, this would not be cruel.

The first round of hearings went against Cockran and his client. Edison himself testified on July 23. He said that he had conducted experiments on his 250 employees to determine the electrical resistance of a human body, and he could guarantee that death could be caused instantly and universally with an electric shock. But you would have to be careful not to use too much power, as that might burn the body.

"Have a nice little bonfire with him, would you?" asked Cockran.

"Oh no, just carbonize him," Edison replied.

At a lower power setting the results would be less spectacular.

"His temperature," said Edison, "would rise three or four degrees above the normal and after a while he'd be mummified. The heat would evaporate all the fluids in his body and leave him mummified."

But Edison was adamant that if the current was correctly controlled, instant death would result without the distressing side effects. Cockran lost the first round, and appealed to the Supreme Court of New York. While that appeal was pending, Brown installed the first electric chair at Auburn. He was assisted by Edwin Davis. Davis, who was in his early forties at the time, would soon be appointed the state's electrician and would oversee 240 executions before his retirement in 1914.

On December 30, the Supreme Court handed down their decision, agreeing with Judge Day in the lower court that the execution by electrocution was not a cruel and unusual punishment. In February 1890 the Court of Appeal heard and rejected the final pleas on behalf of the condemned man. On March 31, Kemmler was told that he would be executed during the final week of April.

He said, "I am guilty and must be punished. I am ready to die. I am glad I am not going to be hung. I think it is much better to die by electricity than it is by hanging. It will not give me any pains."

Final adjustments were made to the chair. It was smaller and neater than originally envisioned, with a high back and a comfortable seat, and a footrest.

But there was one final throw of the dice. Westinghouse had hired Roger Shermann, a high-powered attorney, who obtained a writ of habeas corpus demanding Kemmler be produced at the Circuit Court of New York on June 10—in layman's terms, a stay of execution. And there was more hope—a bill was introduced before the New York Assembly abolishing capital punishment. The bill passed in the Assembly but lost in the Senate. And Shermann failed in his last-minute appeals too, losing out in the Supreme Court. By June 23, all avenues had been exhausted, and all barriers to the execution removed.

On the morning of July 12, 1890, William Kemmler was led from Auburn prison to a train, which brought him to Buffalo. Dressed in a dapper gray suit, with a "natty black derby hat," he sat before Judge Childs, who said that he hoped the long delay in the appeals process had given Kemmler time to reflect on the enormity of his crime and the justice of his conviction. He then ordered the execution date for the first week of August at Auburn Prison.

The New York Assembly issued a gag order on reporting of the new execution method, banning reporters from being present among the witnesses. But Warden Durston allowed Frank W. Mack of the Associated Press and George G. Bain of the United Press to witness first execution as private citizens. Though they were not there in an official capacity, they would be allowed publish their impressions. Their reports were widely circulated and shared among the nation's papers. On August 7, the *New York Herald* reported the previous day's proceedings, saying: "The killing of Kemmler marks, I fear, the beginning and the end of electrocution, and it wreaths in shame the ages of the great Empire State who, entrusted with the terrific responsibility of killing a man as a man was never killed before, brought to the task imperfect machinery and turned an execution into a horror."

Predictably, it had not gone according to plan.

"The scene of Kemmler's execution was too horrible to picture. Men accustomed to every form of suffering grew faint as the awful spectacle was unfolded before their eyes. Those who stood the sight were filled with awe as they saw the effects of this most potent of fluids, which is only partly understood by those who have studied it most faithfully, as it slowly, too slowly, disintegrated the fiber and tissues of the body through which it passed.

"The heaving of a chest which, it had been promised, would be stilled in an instant peace as soon as the circuit was completed, the foaming of the mouth, the bloody sweat, the writhing shoulders and all the other signs of life.

"Horrible as these were, they were made infinitely more horrible by the premature removal of the electrodes and the subsequent replacing of them for not seconds but minutes, until the room was filled with the odor of burning flesh and strong men fainted and fell like logs upon the floor."

The procedure had begun at five o'clock in the morning, when the chaplain and Reverend W. E. Houghton (Kemmler's spiritual adviser) went to Kemmler's cell where they found him up and awake. He was dressed in a new, dark gray suit with a vest and checked tie. He looked spruce and natty—though in the seat of his trousers a large hole for the electrode was visible. Kemmler seemed cheerful and lighthearted.

Witnesses were led into a small room—mainly doctors and legal professionals. The chair was in another room, dimly visible under gaslight. Warden Durston consulted with doctors about how long the electric shock should last. One said three seconds—another said fifteen. They compromised on ten. Then Durston went to fetch Kemmler.

The condemned man entered the death chamber calmly, walking to the chair with self-possession. He said his last words before he sat: "Well, gentlemen, I wish everyone good luck in this world, and I think

I am going to a good place, and the papers have been saying a lot of stuff that isn't so. That's all I have to say."

Then he handed his suit coat to the warden and began to unbutton his vest, but he was told he could leave that on, so he rebuttoned it. Then he sat and calmly adjusted his neck tie as Durston secured the electrode to the base of his spine through the hole in his trousers. The straps were adjusted, and then the final piece was put in place—the hood and face straps. The hood left Kemmler's mouth free to move and he whispered, "Durston, see that things are right."

"Ready?" asked Durston.

"Ready," replied the doctors who were supervising though not operating the equipment.

"Good-bye," said the warden to Kemmler, who made no reply.

The time was now 6:43 a.m., and the warden stepped to the door of the death chamber and gave the signal to the executioner, Davis. "Everything is ready," he said to the hidden electrician, who duly flicked the switch.

Suddenly the body of Kemmler convulsed in the chair, straining against all the straps. Dr. McDonald, looking at his stopwatch, called stop after ten seconds. Durston repeated the command, louder. The current was switched off, but Kemmler remained rigid in the chair. His nose appeared dark red and a fly landed on it and walked about unconcernedly.

"He's dead," two doctors (Edward Spitzka and Carlos McDonald) proclaimed. But then a third doctor, Dr. Balch, spotted a cut on Kemmler's thumb that was pumping blood in small spurts. That was a sure sign he was still alive—his heart still beating. A low cry of horror went through the crowd of witnesses.

"Turn on the current; this man is not dead," cried Dr. Spitzka.

Kemmler began to groan, the sound growing in the small room. His chest began to heave.

The District Attorney hurried from the witness room and began to walk down a corridor to get away from the horror. A sensitive man, he stumbled and fainted and needed to be revived. He did not reenter the witness room for the conclusion of the execution.

The second time, Davis stepped up the current to 2,000 volts, and he held it far longer than the ten seconds recommended by the doctors. Kemmler stopped groaning immediately but drool continued to drop from his lips down to his beard. Still the current flowed, and then the witnesses could hear a sizzling sound, as the flesh around the electrode began to cook. Smoke began to fill the small chamber, and it reeked of burning hair. Durston yelled to turn the current off.

The body remained frozen in its final throes.

Dr. Fell was the first to speak. Despite what he had witnessed, he said, "The man never suffered a bit of pain."

Dr. Spitzka agreed, saying, "The man was killed instantly, I think. Those were only muscular contractions, and the fellow never suffered any pain. That's one sure thing about it."

When he had time to reflect upon it, Spitzka was less sure, refusing to endorse the new form of execution: "For me, first the guillotine, second the gallows, and last of all, electrical execution. Never before have I felt just as I do now. What I have seen has impressed me deeply, not exactly what you would call horror, but rather with the wonder of doubt. I have seen hangings far more brutal than this execution, but I have never seen anything so awe inspiring. What I have seen satisfies me that the scale of capital punishment is first the guillotine, second the gallows, and far in the rear, the electrical execution.

"I do not regard the execution as a failure, but it did not appear to be what it had promised to be."

Westinghouse did regard it as a failure and was quick to condemn the whole experiment, telling newsmen, "I do not care to talk about it. It has been a brutal affair. They could have done better with an axe. My predictions have been verified. The public will lay the blame where it belongs and it will not be on us. I regard the manner of the killing as a complete vindication of all our claims."

Westinghouse proved to be wrong. There were severe reporting restrictions on the first execution, with only two reporters witnessing the procedure. And the version of the officials, that it had gone smoothly, became accepted. Electrocution was here to stay. But Westinghouse was also wrong in his fears that the chair would forever associate AC with death. The public did not care which form of current was used to kill condemned prisoners. And his AC system went on to win the War of the Currents. It is now used worldwide, while DC has dwindled to a few specialty uses. Edison won the battle to get his rival's current used in the chair, but he lost the war.

7

THE SPREAD OF THE CHAIR

Despite the evidence furnished by their eyes, ears, and noses, the observers at Auburn proclaimed themselves satisfied that William Kemmler had not suffered during the botched execution. Electrocution was given the green light to be rolled out across the prison system in New York. Following Kemmler, six more convicts were executed over eighteen months as authorities perfected the system. The gag order on the press was still in effect, so executions were carried out in secret. Little is known about them aside from the official reports, which, like the first, show them proceeding smoothly.

But in February 1892, new governor Roswell Flower repealed the gag order. Now the warden could invite members of the press to be among the twelve neutral observers at each execution.

The seventh victim of Old Sparky was Charles McElvaine, a nine-teen-year-old hoodlum from one of the rougher neighborhoods of Brooklyn, New York. On August 21, 1889, he got married. Two days later, he met with two young associates and broke into a neighbor-hood grocery store. The store owner, Christian Luca, who lived above the shop, woke up and disturbed the three burglars. He confronted them, but McElvaine had a knife. He ran at Luca and drove the knife repeatedly into his chest. The grocer was stabbed several times before falling to the ground, dead.

McElvaine turned to Luca's wife, who was screaming at the sight of her dying husband on the ground. He was about to attack her too when the noise alerted a passing patrolman, and McElvaine was arrested at the scene.

The *Pittsburgh Post-Gazette* reported the crime like this:

McElvaine had entered the passageway to the bedroom when Mr. Luca was awakened by the noise. He went out into the passageway where he came face to face with McElvaine. He grappled with the burglar and would have easily overpowered him, as Mr. Luca was a large, powerful man, while McElvaine was small and weak, had he not been met with a murderous knife. As soon as Luca seized the intruder a terrible struggle ensued. The noise awakened Mrs. Luca, who rushed into the room only to see her husband down on his knees by the window, and McElvaine literally hacking him to pieces with a big knife.

Caught red-handed, his conviction was a formality. But the appeals process took a full two years, during which time he was granted a retrial and once again convicted and sentenced to death. Finally the day loomed for the execution, which was to be held in Sing Sing, about thirty miles up the Hudson River from New York. The warden, W. R. Brown, invited eight reporters to witness the event, on February 7, 1892.

Once again Edwin Davis was the executioner. He was being paid his usual fee of $150 for pulling the switch. Davis was a reclusive man, unwilling to speak to reporters or allow his picture to be taken. As the years passed, he became odder and odder, as his concern for his personal safety grew. He was so worried about relatives of Old Sparky victims seeking him out that he changed his address frequently. He did not even allow the prison authorities to know where he lived by the end of his tenure as New York State Electrician. When they had a job for him, they had to post a cryptic personal advertisement in a newspaper and he would get in touch. He had an arrangement with the rail company that he would not get on board at the platform but would jump on the slowly moving train a bit outside the station.

Despite his oddities, Davis was conscientious about his job and determined to do his best to execute men cleanly and painlessly. He carried his own electrodes, which were always in immaculate condition, and he made several refinements to the chair to improve its efficiency. In fact, to this day he is the only person who has patents registered on the chair. It is very much old technology; it has not changed in over a hundred years.

For the execution of McElvaine, the authorities decided to try an experiment to improve the device. Since Kemmler's execution, the only change that had been made was the positioning of the bottom electrode. Instead of placing it at the base of the spine with the second electrode attached to a shaven spot on the victim's skull, they were now attaching the lower electrode to the victim's calf. This seemed to improve the efficiency of the device, as the skin was thin and there was nothing to impede the flow of current through the body.

But for McElvaine's execution they tried a suggestion of Edison's. He had always felt that the key to an execution was making clean contact with the electrodes. From the start Edison had suggested that the prisoner have his hands in two basins of brine. The salty water was a very good conductor of electricity but would also keep the temperature at the point of contact with the electrodes down. The theory was that the current would flow from hand to hand across the torso, stopping the heart but preventing the burning and the horrible smell of cooking flesh that was a feature of the first six electrocutions.

The chair had been modified to accommodate the new method. The arms of the chair were higher up and sloping downwards. Instead of McElvaine's arms being strapped on top of the chair arms, they were to be strapped beneath them, hands dangling free. Both his hands would then be placed in small jars containing salt water. But the electrodes for the head and legs were also in place, in case the new method did not work.

Dr. Carlos McDonald, who had been present at Kemmler's execution, was the main medical man now. He quickly explained to reporters that the new method should result in a swift and painless death: "The current will not be applied this time as before. Edison and other men have suggested that the current should be applied through the arms. We are going to test that method."

McElvaine had appeared relatively unconcerned when woken that morning and had his last breakfast of toast and milk, which he only picked at. But by execution time, his nerves were showing.

The room went quiet as McElvaine was led into the death chamber and across to the chair. He was accompanied by two Catholic priests and seemed to be nervous. He walked to the chair, clutching a brass crucifix tightly in clenched fists, mumbling, "Oh Jesus, help me. Oh Lord, I am sorry that I have offended thee. Oh Almighty God, I despise my sins. Oh Christ, have mercy. Help me, Oh Lord," a simplified version of the Catholic Act of Contrition.

As the guards began strapping him to the chair, he pressed the crucifix to his lips one final time. He appeared terrified by now; his hands were placed in the two jars of cold water. The warden dropped his handkerchief—the agreed signal—and Davis threw the switch.

The *Pittsburgh Post-Gazette* reported:

'Let her go,' shouted McElvaine and he braced his body for the shock. There was a slight grating sound as the lever moved. Electric sparks flashed up, indicating that the current was there. Then the lever passed to its last notch. The current of 1,600 volts passed into the boxes of salt water and into McElvaine's arms.

There was a convulsive movement. The prisoner's chest and body raised up an inch or two. The chest expanded. There was no sound. Part of the face that was visible turned first white, then blue. McElvaine looked like a statue. The current was kept on 43 seconds, as near as could be judged by witnesses. The official time was not announced.

'Shut it off,' cried Dr. McDonald. The lever was switched back There was a wonderful effect upon the body. From its rigid, statue-like appearance it collapsed and seemed to sink

back in the chair, limp and lifeless. The chest relaxed, and
foam began to drip from the mouth.

The silence in the execution room lasted ten seconds.
Then there was a rattling in the dead man's throat. Was it a
reflex action, or was there still life? The doctors said the former, but it was evident they were not certain, for the electrician stepped forward and, disconnecting the wires that ran into
the boxes of salt water, fastened them to the head and the leg.

The prisoner's wrist was felt, and there was a pulse.

The current was now applied in the traditional way and quickly
steam began to rise from the leg and head of the prisoner. But
Dr. McDonald assured the witnesses that it was not burning flesh, just
steam from damp electrodes.

When the power was switched off, the attending doctors pronounced McElvaine dead. McDonald concluded: "I think Mr. Edison
is right. The current should be applied through the arms. This is certainly the most successful execution that has yet taken place. Death was
instantaneous and painless beyond question. The current was turned on
the second time only to make certain."

However, in hindsight the execution was not judged such a success,
and the experiment of driving the current across the body through the
arms was never repeated. From then on, the electrodes would always be
placed on the lower leg and the crown of the head.

In addition to the eight press witnesses at the execution, there were
four civilian witnesses. One of these was Assemblyman Myer J. Stein,
who said, "It was horrible, the most sickening sight I ever witnessed."

He was so shocked that he tried to introduce a bill to the Assembly
replacing electrocution with hanging, but this failed. Electrocution had
become the accepted method of execution in the state. Soon the method
began to spread. In 1896, Ohio was the second state to build an electric chair. Massachusetts followed two years later. It was a decade before
another state switched, but the floodgates were opened. In 1907, New Jersey built their own chair. Virginia followed in 1908, and North Carolina
in 1909. Kentucky began electrocutions in 1910, South Carolina in 1912,

and Arkansas, Indiana, Pennsylvania, and Nebraska in 1913. It spread throughout the Union, with West Virginia becoming the twenty-sixth and final state to replace the gallows with the electric chair in 1949.

However, aside from a brief period in the Philippines during US rule, the electric chair was never used outside the United States. It remains a peculiarly American innovation.

New York was the state that used the electric chair more than any other. It began there, and the state initially built three chairs, one for Auburn, one for Sing Sing, and one for Dannemora. The three chairs were used until 1914, when it was decided to have only one death row prison. Sing Sing was chosen. From then on all executions took place there, with prisoners being moved to Sing Sing for their final months.

There are many rumors about what happened to the two other chairs. One of the most intriguing is that the famous magician and escape artist, Harry Houdini, bought the chair that fried Kemmler—the original electric chair. The story was widely reported.

Houdini had begun his career in the carnivals and freak shows in places like Coney Island and had always retained a love for that form of entertainment. He used to visit shows all the time, even when he became a world-famous name. One day, after performing with his wife and assistant, Bess, at Huber's Dime Museum on Coney Island, he mingled with the freaks and specialty acts—Big Alice, the Fat Lady; Emma Schaller, the Ossified Girl; and Unthan, the Legless Wonder were among the company. That day, the company was fascinated with a new exhibit, an electric chair. They were told that it was the original chair from Auburn, which had been used in Kemmler's execution. Houdini was fascinated with death and with new technology. It appealed to him on both counts. So when Huber's Dime Museum closed in 1910, he stepped in and purchased the chair, which he put in his Manhattan home. Bess hated the chair and put it out of sight whenever he was away.

After a number of years, Houdini gave the chair as a gift to a fellow magician. Walford Bodie was a Scottish showman who did a bit of everything—hypnotism, ventriloquism, and magic. But he was best known for his electric show. As part of this show, he would stage a mock execution in a replica electric chair. While the current was supposedly flowing through him, his hair would stand on end and sparks would fly. He would hold bulbs and they would light. He was a close friend of Houdini and, perhaps at Bess's insistence, Harry gave Bodie the Auburn chair in 1920. The Scottish man exhibited the chair, and during his show he condemned the practice of electrocuting prisoners, instead urging people to return to the humanity of the English gallows.

What neither Houdini nor Bodie realized was that the chair from the Huber Dime Museum was not the original chair. That was still in Auburn. During its years of use, it claimed the lives of fifty-four men and one woman. It was stored in the prison, unused, after 1914. But during a prison riot in 1929, it was destroyed by fire. Houdini's chair was a well-made fake.

In all, New York electrocuted 686 men and 9 women, with the last victim going to the chair in 1963. That was Eddie Lee Mays, an African-American from North Carolina. He had shot to death a female customer at a bar in New York during an armed robbery on March 23, 1961. She was slow to open her purse and once opened, it was empty. So he calmly put the gun to her head and killed her. He was executed on August 15, 1963, by State Electrician Dow Hover, who had held the position for a decade. A reserved man (who died by suicide several years after his retirement), Hover oversaw forty-four executions in Sing Sing, as well as a number of outside jobs for neighboring states. He was paid $150 per execution, the same as his predecessors. Not only had the chair not changed with advancing technology, the executioner's fee had not kept pace with the modern world either.

In 1965, New York removed the death penalty. It was not put back on the statute books until 1995, after a thirty year absence. But Old Sparky was never used again in the state. Now the death chamber is located at the Clinton Correctional Facility at Dannemora and lethal injection is the approved method. Since 1971, Old Sparky has been lying idle in storage at the Green Haven Correctional Facility. It will never be used again.

Throughout the United States, more than 4,300 people have been electrocuted via the chair. Through most of the twentieth century it was the most popular form of execution. But since the lifting of the moratorium on executions in 1976, it has gradually been replaced by lethal injection, which is seen as a more humane alternative. Every time someone opts for electrocution—some states give prisoners the choice of either that or the needle—the press speculation grows that this might be the last judicial electrocution. A betting man would not wager on Old Sparky ever being fired up in anger again.

A colorful though brutal period of American history is now almost certainly consigned to the past.

8

A CABINET OF CURIOSITIES—SIX NOTABLE AND UNUSUAL EXECUTIONS

Each execution follows a well-worn path. Procedures are laid down and followed by officials. Prisoners are prepared in roughly similar ways, and no matter what the method of execution—hanging, electrocution, needle, or bullet—the officials do their best to ensure that the process runs as smoothly as possible and that the prisoner meets a swift and relatively humane end.

But within these parameters, every execution is unique. Each prisoner has his or her own story, and the ripples of every action spread wide. In this chapter we will look in detail at some of the more unusual executions in the century-long history of Old Sparky. These are the stories of the youngest, the earliest, and the most unusual victims of the electric chair, from a fourteen-year-old boy to a three-ton elephant.

ONE: WILLIE FRANCIS, THE MAN WHO WAS ELECTROCUTED TWICE

One of the objectives of the electric chair was to produce an execution machine that would not permit revival. There were occasional stories of convicts being cut from the gallows and revived by their friends or families after the execution. That had to be made impossible.

Yet, in this, the electric chair failed at least once. One man survived his execution, battered, bruised, and badly burnt, but very much alive. But the story of the man who survived the electric chair had no happy ending. His execution was merely rescheduled, his survival buying him nothing more than a year of extra time.

Willie Francis was born in Louisiana in 1929. A poor African American, he finished high school early and became a clerk in a local drug store in St. Martinville. There is some suspicion, based on his later statements, that while he was employed there the store owner, Andrew Thomas, may have sexually abused the young teen. He did not remain long in the job, eventually moving on. But in 1946, an intruder broke in the home of Thomas and shot him five times as he lay in his bed.

Local cops investigated the crime but no leads showed up. Nine months passed and the crime became a cold case, unlikely ever to be solved. But then Willie Francis was in the wrong place at the wrong time. He had moved to Texas and was in the vicinity of a drug bust. He was arrested and searched. While it was obvious that he had no connection to the drugs, the cops found a wallet in his possession which belonged to Andrew Thomas. The police in St. Martinville were called, and Francis was sent home.

During the course of an extensive interrogation, Francis, a quiet man with a pronounced stutter, tried to implicate several other local youths in the killing. But eventually he made two written statements confessing that he was the gunman. In one statement, he wrote, "It was a secret about me and him." This ambiguous statement was taken by later researchers to imply that there had been some sexual abuse, though this has no other foundation than the statements of Francis.

One bit of evidence did not point to Francis: the gun used in the killing had been recovered and belonged to a cop, a deputy sheriff, who had a grudge against Thomas and who had once threatened to kill him. Conveniently, this gun, along with the bullets, disappeared from evidence shortly before the trial. To this day, motive is unclear and there is speculation that the deputy sheriff gave his gun to Francis or left it where Francis could get his hands on it. The victim was a well-known womanizer who had slept with the deputy sheriff's wife.

The trial lasted eight days. This was a lengthy trial in that era, slowed in part by the fact that Francis pleaded not guilty, despite his two written confessions. Francis could not afford proper legal representation so was represented by a court-appointed lawyer who offered no witnesses and presented no rebutting evidence. The jury had no difficulty convicting Francis and he was sentenced to the electric chair. He would not turn seventeen until close to the execution date.

Louisiana used a chair nicknamed Gruesome Gertie. During the war years the state made the decision to make Gertie mobile, so that the chair would be brought to the prison where the condemned man was being held, rather than having all the condemned men waiting on death row in one facility. The chair was a 300-pound monstrosity of heavy oak construction. It was dismantled and transported by truck from prison to prison. Two men accompanied it—an experienced guard and a prison trustee who helped with the construction. State prison warden Dennis Bazer normally traveled from the Louisiana State Penitentiary in Angola with the chair, but couldn't this time as he had an important meeting with the state governor the same day as the execution. So he sent Captain Edward Foster, a prison officer, and Vincent Vinezia, an Angola prisoner who was a trustee.

The two arrived in St. Martinville two days prior to the execution and set up the chair, connecting it to a generator running off the van engine. They tested it, and it was delivering sufficient power to get the job done. Then they adjourned to a nearby tavern and went on a two-day bender. By execution day, according to witnesses, the two men reeked of whiskey, but they seemed to be methodically connecting all the wires and electrodes and all seemed to be in order.

On the morning of the execution, a prison barber came into the New Iberia Courthouse, which had a prison wing. This was where Francis had been held since the trial. The barber shaved Francis's head. As he put away his scissors and razor afterward, he joked: "I guess that's one haircut you won't have to pay for."

Francis laughed loudly. He knew that the barber, a fellow prisoner, was trying to break the tension and put some normality into the day, and he appreciated it. Although he was doing his best to make a good show, he was terrified. A few minutes later, the sheriff and a priest arrived and Francis was put in the back of a black Ford sedan for the ride from New Iberia to the St. Martinville Prison, where Gertie had been set up. The prison was a small, red-brick structure. Outside, as the church bells tolled the hour, a large crowd had gathered. The local *Weekly Messenger* had proclaimed, in large headlines, "Negro Murderer to Die Here Today."

The sheriff did not drive directly to the prison, but took a brief detour so that Francis could see the home he had grown up in one last time. His mother was inside, but was in bed sick (perhaps from worry about her son). He did not see her, but he sighed nostalgically as the car cruised past. Then they turned towards the prison, and the final walk. Francis had been given a pair of shiny new leather shoes that morning and realized he was not going to get a chance to wear them for much more than a few yards.

The car drove past the crowd and into the prison, and then the terrified boy was led to the chair and strapped securely in. A black hood was drawn over his head and the guards left the chamber. The engine of the van outside was fired up to power the generator. The room got noisy. At 12:08 p.m. the switch was thrown and Francis's body stiffened and convulsed as expected. There was the usual low hissing of the electrical circuits. Then the scene was shattered by a scream from the electric chair.

"Stop it! Stop it! Let me breathe!" shouted Francis, shocking the witnesses. One shot back: "You're not meant to breathe."

For about thirty seconds this went on. The chair shuddered and began to slide along the polished floor, despite weighing almost 300 pounds. Then the indicators on the voltmeter dropped to zero. Foster frantically shouted to Vinezia for more power and Vinezia gunned the van, but the dials were registering nothing. After a minute, the power was switched off and the prison authorities confirmed what everyone knew. Not only was the prisoner still alive, he was conscious and screaming in agony.

The first jolt normally produced unconsciousness and no one had ever heard someone cry out from the death chair. But clearly Francis was still very much alive. They decided to try one more time. This time, when they threw the switch Francis stiffened, but it was obvious this was fear. There was no electricity going through his body.

"I'm not dying!" he bellowed, as he struggled against his restraints.

It was decided immediately not to proceed with the electrocution. Something had clearly gone wrong. A subsequent examination of the equipment revealed what had happened. Those responsible had neglected to ground the chair. Francis had escaped death, but as Sheriff E. L. Resweber said, "This boy really got a shock when they turned that machine on."

The first jolt had been sufficient to cause intense pain, leaving his heart racing. But it had not even burned his skin.

Following the failed execution, the prison governor informed Francis that they would reschedule the execution for six days' time, before having the teen led back to his cell. But a local lawyer, Bertrand DeBlanc, stepped in and took over Francis's case, lodging an immediate appeal. This was unpopular in the small Cajun town, especially as the lawyer had been a good friend of the murder victim. But DeBlanc had a strong sense of duty and knew that the young, black defendant was entitled to a proper defense. He took it all the way to the Supreme Court, arguing violations of Fifth, Eight, and Fourteenth Amendment rights (equal protection, double jeopardy, and cruel and unusual punishment). By a narrow margin his appeal failed. One of the judges who rejected the appeal actually tried to petition the governor for the sentence to be commuted to life in prison but was unsuccessful.

That Supreme Court ruling set an important precedent. It was not cruel and unusual punishment to have to be executed twice. If someone escaped the chair, the state could try again without violating the prisoner's constitutional rights.

On May 9, 1947, Francis was once again prepared for the execution chamber. This time the men responsible were sober and had tested every wire and connection. There was a lot more public scrutiny on the whole procedure. A crowd of five hundred had gathered outside the prison. Most were in favor of the second execution, but some friends and family members of Francis were also there, including his tearful mother. For the first attempt, Francis had been in his prison uniform, despite his shining new shoes. This time he was dressed in formal slacks and a spotless white shirt. He was taken from New Iberia early in the morning and driven straight to St. Martinville Prison, where he was placed in a cell for a few hours. Several members of his family came to say their last good-byes.

His last meal was prepared mid-morning. He'd have loved to have had fried chicken, his favorite, but he was a Catholic and Catholics are not allowed meat on a Friday. Instead, he asked for fried fish and potatoes and finished the plate.

When he arrived at the death chamber there were unfamiliar faces in charge. The State of Louisiana was taking no chances and had brought in an expert. Grady Jarrett was a Texan who had overseen dozens of executions, and he would make no mistakes. Local priest Father Hannigan accompanied Francis, but at the last minute the condemned man asked the priest to leave him so that he could walk to the chair unaided. He did not want to show fear or weakness. He crossed the thirteen steps to the bulky wooden structure, turned, and sat. Jarrett quickly began preparing him, tightening the straps and cutting a slit in the new trousers so that he could attach the electrode to Francis's leg. When all was ready he straightened up, then asked the prisoner if he had anything to say.

"Nothing at all," replied Francis.

Francis had entered the death chamber at 12:02 p.m., two minutes behind schedule. It took three minutes to strap him in and secure the electrodes. At 12:05 p.m. Jarrett threw the switch. They had increased the voltage from the previous time, and 2,700 volts shot through the seventeen-year-old's body. He stiffened, but nothing more. He didn't move—didn't struggle at all. It is probable that death came instantly the second time.

But the state was taking no chances. After a minute, the power was switched off, and then quickly a second jolt was administered to be sure.

At 12:10 p.m. Jarrett pronounced the prisoner dead. The man who had escaped the electric chair was not able to repeat that lucky performance.

TWO: MARTHA PLACE—FIRST WOMAN TO THE CHAIR

More than a thousand people have sat in the hot seat but less than thirty have been women. America has always shown glaring bias when it comes to the death penalty. African-Americans were more likely to be executed than whites, though that is changing. Working class are more likely to fry than middle class, poor more than rich. But the most glaring inconsistency is when it comes to women. Only twenty-six have sat in Old Sparky.

The first was Martha Place.

Martha Garretson was born in New Jersey in 1849. At the age of twenty-three she was in an accident, being struck on the head by a sledge. It concussed her and family members said that she never completely recovered from the head injury. She became mentally unstable and was subject to mood swings. But it was not bad enough to seriously affect her life. She married and had a young son. But then she separated from her husband after four years and gave the young boy to an orphanage, unable to raise him herself. The abandonment of her son preyed on her mind for years.

She set up a dressmaking business with her sister, but upon her sister's death she gave that up. At the advanced age of forty-four, Martha, a tall, sharp-faced woman, met a widower, William Place, and began working for him as a housekeeper. He had an eleven-year-old daughter, Ida, from his earlier marriage and was struggling to cope. Over the months, a friendship grew between employer and housekeeper and eventually romance blossomed. William asked Martha to marry him and the three set up home together in Brooklyn. He had hoped that Martha would help him raise his girl but from the start there were tensions in the house, and on at least one occasion things grew so tense that William had to call in the police. Martha had threatened to kill Ida.

She was jealous of the affection William showed for his daughter, who never bonded with her stepmother.

That row blew over and William put it out of his head. Tensions remained, but things seemed to be going better. Then, on February 7, 1898, over breakfast there was a blazing row in the house and Ida sided with her father against Martha. William Place picked up his hat and left the house to go to work and didn't think any more of it. He was growing used to the angry words.

But once he left the house, Martha turned on Ida, now seventeen. She got some acid and threw it into the face of the young woman, burning her eyes badly. Then she knocked Ida to the ground and tried to force the acid down her throat. When Ida struggled, Martha picked up an axe and used that to finish the job, hacking her stepdaughter to death. She then dragged her body under a bed.

When Place arrived home at lunchtime, Martha flew out the door at him, attacking him with an axe. Before he had a chance to react, she brought the axe down on his head, shattering his skull. But she failed to knock him out with that blow and he ran. Neighbors came to his aid and someone ran for the police. When they arrived, the police found Martha unconscious in the kitchen. She had turned on the gas in an attempt to kill herself. Upon searching the house they were shocked to discover the bloodied body of Ida under the bed. Her death had been horrendous. She had been forced to drink acid, then smothered, in addition to being struck with the axe. Her mouth and face were burnt from the acid.

Both William and Martha were brought to St. John's Hospital in Brooklyn. William's badly fractured skull needed surgery, with fragments of bone being removed from a hole cut in what remained of the skull. He eventually recovered. Martha was unconscious, but as the newspaper *The World* noted: "Doctors found that there was little the matter with her; that she had not inhaled enough gas to stir the pulse of a baby."

The following day she made a partial confession, admitting to throwing acid at Ida, but stopping short of admitting the murder.

Despite this partial confession, from the start Martha pleaded not guilty. She claimed insanity, citing her earlier accident with the sledge. The horrific nature of the crime and her immediate attempt to commit suicide were considered, but she was declared sane. Once this was out of the way, the trial was uneventful. The chief witness for the prosecution was William Place, who had recovered enough to testify. The jury had no difficulty in finding Martha guilty. She was sentenced to die.

She was sent to Sing Sing Prison, on the banks of the Hudson River, north of New York City. She was held there for the weeks preceding her date with death. She did not handle her time in Sing Sing well, and she was often subject to hysterical outbursts and fits of weeping. When she heard that her request for a retrial had been rejected, she lost all hope and sank into despair. But she had constant access to a priest, and under his guidance she regained some self-control and accepted her fate.

There was no great public sympathy for her, given the nature of her crime. One newspaper cruelly described her as "homely, old, ill-tempered, not loved by her husband." But no one was comfortable with the idea of a woman going to the electric chair—no matter how well deserving of it she was. Another journalist wrote: "It was a murder so shocking that nothing worse could be thought of—that is to say, only one thing worse could be thought of, and that was the electric killing of the old woman."

There was an attempt to get a reprieve, but the governor of New York, Teddy Roosevelt, was adamant; there would be no last second change of heart. The sentence of the law would go ahead.

In a break from normal tradition, Martha was not given a time for her death. She was merely told that there was no hope for a reprieve and that she should ready herself for the call at any time. Whether this was done to show kindness is not known. She spent her last few days living an unusual life in the prison. She ate each day in the chief warden's quarters, almost more like a guest than a prisoner, and she saw her priest regularly.

On March 20, 1899, a little over a year after the murder of Ida and attempted murder of William, the call came. The electric chair in Sing Sing, one of three in New York State at the time, was ready.

State Electrician Edwin Davis was in place, and the execution was to be carried out immediately. Davis had overseen the first ever electric chair electrocution and actually held patents on some parts of the chair. He was the most qualified man to do the job at the time and would eventually oversee 240 executions before his retirement fourteen years later.

A female guard was assigned the task of leading Martha Place to the death chamber. She accompanied her to the chair, and Place sat calmly, not offering any resistance. She was dressed in a plain and drab dress and clutched a bible in her lap. As one guard stood behind her and began cutting her hair short, another slit the back of her dress so that they could attach the electrode to her leg. Once this was done, a patch on the back of her head was shorn. This was normally done several hours before the execution, not in the death chamber itself, but this was the first time any of the staff had overseen the electrocution of a woman.

The last woman to be executed in Sing Sing had been hanged, and the execution had been botched badly, leaving her to choke to death for over fifteen minutes on the noose. Nobody wanted another mistake with this execution.

Once both electrodes were in place, the death chamber was cleared and the generator fired up. When Davis threw the switch, 1,760 volts shot through Mrs. Place. This voltage was maintained for about four seconds, after which it was reduced for a further minute, before finally being switched to full power again for another few seconds. Then he switched the fearsome apparatus off.

Martha Place had not struggled or cried out. After the initial contraction of the body against the restraints, there had been no movement and when the current was switched off, she slumped. Geoffrey Abbott wrote in his *Amazing True Stories of Female Executions* that a female doctor, elegantly "dressed in the height of fashion, immaculate in a gray dress and a huge hat with pronounced crimson trimmings" stepped forward and placed her hand under the dark hood which concealed Place's face. She felt on the neck for a pulse and found none.

The execution of the first woman to face the electric chair had gone flawlessly.

THREE: GEORGE STINNEY—THE CHILD WHO FRIED

The idea of sending a child to the electric chair is revolting. The added fact that he was probably innocent of the crime for which he was convicted makes it doubly so. Welcome to the world of Jim Crow America.

Opponents of the death penalty say that one of its problems is that it is unevenly applied. If you are black and educationally challenged, you are far more likely to go to the chair than if you are white, middle class, and well educated. The statistical evidence reflects this to this day—though in the past it was an even greater bias and a bigger problem. Another problem is that innocent people occasionally are wrongly imprisoned and executed.

Actually, innocent people go to the chair more often than people suspect. Independent analyses of the records bears this out. University of Michigan law professor Samuel Gross and his team looked at the statistics and estimated that 4.1 percent of the people on death row were and are innocent. One in twenty-five—that is a huge number of wrongful deaths to justify or ignore.

Abolitionists looking for ammunition need look no further than the case of George Stinney for their proof. Stinney was the youngest-ever victim of the electric chair, a child of fourteen wrongly convicted and executed in the Deep South during the old Jim Crow days.

Looking at the case today, one cannot avoid the conclusion that Stinney was not executed; he was lynched by the state of South Carolina.

It all began on the sunny afternoon of March 24, 1944, in Alcolu, a small town in Clarendon County, fifty miles east of Columbia. Two girls—eleven-year-old Betty June Binnicker and her friend, eight-year-old Mary Emma Thames, set out to pick flowers. They had a bicycle but walked as often as they pedaled. On their way along a forested path they saw a fourteen-year-old "colored" boy, George Stinney. They knew him well; it was a small community. They exchanged greetings and asked him for directions.

Stinney was the last person to see them alive.

Within a few hours, the families of both girls were becoming anxious. They were good children who did not stay out longer than they should. And they knew the local area well, so they could not have gotten lost. A search party was put together. The local lumber mill organized the search and the whole town got involved, black and white. Stinney was one of the many volunteers searching, along with members of his family. He told people that he had spotted the girls shortly before their disappearance. They searched through the night, with no success. But at seven thirty the following morning, as light slowly returned, one of the men spotted small footprints in the soft ground. They followed the trail and came across a pair of scissors belonging to Betty June. Within minutes they reached a waterlogged ditch where the undergrowth was broken and trampled. Under the water they could make out a small bicycle. Then one of the searchers screamed; the bodies had been found.

Men jumped into the muddy hole and both bloodied bodies were drawn forth. They had been savagely beaten with a blunt object and their skulls crushed in.

There were no clues and no indications of what had happened. But as the investigators began to piece together the events of the previous afternoon, they remembered that one person had seen the girls after everyone else. In a community where racial prejudice lurked very close to the surface, it did not take long for the cops to decide that the young black boy was not a witness; he was a killer.

George Stinney was arrested. The illiterate son of a local mill worker, he had just turned fourteen. There was no question of following due process. Stinney was questioned without his parents and without a legal representative. He was just a frightened black child facing a tough, white police force. They played good cop, bad cop. While some bullied the boy, others offered him ice cream if he admitted to the offense. In the end, confused and frightened, he gave the cops the confession they were looking for.

The police alleged that Stinney led them voluntarily to the murder scene and showed them where he had concealed the iron spike he had used to beat in the girls' heads. The fact that he wasn't strong enough to lift the twenty-pound spike over his head effectively didn't bother the men; they were looking for a simple solution and a scapegoat. The crime had caused outrage, and the cops needed a quick arrest.

According to the confession they forced from him, Stinney had killed the younger girl, Mary Emma, because he wanted to have sex with Betty June. Then he killed Betty June because she struggled. When word of this version of the killing got out, a huge crowd gathered outside the county jail. There was going to be a lynching if the crowd had their way. In one of the few proper moves the authorities made, they got him out of the jail in time and into a cell in nearby Columbia.

On April 24, just a month after his arrest, Stinney was facing judge and jury. He faced them alone, as his parents had been driven from the locality by angry neighbors. His court-appointed attorney, Charles Plowden, had political ambitions, so he did the bare minimum and made no real attempt to defend the unpopular Stinney. There were fifteen hundred spectators—each one a potential voter. A jury was selected, without a single black member. The cards were stacked against Stinney. The prosecution presented their side. Plowden shrugged and said that Stinney was too young to be held responsible for his crimes. He offered no evidence in rebuttal of the state's case. The case opened at two thirty in the afternoon and was finished, sentence and all, by five thirty.

"The jury [all white] retired at five minutes before five to deliberate. Ten minutes later it returned with its verdict: guilty, with no recommendation for mercy," according to one contemporary account. Under three hours—the town was getting their lynching. Stinney would face the electric chair on June 16, 1944.

The town of Alcolu was happy, but as word of the travesty of the investigation and trial began to spread, pressure mounted for a review. The National Association for the Advancement of Colored People (NAACP), churches, and unions petitioned the governor, Olin Johnston, to show mercy. The governor was unmoved, despite hundreds of letters and messages. Mercy is not part of the lynching process.

Stinney languished in prison in the South Carolina State Penitentiary in Columbia. During the two short months he had left, he wrote to his parents, assuring them of his innocence.

On the morning scheduled for his execution, Stinney made his last walk from his cell to the death chamber. A slight figure, at only five feet one inch and less than ninety pounds, he looked like a lost and bewildered child in the midst of the large guards. He clutched a bible to his thin chest as they shuffled him along. When they got to the chair, they realized they had a problem; he was too small for the device, which had never been designed to kill children. The guards struggled to strap him in place and were unable to tie his arms and legs as tightly as they normally would.

They lowered the electrode onto his shaved skull and secured it as well as they could. This was the moment of his last words, and all the witnesses waited tensely, expecting a final confession. One of the guards prompted him, asking whether he had anything to say to the families. But Stinney said nothing.

"Stinney refused to make any statement when given the opportunity by prison officials," the *Daily Item* reported.

The guards pulled the death mask down over the young boy's face, but it was too big and didn't fit properly. They did their best to cover his face, and then stepped back. The order was given; the switch was thrown. Immediately Stinney's thin body convulsed and jerked. Because he was tied so loosely, his body moved more than most convicts and his head moved sharply, dislodging the mask. His face was exposed to the viewing gallery. His eyes were wide and staring, with tears coursing down his face. Spittle dribbled from his mouth. The sight of the frightened eyes of the child about to die would haunt many of the witnesses for months to come.

Twenty-four hundred volts were applied three times in quick succession.

It took less than four minutes before a doctor stepped forward, did a quick examination, and pronounced Stinney dead. From the time of the crime he probably did not commit to the final execution had taken just eighty-one days, unseemly haste compared with today's more careful trial and appeal processes.

George Stinney was the youngest person ever to sit in the electric chair and the youngest person to be executed in well over a hundred years. Unlike Britain, America had never had a culture of executing children. Since the seventeenth century, 365 juveniles have been executed—compared to thousands in the United Kingdom. The earliest was a sixteen-year-old, Thomas Graunger, hanged in Plymouth Colony, Massachusetts, in 1642 for the crime of bestiality, committed with a mare, a cow, two goats, two calves, several sheep, and a turkey. The youngest was a twelve year old Indian girl, Hannah Ocuish, hanged in 1786 for murdering a six year old girl.

Stinney was the youngest executed in the twentieth century, though currently there are approximately seventy juvenile offenders on death row. Following a Supreme Court ruling in 1988, those who committed a crime before reaching the age of sixteen cannot face the chair. That ruling came decades too late for Stinney. There is some speculation that the real killer was a well-off white man, who allegedly gave a death-bed confession. At this point there is no way of proving or disproving that. We do know, however, that Stinney was innocent. That has been acknowledged at last by a retrial granted in 2014. Surviving members of Stinney's family testified that he had been with them on the day in question and had an alibi for the time of the murders. They also testified that they could not afford to mount a proper defense for the boy and had to leave town for fear of reprisals from their white neighbors. The case was heard before Circuit Judge Carmen Mullen in December 2014 and the judge vacated the boy's conviction, effectively clearing George Stinney's name.

The judge ruled that Stinney's confession was likely to have been coerced and so was inadmissible, especially as he later denied it. She said the confession was: "due to the power differential between his position as a fourteen-year-old black male apprehended and questioned by white, uniformed law enforcement in a small, segregated mill town in South Carolina.

"This Court finds fundamental, Constitutional violations of due process exist in the prosecution of George Stinney Junior, and hereby vacates the judgment."

She said that there had been a number of violations of the boy's procedural due process rights, which tainted the prosecution. She listed these—the fact that the trial lasted just three hours and no witnesses were called on Stinney's behalf; his court-appointed lawyer was a tax commissioner who had never worked a criminal trial before; no prosecution witness was cross-examined. On top of all that, no appeal was filed after the death sentence was imposed.

"It is never too late for justice," said filmmaker Ray Brown, who is making a film on the Stinney case. "South Carolina got it right this time. During a period of time in our nation where we seem to have such a great racial divide, you have a southern state that has decided to admit they made a mistake and correct it."

It was too late for one boy lynched by a corrupt and uncaring system. Executioners, like doctors, bury their mistakes. But at least, under current legislation, no child will ever be allowed go to the chair again.

FOUR: VIRGINIA CHRISTIAN—MAID FOR THE CHAIR

Many states show no scruples about executing juveniles. But under current legislation someone must be sixteen or older at the time of his or her crime to be in danger of the death sentence. It was not always the case, with children as young as fourteen being sent to the chair in the past.

As with most statistics, juvenile women are far less likely to face the chair than juvenile men. In fact, in more than a hundred years, only one girl has been given the frightful sentence. Virginia Christian made history by being the first woman to be executed by the state of Virginia in the twentieth century and the only juvenile girl to be electrocuted.

Born in 1895, Virgina came from a poor, black family. She had some education but left school at an early age, and in her teens was working as a maid and washerwoman for a well-off white widow, Ida Virginia Belote, of Hampton. Ms. Belote was the daughter of a prominent local grocer and was well respected in the community. A small, frail woman of fifty-one, she had a violent temper and often mistreated Christian.

On March 18, 1912, sixteen-year-old Christian was working for Ms. Belote when the widow accused her of stealing a locket and a skirt. Christian protested her innocence but Belote picked up a spittoon and struck the young girl across the face with it. As Belote continued to strike her, Christian ran into Belote's bedroom and grabbed the first weapon to hand. Belote used two broom handles to prop her window open during the day, and the two women dived for the handles.

Christian was faster and brought the broom handle down sharply on Belote's forehead, knocking her to the ground.

The elderly woman began to scream, and in an attempt to stifle the screams Christian grabbed a towel and stuffed it into her mouth, using the broom handle to push the towel in deep. The cause of death was later determined to be suffocation. Belote's throat was blocked completely by the towel and by chunks of her hair which had also become lodged during the scuffle.

Before Christian fled the house, she stole Belote's purse and a ring. There wasn't much money in the purse, certainly not enough to fund a getaway. Later the body of Ms. Belote was discovered. According to newspaper accounts of the time, she was: "lying face down in a pool of blood, and her head was horribly mutilated and a towel was stuffed into her mouth and throat."

It did not take long for the police to track down Christian. She admitted that she had fought with her employer and openly confessed to having struck her with a broom. But she seemed genuinely shocked when she learned that Ms. Belote had died as a result of the assault. She was arrested and charged with murder.

From the start, it was a case dominated by the race of the victim and the accused. Black Americans were very much second-class citizens, and it mattered little to the local population that Christian had been struck first. Many felt that it was quite all right for an employer to strike a black servant. They were only two generations removed from the slave-owning days. There was an element of lynch-mob mentality in the town, and the police moved swiftly to prevent the law from being taken out of their hands. Christian was arrested.

She did little to cover up her crime, confessing soon after her arrest. The local papers were unabashed in the racial nature of their coverage, with one writing: "Christian is a full-blooded Negress, with kinky hair done up in threads, with dark lusterless eyes and with splotches on the skin of her face. Her color is dark brown, and her figure is short, dumpy and squashy. She has had some schooling, but her speech does not betray it. Her language is the same as the unlettered members of her race."

The *Daily News* went on to report the confession, in their best pastiche of a negro accent:

> She (Mrs. Belote) come to mommer's house dat morning an'
> say she want me to come an' do some washin'. When I come
> home mommer say Miss Belote want me an' I went 'roun'
> to de house. I wen' in de back way an' when she see me she
> asked me about a gold locket she missed. I told her I ain't seen
> it an' don't know nuttin' about it. She also say sumthin' about
> a skirt but de main thing was the locket. She say 'yes, you got
> it an' if you don't bring it back, I'm goin' to have to put you
> in jail.
>
> I got mad an' told her if I did have it, she wasn't goin' to
> git it back. Den she picked up de spittoon and hit me wit it
> ain't it broke. They wuz two sticks in de room, broom han-
> dles. She run for one, an' I for de other. I got my stick furst
> an' I hit her wit it 'side de hade and she felld down. She kep'
> hollerin' so I took a towel and stuffed it in her mouth. I helt
> it there twel she quit hollerin' and jes' groaned. I didn't mean
> to kill her an' I didn't know I had. I was mad when I hit her
> an't stuffed the towel in her mouth to keep her from hollerin'.
> I never meant to kill her. When I lef' she was goranin' and
> layin' on her back.

It is a certainty that a white girl's confession would not have been written up like that.

The trial came just two weeks after the murder, and Christian was never put on the stand to give evidence. So the jury never heard that she had been attacked first. She was defended by a black lawyer who chose not to let her testify, perhaps fearing that her testimony might have inflamed the already tense racial situation in the town. His decision may have prevented rioting, but it also ensured that Christian received no effective defense. She was convicted and sentenced to death.

Her mother wrote to the governor, William Hodges Mann, appealing for clemency. Her letter read:

> My dear mr governor
>
> Please for give me for Bowing low to write you a few lines: I am the mother of Virginiany Christian. I have been pairalized for mor then three years and I could not and Look after Gennie as I wants too. I know she dun an awful weaked thing when she kill Miss Belote and I hear that the people at the penetintry wants to kill her but I is praying night and day on my knees to God that he will soften your heart so that She may spend the rest of her days in prison. they say that the whole thing is in yours Hands and I know Governer if you will onely save my child who is little over sixteen years old God will Bless you for ever . . . If I was able to come to see you I could splain things to you better but I cant do nothing but pray to God and ask him to help you to simpithise with me and my truble
>
> I am your most umble subgeck, Charlotte Christian.

His heart was not moved by the appeal, and the governor declined to commute the death sentence.

On August 15, 1912, Christian celebrated her seventeenth birthday behind bars on death row in Richmond, Virginia. There is no record that the occasion was marked in any way. The following day she was scheduled to die. The Virginia electric chair was quite new, having only been built in 1908. The wood was still fresh and the fittings gleamed. The procedure then was almost as new as the chair, and the final protocol, now well established, had not been worked out fully.

The terrified teenager was led into the death chamber by female guards and strapped to the chair. Then the electrodes were attached to her right and left forearms, rather than the usual head and foot. This meant that the electricity, instead of traveling through the head (knocking out the brain), then through the torso and stopping the heart, would now travel across her body, just frying the internal organs. If death was not instant, the prisoner would remain conscious throughout the ordeal.

The *Daily News* reported: "The usual three shocks were administered by the officer in charge of the electric current. Each time the electric switch was touched, the body of the woman responded with fearful convulsions. Death, it is believed, was instantaneous."

In a final poignant note, Christian's family did not have the money to transport her body back to Hampton from Richmond for burial. So her body was turned over to the state medical school instead.

FIVE: MOST ELECTROCUTIONS IN ONE DAY

Multiple executions used to be a tremendous public spectacle. Crowds thronged Tyburn in London to see up to twenty people hang at a single time, and Madame Guillotine in Paris was always surrounded by her knitting acolytes during the height of the French Revolution. But with the electric chair and the decision to make executions private, such public spectacles became a thing of the past in the United States. Now there are only multiple executions if a number of people are convicted of the same capital crime. It has become rare, but is not unheard of.

Robert G. Elliott was the executioner for six states from 1926 to 1939, and wrote: "Eight times I have been the agent of death for a state which demanded that four men give up their lives on the same day. Thirty times the chair's toll has been three, and on fifty-three occasions I have electrocuted two people within a few minutes."

Elliott was probably the most prolific public executioner in US history, being responsible for nearly four hundred electrocutions, or 10 percent of the total number in the history of the punishment. On Thursday, January 7, 1927, he executed six men in two states, a very busy schedule. In the morning he executed Edward Hinlein, John Devereaux, and John McGlaughlin in Boston for the murder of a night watchman two years previously. Then he caught the train to New York, grabbed a quick dinner and a movie with his family, before heading out to Sing Sing where he executed Charles Goldson, Edgar Humes, and George

Williams. The three, like the first three, had been convicted of murdering another night watchman. He was paid $150 per execution, making that a very lucrative day. In today's money he earned nearly $12,000 on that day.

But Elliott was not in charge on the day that the most men ever went to the chair in the same place.

That happened on July 13, 1928, in Kentucky, when seven men were electrocuted, one after the other—all for murder. Three were black, four were white, and two had committed murder in the course of a robbery. The local *Southwest Missourian* recorded the event almost as a triumph for the state: "EXECUTIONS OF SEVEN SET NEW DEATH RECORD—Kentucky Extracts Supreme Penalty for Numerous Slayings."

The executions were carried out in the state's electric chair, Old Sparky, in Eddyville Penitentiary, and the entire process took just an hour and a half. The *Southwest Missourian* reported:

Four white men, three of them very young, and three Negroes made up the seven whose deaths in the electric chair set a record for Kentucky. Sullen, defiant, and prayerful by turns during their stay in the death house, the condemned men were reduced by fear to a condition bordering upon collapse as midnight approached.

Although there was no clock gong to sound the hours, the prisoners sensed the time and all talk died away long before the death march started at 12:15 a.m. With heads supported in cupped hands, they sat silent, their bodies shaken by chills despite the intense heat in the squat stone house that had been their home in the prison. In plain view was the execution chamber and the chair.

There was no somber darkness in the place. Instead, there was brilliant light and shadow and polished steel.

The men were held together in a cell block, and the order of the executions was revealed about eight o'clock the previous evening.

Most of the prisoners were allowed visits from family and relatives that final evening, but a few hours before midnight everyone was removed, leaving just seven convicts and their guards. All possibilities of reprieves had been exhausted. All that day, and on the previous day, Governor Flem D. Sampson had been swamped with petitions for clemency. He reviewed all petitions conscientiously, but in the end rejected them all.

Even in the face of death, segregation was observed. The four white men went to the chair first. Milford "Red" Lawson led the way. A thirty-five-year-old mountain man from the rural county of Corbin, he had murdered a neighbor. He was taken to the chamber at 12:15 a.m., and quickly strapped into the chair. He looked up and said, "I am ready to forgive everybody." Three minutes later he was dead, and a team of guards, holding their noses against the stench of burning flesh, rushed into the chamber and removed his body.

Next up was Orlando Seymour, just twenty-one. A native of Louisville, he was a factory worker who had murdered a local merchant during the course of a robbery. He had hopes of a last minute postponement of his sentence, and when he had heard a few hours earlier that the hoped-for reprieve was not coming, he had sunk into a stupor. He seemed to be in a daze as he was led into the chamber and strapped to the chair. The execution was swiftly concluded and his body removed to make way for the next victim.

The third man to face the chair was also just twenty-one years old. Hascue Dockery was from Harlan and had killed two women and a man. He remained brazen up until nearly the end. Four hours earlier he had been told by Warden Chilton that he was the first to face the chair that night, and he had merely sneered and flicked the ashes from his cigarette at the official. But just before the executions were due to start, as the hum from the electric dynamo filled the cell block, he panicked and asked to see the Catholic priest. He told the surprised cleric that he wished to convert to Catholicism before his death. This would require a few minutes, so he was switched to third on the list.

The priest had hastily performed the baptism. Catholic baptism does not require total immersion in water. A small amount of holy water is sprinkled over the acolyte's head and a few prayers are said. It only takes a few minutes. Dockery was ready when his name was called.

But the cockiness of a few hours earlier was gone. He was silent when his time came, and unresponsive, and had to be dragged to the chair, where he sat without a word as the straps were tightened. Then, as the hood was lowered over his face, he began to mutter some prayers. Death came swiftly.

The final white man called was Charles Paul Mitra, twenty-three, from St Louis. He was a laborer who had murdered a grocer in the course of an attempted holdup. A punk to the end, he had a disdainful attitude towards the guards and was aloof from the other six who awaited their deaths. He was led into the chamber and sat without a word. He was strapped down, the electrodes placed, the switch thrown, and death pronounced in three minutes. It was clinical and precise.

Finally it was the African Americans' turns. The newspaper noted: "The Negroes, apparently crushed earlier in the night by the nearness and certainty of death, recovered their spirits to a greater degree than the white men before the time came for them to pass down the corridor of steel and stone that connects the death house with the chair room."

Willie Moore from Louisville, a forty-five-year-old, was the first to make the short walk. He said nothing, and the execution proceeded swiftly. Next to die was James Howard, a twenty-two-year-old also from Louisville. He was in remarkably good spirits, singing as he was led to the chamber. He had a rich voice, and the words of "Lily of the Valley" filled the chamber and the nearby witness room. He sat back in the chair and settled comfortably as the guards began securing the straps.

Looking over at the witnesses, he said, "Gentlemen, how are you all feeling tonight?"

A lot better than he felt moments later when the volts coursed through his body.

The final man to face execution was Clarence McQueen. The thirty-eight-year-old from Cynthiana was a moonshiner, a distiller of illegal alcohol. He hummed a song as he was led to the chair and seemed to show a great curiosity as the straps were tightened. He met his end with cheerfulness and dignity.

The last execution was concluded by one thirty in the morning, and the relatives, many of whom had spent their final few hours with the condemned men, were able to collect the bodies for burial the following morning.

On the same day in Mississippi, two convicts, both black, were hanged in Jackson. One, Green Kirk, had killed two cops, and the newspaper noted that he had been in fear of mob action—a lynching — since his arrest. So the hanging saved him from a hanging. And in Milledgeville, Georgia, two more men faced the electric chair, making that day in July 1928 the blackest day in modern US history for the death penalty.

SIX: TOPSY—ELECTROCUTING THE ELEPHANT

When the legend becomes fact, print the legend. That is the famous quote from John Ford's "The Man who Shot Liberty Valance," and it can be an accurate reflection on how the media works. Some stories gain such currency that they are accepted without question. We all "know" that there was a second man working with Lee Harvey Oswald when he assassinated President Kennedy in Dallas. He was hidden behind the grassy knoll. Many of us have a shaky grasp of what a "grassy knoll" actually is, but we know the guy was there. That is an example of the legend becoming fact.

Great men attract such embellishments: that Einstein invented the atomic bomb, that Dr. Guillotine was a victim of the execution machine he invented, that Thomas Edison electrocuted an elephant to prove the electric chair would work. The legends are believable because there is a grain of truth in them. Einstein was not a nuclear physicist, but he did write a letter to the president urging him not to fall behind in the development of the bomb. Dr. Guillotine was not executed (he also did not invent the beheading machine, just popularized it), but his nephew was guillotined. The grain of truth makes the legend believable.

The Edison legend is quite simple. During the current wars, Edison wanted to prove the danger of alternating current, so he regularly staged press conferences and public talks at which dogs, cats, donkeys, and other animals were sacrificed on the table of science. And according to the legend, he once electrocuted an elephant to demonstrate that even a big animal was susceptible to the dangers of alternating current.

So what is the truth behind the Edison legend?

An elephant was indeed electrocuted. And the Edison name was all over it. But it happened long after the current wars and Edison had no direct involvement in the affair. And it had nothing to do with proving his point.

The elephant in question was Topsy, a top attraction at the Luna Park Zoo on Coney Island, New York. And she was condemned to die after stomping a man to death.

Topsy was a female Asian elephant, born around 1875. As a calf she was captured by elephant traders and sold to Forepaugh Circus. The circus, ever conscious of a marketing opportunity, smuggled the baby animal into the United States. They then released the information that they had the only baby elephant born in captivity in America. Their rivals, Barnum and Bailey, might have had the biggest elephants, but Forepaugh had the cutest.

She was named Topsy, after a slave in *Uncle Tom's Cabin*.

But as Adam Forepaugh boasted that he had "the only baby elephant ever born on American soil," the animal dealer who sold him the beast tipped off P. T. Barnum about the deception. Both sides milked the controversy for all it was worth. Topsy was a headliner from the start. Soon, she outgrew her cuteness, becoming a full-grown elephant. Her publicity material indicates she was ten feet high and weighed six tons. But the average height of Asian elephants is a little over seven feet and they typically weigh around three tons. So she was probably a bit smaller than advertised. Still, she was a big draw for the circus. But her temper could be uneven. Elephants are highly intelligent animals and can be trained to a surprising extent. In the Far East they are used as work animals, but early western circuses had a bad record for mistreating animals. Training was a matter of instilling fear into an animal, and the only way of instilling fear on an animal the size of Topsy was by beating her severely. No wonder she was prone to fits of temper. And when three to six tons throws a tantrum, it is best not to be there.

She gained the reputation as a killer in 1900 after two incidents in Texas. It was said that she killed two circus workers, one in Waco and the other in Paris, Texas. This reputation drew in the crowds when Forepaugh & Sells Brothers' Circus came to Coney Island. However, like her size, there was an element of exaggeration. A circus worker had been injured in Paris, but he made a full and speedy recovery. And there was no injury in Waco. However, the bad temper was no exaggeration.

Things came to a head on the morning of May 27, 1902. The circus was in Brooklyn. A drunk keeper, James Fielding Blount, wandered into the menagerie where all the elephants were tied up together. As he staggered down the line, he teased the massive animals, waving a bottle of whiskey under their trunks. Not getting enough of a reaction, he threw sand into Topsy's face, then offered her a treat—a lit cigar. The trunk of an elephant is highly sensitive, and this must have caused her agony. Topsy lashed out with her trunk, tossing Blount to the ground. She then stood on his head, crushing his skull and killing him instantly.

Newspaper accounts, of course, exaggerated the incident. The elephant had gone on a rampage and savaged Blount with her tusks. Female Asian elephants do not have tusks, but why let the truth spoil a good story. Accounts also surfaced claiming that Topsy had killed twelve people in total. The truth was one death and one injury. But it was enough to make the circus a huge draw. There were full houses for weeks after the death of Blount, with everyone eager to see the rogue killer elephant.

But a few weeks after the death, there was another incident. The circus had moved on and was pulling into Kingston, New York. The train stopped at the platform and the carriages opened. As the elephants were being led from the station to the field, a spectator with a stick, Louis Dodero, raised the stick and tickled Topsy behind the ear. She whirled rapidly and seized Dodero around the waist with her trunk. She hoisted the startled man into the air and slammed him into the ground. Immediately her handlers surrounded her and brought her under control.

Beyond minor injuries, no harm was done. But the circus knew they could no longer tour with the temperamental elephant. The owners decided to sell Topsy.

Back then there was a demand for elephants. Coney Island's Sea Lion Park was glad for an addition to their lineup. Topsy came with her handler, William Alt. But when the Sea Lion Park went bankrupt, the whole concern was sold to Frederick Thompson and Elmer Dundy, who wanted to develop a far larger attraction—Luna Park. Luna Park was a large amusement park with spectacular rides and attractions, as well as shows and animals. It was due to open in May 1903, and the owners wanted to stage a spectacular event to announce its arrival.

They decided that Topsy could help. They used the elephant during the construction phase, allowing newspaper men to photograph her hauling large loads of lumber. They said it was part of her "penance" for killing a spectator. But her handler, William Alt, was drinking heavily and was losing control of his charge. He turned the elephant loose in the streets one day, and on another day tried to break into a police station on top of the elephant. He was fired.

Now there was no one who could control the elephant who had a reputation for irascibility. The park owners decided that they would have to move her on, but with her reputation no one would take her. There was only one solution; they would have to put her down. This presented a tremendous marketing coup; they could make her execution a public spectacle.

The date was set for January 4, 1903. It would be a big after-Christmas attraction, an event for the whole family. Luna Park would charge twenty-five cents a head. Previous executions of elephants in other parts of the country had been big draws. Elephants had been hung, strangled by ropes tied to other elephants, poisoned, and shot. There had even been an attempt to electrocute an elephant, but the current didn't seem to have any effect on the massive animal, so Luna Park dismissed that idea. They opted for hanging. An industrial crane would be used. Their press agent swung into action, publicizing the execution. Posters were put up all over the city, advertising both the hanging and the opening of the park a few months afterward.

But the American Society for the Prevention of Cruelty to Animals was horrified and protested. So Luna Park decided to use the more humane execution method of electricity, which had replaced hanging for people. Now it was going to replace hanging for animals. They also agreed not to charge for the spectacle.

Power in that part of New York was supplied by the local Edison Electricity Light Company. The power plant still bore the Edison name, but the inventor was no longer involved in the electricity supply business. But now his name was linked to the elephant execution. A team from the park liaised with the plant engineers. They began by stringing a wire the nine blocks from the substation to carry the power needed. Secretly, the park owners decided to administer a poison just to help things along. The previous attempt to electrocute an elephant had been a spectacular failure, and they wanted to get this one right.

On the morning of the execution, Topsy was led from her pen into the unfinished park. There was a raised platform near the edge of a lagoon where the execution would take place. The spectators—1,500 of them, alongside 100 press photographers—were on the other side of the lagoon. Topsy was led through the crowd and onto a bridge across the lagoon. But she refused to cross the bridge, even when bribed with apples and other treats. Someone was sent to fetch William Alt, the fired trainer, but he was too attached to the elephant and refused to come. They offered him twenty-five dollars, nearly $700 in today's money. But he said he would not come for even $1,000.

Unable to get the elephant to the electrocution platform, the park was forced to improvise. They hastily tore down the platform and moved it across the bridge to the spectator side of the lagoon. The electricians managed to get a copper-lined sandal onto Topsy's right forefoot and another on the rear left foot. Once these were connected, power would flow through the entire torso of the elephant, frying the vital organs. Then, at the last minute, Topsy was given a bunch of carrots—laced with 460 grams of potassium cyanide.

The call went through to the power station nine blocks away and the power was turned on. Luna Park chief electrician Hugh Thomas threw a switch at his end, and 6,600 volts shot through Topsy's body for ten seconds. The massive creature stiffened instantly and smoke billowed from both copper plates. Then the back leg flashed bright as it caught fire. The flames shot up about a foot high, and then the hind leg came up off the ground, and Topsy, her body rigid, fell over onto her side, her legs sticking up in the air. It took only seconds. Veterinarians on the scene ran forward and quickly gave assurance that the elephant had died instantly. But they were taking no chances. A noose was placed around Topsy's neck and pulled tight, the pressure being maintained for ten minutes. At the end of that time it was obvious that the elephant would not be getting up again.

The *Commercial Advertiser* wrote the following day: "Topsy, the ill-tempered Coney Island elephant, was put to death in Luna Park, Coney Island, yesterday afternoon. The execution was witnessed by 1,500 or more curious persons, who went down to the island to see the end of the huge beast, to whom they had fed peanuts and cakes in summers that are gone. In order to make Topsy's execution quick and sure, 460 grams of cyanide of potassium were fed to her in carrots. Then a hawser was put around her neck and one end attached to a donkey engine and the other to a post. Next wooden sandals lined with copper were attached to her feet. These electrodes were connected by copper wire with the Edison electric light plant and a current of 6,600 volts was sent through her body. The big beast died without a trumpet or a groan."

The entire event was filmed by the Edison Manufacturing Company, who shot many shorts of animals and other subjects. The footage, entitled "Electrocuting an Elephant," was shown in cinemas throughout the country but was not very popular, so it was eventually removed from circulation. It is now available on YouTube. That film forever linked Edison with the electrocution of an elephant, and eventually the legend replaced the truth—the truth being that Thomas Edison never killed an elephant to advance his cause during the current wars.

9

LAST MEALS

In the summer of 2014 someone in London, England, had a great idea for a pop-up restaurant. The whole country reacted with predictable horror. "Death Row Dinners" closed before it even opened. Yet the fledgling venture got great publicity. Everything surrounding the death penalty has a visceral power over us.

The last meal is one of the enduring traditions surrounding execution, like the last cigarette before a man faces the firing squad. The last cigarette is a thing of the past. In these days of health consciousness smoking has been banned in prisons, and the condemned man is not allowed his last nicotine hit. He has to remain healthy for the bullet. But the last meal has endured in most states.

The history of the last meal does not stretch back nearly as far as people imagine. In fact, it is less than a hundred years old in America as a formal part of the execution ritual. But it has roots stretching back to medieval European superstitions. In that era they believed that the last meal was a symbolic act. When the condemned man accepted the freely offered food, it was a sign that he was making peace with those who had condemned him to death. In accepting the last meal he was symbolically forgiving the judge and executioner. With luck his spirit would not come back to haunt them all afterward.

In France, the prisoner was even offered a small shot of rum a few minutes before the execution. This was not just a kindness—a slightly inebriated prisoner was easier to handle.

The one place where considerations such as a last meal were not a feature of executions was in England. The law was clear: "During the short but awful interval between sentence and execution, the prisoner shall be kept alone, and be sustained with only bread and water." (*Blackstone's Commentaries on the Laws of England*, 1765).

The tradition of the last meal was formalized in America in 1924. Texas was the first state to introduce it, and it quickly caught on. Prior to 1924, executions were carried out on a county by county basis, and last meals were organized locally. In 1924 the state took over executions, and last meals became a fixture of the procedure. But last meal is a misnomer. It isn't always the last meal served to the prisoner, because hours away from execution many cannot face it. Sometimes the meal—called a "special meal"—was served a few days prior to the execution.

Each state does it in its own way, but almost always alcohol and tobacco are denied the prisoner. Unusual items are not always available and often substitutes are used. Some states have tight restrictions on what may be ordered. For instance, Florida limits the budget to forty dollars and the ingredients must be purchased locally. Oklahoma is even stingier, limiting the budget to fifteen dollars. Occasionally, family members are allowed eat with the prisoner. In Louisiana, the prison warden traditionally joins the condemned prisoner. On one occasion, the warden actually paid out of his own pocket for the two of them to enjoy a lobster dinner.

A certain latitude is often allowed. Francis "Two Gun" Crowley, a New York gangster who went to the chair in Sing Sing in 1932, was allowed to share his last meal with John Resko, a murderer also on death row. Resko never got his own last meal; his sentence was eventually commuted to life imprisonment. Raymond Fernandez, the Lonely Hearts Killer, was fried in 1951. He requested that his last meal be distributed among the other inmates in the prison. They got his omelet and fries.

It is impossible to go through every last meal request, but some do stand out. Here are some of the highlights of the last meals of those who went to death in the electric chair.

Ruth Snyder was famously photographed in the electric chair by a reporter who used a concealed camera. The shocking image was front page news in 1928 when she was executed for the murder of her husband. Ruth's final meal was chicken Parmesan with alfredo pasta, followed by ice cream, and washed down by two milkshakes and a twelve-pack of grape soda.

"Two Gun" Francis Crowley was a punk Irish gangster in Prohibition-era New York. During a three-month murder and robbery spree he killed a number of times. He was caught after a two-hour shootout, during which cops fired over seven hundred rounds into the apartment he was holed up in. His last meal, in 1932, was steak and onions with french fries, followed by apple pie and ice cream. He shared it with a fellow prisoner. His last words were to ask for a cloth to wipe off the chair, as it had been used in a previous execution.

Bruno Richard Hauptmann, convicted of the kidnapping and murder of the Lindbergh toddler, was executed in 1936. He asked for a last meal of celery, olives, chicken, french fries, buttered peas, cherries, and a slice of cake.

The "Lonely Hearts Killers," Raymond Martinez Fernandez and Martha Jule Beck, murdered as many as twenty women for their savings between 1947 and 1949. They were executed in Sing Sing, New York, on March 8, 1951. Fernandez had an onion omelet and french fries, followed by a chocolate candy bar and a cigar. He asked that the meal be shared among his fellow prisoners.

Original teen "rebel without a cause" Charles Starkweather was executed in Nebraska in 1959 for a series of murders committed with his teen girlfriend. He declined the usual steak dinner and opted for a plate of cold cuts instead.

Joseph "Mad Dog" Taborsky was sentenced to death in 1950, partly on the testimony of his brother. But when his brother was declared insane and institutionalized, Taborsky appealed and was released from prison after serving just three years. In 1955, he went on a crime spree, killing six people in a series of brutal armed robberies. He was executed on May 17, 1960, at Wethersfield Penitentiary, Connecticut. His accomplice in the six murders got a life sentence, in part because he had protected a three-year-old who Taborsky had wanted to kill. Taborsky asked for a banana split and a cherry soda, followed by coffee, before going to the chair. He also asked for a pack of cigarettes.

Richard Kiefer, from Fort Wayne, Indiana, grew tired of his wife's nagging about his fishing and drinking, so he took a hammer to her in 1957. When his five-year-old daughter tried to break up the fight, he killed her too. His final meal, before being executed in 1961, was fried chicken and french fries, followed by banana cream pie and vanilla ice cream.

Ralph Hudson went to the chair in Trenton, New Jersey, in 1963. He was the last person executed by that state, for the crime of stabbing his estranged wife to death. His last meal was prime rib steak and ice cream, followed by a good cigar.

Ted Bundy was the handsome boy-next-door who killed thirty women. He was executed in Florida in 1989. When it came time to face the chair, his courage—or at least his appetite—failed him. He declined a last meal, and was instead given the standard steak (medium-rare), eggs (over easy), hash browns, toast, milk, coffee, and juice. But he didn't eat any of it.

Allen Lee Davis was a huge man with a huge appetite. He had bludgeoned a pregnant woman to death and had killed both her young daughters. Weighing 344 pounds, he requested a feast—a lobster tail, half a pound of fried shrimp, six ounces of fried clams, and a side of fried potatoes. He also had half a loaf of garlic bread and washed it down with root beer. When he was electrocuted in 1999, he bled profusely from the nose and suffered severe burns to his groin and legs. There was an outcry, which Governor Jeb Bush dismissed, saying, "Everybody's getting all worked up about a nosebleed." But the horror of his execution caused Florida to switch to lethal injection immediately afterwards.

James Neil Tucker was a rapist and career criminal, convicted of shooting two women in the head during two burglaries. He was executed in South Carolina in 2004. For his final meal he chose a pizza, two BLT sandwiches, and Mountain Dew.

Some last meal requests are denied by the state. Philip Workman was facing lethal injection in Tennessee when his final request was turned down. He had been convicted in 1982 for the murder of a police officer during a botched armed robbery. After serving twenty-five years—more than a life sentence in most developed countries—he was finally strapped to the gurney on May 9, 2007. He had asked that his last meal—a vegetarian pizza—be given to a homeless person. It was a selfless gesture, but one the prison authorities decided was not possible. So he refused any last meal. But his attempt to give a pizza to a street person got widespread media coverage. The attempted gesture seemed to tug at people's heartstrings in some way, and in the hours following his execution local homeless shelters received several hundred pizzas. They were not all vegetarian, but it is the thought that counts. One woman donated $1,200 worth of pizzas to Nashville's Rescue Mission. An employee of the mission, Marvin Champion, told *The Tennessean*: "I used to be homeless, so I know how rough it gets. But we got pizza to feed enough people for a while." PETA (People for the Ethical Treatment of Animals) president Ingrid Newkirk donated fifteen veggie pizzas, saying, "Workman's act was selfless, and kindness to all living beings is a virtue."

Perhaps the most unusual last meal request was from Victor Feguer, a drifter who kidnapped a doctor and killed him for whatever drugs he had in his possession. He was hanged in Iowa in 1963, the last execution in that state. His final meal was a single olive, with the stone still in it. Robert Buell, a serial child rapist and murderer executed in Ohio in 2002, enjoyed the same last meal.

James Edward Smith, executed in Texas in 1990 for the murder of an insurance clerk, claimed to be a voodoo priest, having been obsessed with black magic and voodoo since the age of six. He asked for a plate of dirt but was given a yogurt instead. There were questions about his mental competency, but the execution went ahead none the less.

The reason he asked for dirt was because he believed it would prevent his spirit from coming back as a ghost. When his request was denied, he told officials that his ghost would haunt the facility at Huntsville for the next three hundred years.

Ricky Ray Rector, executed in Arkansas in 1992, was severely mentally disabled (as a result of an attempted suicide, when he shot himself in the head). He enjoyed most of his last meal but left the pecan pie on the plate, telling stunned warders that he would eat it later, after the execution. Many people felt great unease at his execution due to his poor grip on reality and obvious disability.

Not every prisoner requests a last meal. For those who don't, they have two options. They can have whatever is on the menu on the day of their execution in the general body of the prison, or they can have the generic last meal, which is quite a substantial feast. For those unable to make up their minds, they get a steak, medium rare, eggs over easy, hash browns, and buttered toast. They follow this with jello, and may wash it down with a glass of milk and a glass of juice.

The most gruesome of all last meal requests came from Doug Stephener, a huge evil-looking monster with a face that could have come from a Lon Chaney movie. According to reports that circulated widely, this fiend was a pedophile who had eaten parts of his victims. He was scheduled to die by lethal injection in Texas in the fall of 2014; however, there was worldwide revulsion at his apparent request. He said he wanted to eat a young boy, under the age of eight, and a non-Asian, for his final repast. Of course it was an Internet hoax, though it took in many people. Had they done their research they would have realized immediately it could not be true. Texas had abolished the tradition of the last meal three years earlier, in September 2011.

The reason for abolishing the last meal was that one prisoner abused the privilege, at least according to Texan officials. Lawrence Russell Brewer was a vile white supremacist, who took part in one of the most horrific race killings in living memory. Along with two companions, he picked up a black man, James Byrd Jr., in Jasper, Texas. Byrd was looking for a lift, but the three men chained him to the back of their pickup truck and dragged him to his death. He was alive for about a mile of the ordeal before his head struck something on the road and was torn from his body. The forensic evidence was clear that he was alive up to that point. When Brewer was executed in 2011, he used the occasion to give one final middle finger to the world. He requested a triple bacon cheeseburger, two chicken fried steaks with gravy and onions, a cheese and beef omelet, tomatoes, a meat lovers pizza, some bell peppers and jalapenos, a bowl of okra, a pound of barbecued meat, half a loaf of bread, and three fully loaded fajitas. He also ordered three root beers, a pint of ice cream, and a slab of peanut butter fudge.

On the day that he was to enjoy this banquet, the general body of the prison were getting sloppy joes, navy beans, creamed corn, and sliced bread. The prison provided the huge feast for Brewer, despite the fact that no ordinary man would have a hope of making a serious dent in such a meal. When the meal arrived, Brewer refused to eat a bite. The food was eventually thrown out. In reaction both to the flagrant waste and the vile man who had created the waste, Texas Senate Criminal Justice Committee Chairman John Whitmire wrote to Huntsville Penitentiary Chief Brad Livingston: "It is extremely inappropriate to give a person sentenced to death such a privilege. Enough is enough."

He went on to describe the last meal as "ridiculous" and pointed out that Brewer had not allowed James Byrd the privilege of a last meal or any other merciful consideration. Forks down; the last meal was over.

Livingston pulled the plug on last meals in Texas, immediately announcing that from that day on convicts on death row would eat whatever was on the prison menu on the day of their execution.

There was a liberal backlash, with Elizabeth Stein, producer of "Execution Watch" for KPFT-FM radio station, telling the *Houston Chronicle*: "I think it's sad that our elected and appointed leaders are wasting their time talking about menus on death row when we have important issues like potential innocence and the validity of the entire death-penalty system that desperately need to be looked at."

Former prison chef Brian Price prepared over two hundred last meals for Texas death row and wrote a book about his experiences, *Meals to Die For*. He tried to introduce an element of reality into the fray, denying that last meals were an extravagance.

"They only get items in the commissary kitchen. If they order lobster, they get a piece of frozen pollock. They quit serving steaks in 1994. If they order a hundred tacos, they get two or three," he pointed out. "Whitmire's just getting on a political soapbox."

Soapbox or no, Whitmire got his way, and Texas, the state responsible for more than a third of all US executions, no longer honors the age-old tradition.

10

A MORATORIUM ON EXECUTIONS

When forty-eight-year-old Luis Josè Monge went to the gas chamber at Colorado State Penitentiary in Canon City on June 2, 1967, he made history of a sort. He was the 101st convict to be executed in Colorado, missing out the landmark century by one. He was also the 14,489th person to be executed in the United States since 1607. But it was not for this that he was noteworthy. Monge was the last person executed before a moratorium on the death penalty stopped all executions for more than a decade. The moratorium ended the golden era of the electric chair; when executions eventually resumed, the chair had gone into a decline, replaced by lethal injection.

Monge was a salesman, originally from Puerto Rico. He grew up in New York, then settled in Denver with his wife. They started a family and didn't know when to stop. They eventually had ten children. But Monge began an incestuous affair with one of his elder daughters. When his wife Leonardo discovered the affair, it was the trigger that pushed him over the edge. He waited until evening, then beat his pregnant wife to death with a steel bar. He then killed three of their children: Alan, aged six; Vincent, aged four; and Teresa, just eleven months old. He stabbed Teresa, choked Vincent, and bludgeoned Alan. As he sat in his home surrounded by the carnage, he picked up the phone and called the police.

Monge had no previous felony convictions and there was little in his past to indicate the violence that he was capable of. The only anomaly in an otherwise conventional life was that he had walked out on the family for a brief period in 1961 and ended up in county jail for vagrancy.

At the trial, Monge pleaded not guilty by reason of insanity, a notoriously difficult defense. A team of psychiatrists evaluated him for the court and found him sane. After that, he stopped protesting and changed his plea to guilty of first-degree murder. The jury recommended the death penalty and his appeal was rejected.

Events from the outside world almost intervened. In January 1966, Governor John Arthur Love suspended all executions in Colorado pending a referendum on capital punishment. Monge's sentence was on hold, with a reasonable chance it would end up commuted to life in prison. But on November 8, the voters decided overwhelmingly to retain the death penalty. Monge was back on death row.

He decided to go out with a flourish and garnered national headlines when he requested that he be hanged—at high noon—on the front steps of the Denver City and County Building. Not surprisingly, this request was denied. He would go to the gas chamber like everyone else. In the late sixties the appeals process was not as prolonged as it is now, but it was still lengthy. But Monge short-circuited the process by firing his legal team and chose that no attempts should be made to save his life. He wanted to be executed. His surviving seven children appealed for clemency, but to no avail. A week before the execution, he was allowed to share a final meal with the children, a poignant affair. Then, on June 2, 1967, he went to the gas chamber. Seventy members of the Colorado Council to Abolish Capital Punishment protested on the steps of the State Capitol building in Denver in the hours leading up to the execution.

One of Monge's final requests was that his cornea be transplanted in order to save the sight of a teenage reformatory inmate.

The gas chamber, not used since Monge's execution, is now on permanent exhibit at the Museum of Colorado Prisons in Canon City. Its retirement came a little late for Monge and was a response to a nation-wide campaign that eventually ended up before the Supreme Court. The court agreed to consider whether the death penalty in a number of cases was unconstitutional. While the cases were being reviewed, lower courts in all states stayed all pending executions. This created a moratorium on the death penalty throughout the country. This unofficial moratorium began with the execution of Monge and would last a decade.

The key case that the Supreme Court considered was *Furman v. Georgia.*

William Henry Furman was a poorly educated black man, described as "emotionally disturbed and mentally impaired." He left formal education at sixth grade (age twelve) and was barely literate. He drifted into a life of crime. On August 11, 1967, he broke into the home of twenty-seven-year-old Walter Micke in Savannah, Georgia. He intended to rob the house, but Micke woke up and disturbed him. Furman gave differing accounts of what happened next. His first statement said that when Micke disturbed him, he fired blindly into the dark and ran. His next statement said that he turned and ran, then tripped over a piece of furniture and his handgun went off. The bullet accidentally struck the victim. The first account is more probable; the later account was an attempt to lesson his responsibility. But, in either case, he did not intend to kill the homeowner.

Such niceties do not concern the law. The killing occurred during the course of a felony, so it was first-degree murder whether Furman intended to shoot or not. At the end of a one-day trial, he was sentenced to death. That was in September 1968. Fifty years earlier, he would have been on death row in hours and have sat in the chair within weeks. But by the late sixties the appeals process had become prolonged. It would be a year or more before he was due for execution. His legal team had plenty of time to play the courts and buy him extra precious months.

A few years previously, in 1962, the Supreme Court had handed down a decision in *Robinson v. California.* Robinson had been stopped by a traffic cop, who spotted needle marks on his arm, indicating drug use. He was jailed for ninety days as a drug addict. The Supreme Court decided that being an addict in itself was not enough to justify being jailed, and that to jail Robinson for what was essentially a medical condition (addiction) was cruel and unusual and against his Eighth Amendment rights. This paved the way for other Eighth Amendment challenges.

One of the cards Furman's attorneys played was an appeal to the Supreme Court, where they argued that the death penalty was not applied consistently. A disproportionate number of black men were on death row. In Georgia, of the thirty-three men facing the chair, twenty-seven were black and only six were white. This violated Furman's Eighth Amendment rights as he was essentially being given a harsher sentence because of his color. They also argued that it denied Furman due process, violating his Fourteenth Amendment rights. At the same time, the Supreme Court considered two other cases, *Jackson v. Georgia* and *Branch v. Texas*. They had been due to consider a fourth case, *Aikens v. California,* but the California State Supreme Court had already ruled that the death penalty violated the state constitution, so Aikens found his sentence commuted to life imprisonment.

Jackson was sentenced to death for raping a white woman during the course of an unsuccessful armed robbery. He was a black defendant from Georgia. Elmer Branch was also black. He broke into the home of a widow in Vernon, Texas, and violently raped her, before stealing money from the house. She did not suffer serious physical injuries in the attack but he was condemned to death for raping a white woman. There were definite racial undertones in the case.

The three cases were considered together by the nine-man Supreme Court, but they focused mostly on Furman's case. It was close. The final decision was five to four—in Furman's favor. He would not go to the chair. Neither would Jackson, Branch, or anyone else for the next decade.

The court issued a one-page per curiam opinion, holding that the death penalty in the three cases was a cruel and unusual punishment and violated the Constitution. By a five-to-four majority, the death penalty was struck out for Furman and also in the other two cases considered with it. The per curiam opinion was an indication of how divisive the subject was. Normally the Supreme Court issues a decision with a majority opinion, written and signed by one of the justices. Per curiam decisions are more rare and take the form of a brief and unsigned document. It is always a sign that the court was deeply divided over the decision. In the Furman case, all nine justices wrote a separate opinion outlining their reasoning. The five that agreed to overthrow the death penalty were quite divided on why.

Two of the justices, Brennan and Marshall, believed the death penalty to be unconstitutional in all cases, given evolving standards of decency in society. We had moved beyond such barbaric practices. Others held that the problem was the arbitrary nature with which the death penalties had been imposed, which often showed a racial bias against black defendants. Justice Douglas felt that the inequality in application was what made the death penalty unconstitutional, and this opened the possibility of a return to the electric chair if the inequalities, which condemned more of the poor and the "colored," could be eliminated. Justice Byron White felt that the infrequency of execution prevented capital punishment from serving as an effective deterrent, and thus it was not meeting the legitimate social need for retribution.

The most influential opinion came from Justice Potter Stewart, who said, "The penalty of death differs from all other forms of criminal punishment, not in degree but in kind. It is unique in its rejection of rehabilitation of the convict as a basic purpose of criminal justice. And it is unique, finally, in its absolute renunciation of all that is embodied in our concept of humanity."

He went on, "These death sentences are cruel and unusual in the same way that being struck by lightning is cruel and unusual. For, of all the people convicted of rapes and murders in 1967 and 1968, many just as reprehensible as these, the petitioners are among a capriciously selected random handful upon whom the sentence of death has in fact been imposed. My concurring Brothers have demonstrated that, if any basis can be discerned for the selection of these few to be sentenced to death, it is the constitutionally impermissible basis of race . . . I simply conclude that the Eighth and Fourteenth Amendments cannot tolerate the infliction of a sentence of death under legal systems that permit this unique penalty to be so wantonly and so freakishly imposed."

He rejected the sentences on Furman, Jackson, and Branch, because he believed the sentences had been imposed capriciously. The juries in these cases had been given complete discretion to do what they wished when it came to sentencing, with the result that the death penalty was "wantonly and freakishly imposed." He felt that the death sentence was cruel and unusual in the same way that being struck by lightning was cruel and unusual; it was randomly imposed rather than fairly imposed.

Four justices dissented. These were Chief Justice Burger, and Justices Harry Blackmun, Lewis Powell, and William Rehnquist. All four were recent Nixon appointees. They were more in agreement than the five on the majority side. They felt that capital punishment had always been regarded as appropriate under the legal system in the United States and the British system they inherited it from. It was appropriate for serious crimes such as rape and murder and that the text of the Constitution implicitly allowed the death penalty. There was a reference in the Fourteenth Amendment to the taking of life, in section two: ". . . nor shall any State deprive any person of life, liberty, or property, without due process of law; nor deny to any person within its jurisdiction the equal protection of the laws."

They held that the State was entitled to deprive a citizen of life if there was due process and equal protection.

The bottom line was that individual states, and the national legislature, now had to rethink their statutes for capital crimes, to ensure the death penalty was not administered in a discriminatory way.

The ruling was messy, but sufficient to halt executions immediately.

Upon the verdict being handed down, Furman, Jackson, and Branch had to find new accommodations; they were no longer to be housed on death row. In fact, there was an unofficial moratorium on the death penalty across the country. At the time, there were executions pending in many of the thirty-nine states that permitted capital punishment, and all these were stopped immediately. A total of 697 men and women came off death row. The thirty-nine states faced three choices in response to the split decision from the Supreme Court. They could impose mandatory death sentences for certain classes of crime, which would have to be carefully defined and not open to discretion; they could develop proper and fair jury guidelines to prevent jurors acting improperly or arbitrarily; or they could abolish capital punishment.

The decision was handed down in 1972, but the moratorium had been in place since 1967, as states watched and waited for the verdict. In the four years following the decision, thirty-seven states introduced new legislation aimed at overcoming the concerns of the Supreme Court. One of the solutions explored by several of the states was splitting the trial process into two sections. There was the first phase, when guilt or innocence was established. If the defendant was found guilty, they moved on to a second, and separate, sentencing phase. Other states imposed standards on judges to ensure that the death penalty, if it was ever imposed again, would be applied consistently and never again along racial lines.

It would be four years before the Supreme Court tested these new legal processes.

And what of William Furman? He served sixteen years before being released on parole in 1984. He stayed out of trouble for the next two decades, but in 2004 he pleaded guilty to a burglary charge in Bibb County Superior Court, Georgia. He was sentenced to twenty years and is currently in prison.

11

SUPREME COURT CHANGES ITS MIND— EXECUTIONS ARE BACK ON

Troy Leon Gregg has one of the most fascinating stories of all the death row convicts. His case was crucial to the reinstatement of the death penalty—but he escaped the executioner in a unique and tragic-comic manner.

Born in 1948, Gregg was a white career criminal. He was a drifter who stole what he needed and had no compunction about using violence. On the morning of Wednesday, November 21, 1973, he was with a teenage companion, Floyd Ralford Allen, and they were hitchhiking in northern Florida. They were broke—they had just eight dollars between them. A car stopped to pick them up. It was driven by Fred Simmons and Bob Moore. Together they drove north along the Florida Turnpike, but about 240 miles out of Miami the car broke down on the highway. A Florida State Highway patrolman drove Simmons and Moore to an auto dealer, where they bought a 1960 red and white Pontiac. Then they drove back and picked up their hitchhikers.

Gregg realized that the two men had enough money to buy a car and plenty more besides. As they drove onwards, he began to plan ways of relieving them of that stash. Along the way, they picked up another hitchhiker, Dennis Weaver, who got out when they reached Atlanta,

Georgia. The four occupants of the car then drove on again. All were drinking. They got to the intersection of Georgia Highway 20 and I-85 in Gwinnett County, Georgia, where they stopped for a comfort break. Simmons and Moore got out, and then Gregg turned to Allen and told him to get out too, as they were going to rob the two Good Samaritans who had picked them up. He produced a gun and lay in wait behind the car, using the roof to steady his aim. When Simmons and Moore reappeared, Gregg fired three times, dropping the two men. Then he circled around the car and shot both in the back of the head, execution style.

After emptying the wallets of their victims Gregg and Allen got into the car and drove off.

It was an opportunistic crime and they had not thought it out. The third hitchhiker, Weaver, spotted an article in an Atlanta newspaper about the double slayings and went to the police. Gregg and Allen were apprehended shortly afterwards.

At the trial in Georgia in 1974, Gregg was convicted of both murders, which were committed in the course of a robbery. That would traditionally have merited him the death penalty in the pre-Furman days. As a result of changes in the relevant legislation, the court in Georgia felt confident imposing the death penalty. Gregg found himself on death row.

The inevitable result was that the case was thrown on to the Supreme Court, which would pass final judgment on whether the state of Georgia had made enough changes in their legislation to make capital punishment once again constitutional.

Other states also felt they had made sufficient changes to satisfy the Supreme Court and reintroduce the death penalty. Four other cases were considered alongside *Gregg v. Georgia*. These were *Proffitt v. Florida*, *Jurek v. Texas*, *Woodson v. North Carolina*, and *Roberts v. Louisiana*.

Charles William Proffitt broke into a home in Florida, where he stabbed the homeowner, Joel Medgebow, in his bed. He pushed over Medgebow's wife and ran. He had been intending to burgle the house but the homeowner had woken and disturbed him.

Jerry Lane Jurek was convicted of abduction, rape, and murder of a ten-year-old girl in Texas. He was twenty-two at the time and had been drinking all afternoon. After ditching his companions, he went prowling for a young girl to have sex with. He found a ten-year-old girl in a public swimming pool where her grandmother had left her. He abducted and raped her, and then strangled her and tossed her body into a river.

James Tyrone Woodson was convicted of armed robbery and murder in North Carolina. With three accomplices he robbed a grocery store. Two stayed outside as lookouts. Two went inside. Woodson asked for a pack of cigarettes, and as the woman behind the till reached for the pack, he drew his gun and shot her. As he was running out, he bumped into a customer coming in, and he shot the customer too. The employee was killed immediately but the customer survived.

Harry Roberts was an armed robber in Louisiana. As he was robbing a gas station, he shot employee Richard Lowe four times in the head. He was arrested along with three accomplices and convicted of first-degree murder when the three testified against him. The story that emerged was that the men decided to rob the gas station and went there around midnight on August 17, 1973. They pretended to be looking for employment and gained entry to the office, where Roberts stole a pistol. He used this to shoot Lowe in a back room while the others were outside.

All four killers were sentenced to death, and their states, too, were confident that they had made the changes to satisfy the Supreme Court following *Furman v. Georgia.* The last execution had been in 1967. It was now 1976. Would the Supreme Court allow the new executions or shoot them down? Would the decade-long absence of the death penalty in the United States become a permanent feature?

All five cases shared the same basic procedural history. Georgia, Florida, Texas, North Carolina, and Louisiana had amended their legislation to comply with the guidelines laid down by the Furman decision. In all five cases the individual State Supreme Courts had upheld the death penalty. But would the US Supreme Court? The attorneys for the five defendants hoped that this test case would eliminate forever capital punishment in the United States. The crux of the matter was that the Court had declared capital punishment unconstitutional ("cruel and unusual") because there were no rational standards that determined when it was imposed and when it was not. Had the new legislation changed that?

The first thing the Court found during their July 1976 deliberations was that America had not outgrown the death penalty, as some had hoped. Noting that thirty-five states and Congress had adapted legislation to take into account the Furman decision, rather than abolishing the penalty, the court said, "The most marked indication of society's endorsement of the death penalty for murder is the legislative response to Furman." They were also influenced by a referendum in California, when the people voted that the death penalty should not be removed.

Capital punishment served two purposes: retribution and deterrence, and it "comports with the basic concept of human dignity at the core of the Eighth Amendment." The deterrent effect was impossible to measure, but the Court could not dismiss it, as "The possible penalty of death may well enter into the cold calculus that precedes the decision to act."

They also felt that the death penalty was not a disproportionate reaction to murder, saying that although death was irrevocable, that did not make it disproportionate to the crime of deliberately taking a live.

"It is an extreme sanction, suitable to the most extreme of crimes," they judged.

Having said that, it had to be applied rationally and fairly. The first thing the Court determined was that the death penalty could not be mandatory for certain crimes, as it had been in other jurisdictions such as medieval England and as it had been in the United States until the 1790s. Around that time, a distaste for the death penalty had begun to creep in and juries occasionally found someone innocent because they thought it was the lesser of two evils when faced with the prospect of hanging him. Back then there were no jails, so lengthy imprisonment was not an option—it was either hang or walk.

Pennsylvania was the first state to split murder into different degrees, allowing juries to convict of murder in a lesser degree and save someone the noose. That was in 1794. In the 1840s, Tennessee, Alabama, and Louisiana began to allow juries to exercise discretion when it came to capital cases. They could recommend the death penalty or life imprisonment. This development quickly spread, and by the end of that century, twenty-three states allowed jury discretion. Fourteen more states followed in the early years of the twentieth century, and by 1963 all death penalty jurisdictions employed discretionary sentencing. But it had been applied arbitrarily and sometimes along racial lines.

The Court laid down two guidelines that states needed to follow to make the death penalty constitutional. The first was that there must be objective criteria to guide juries or judges in exercising sentencing discretion. The objectiveness and fairness of these criteria would be tested by the appeals system in the state and every death sentence would be scrutinized by the appeals system. The second guideline was that the judge or jury must be able to take into account the character and previous record of the defendant facing the death penalty.

Looking at the five cases before them, the Court decided that in the case of Gregg, Proffitt, and Jurek, the sentencing schemes of Georgia, Florida, and Texas had met their criteria. But in the other two cases (Woodson and Roberts), North Carolina and Louisiana had not.

It is worth looking at the three procedures of the states that passed and the two that didn't, to understand why the death penalty was reintroduced in the United States and how it is applied today.

What Georgia implemented fairly much followed the Model Penal Code, a blueprint drawn up in 1962 to encourage states to update and standardize their laws. There was a two-part trial. In the first part, the defendant pleaded guilty or was found guilty of a capital offense. In the second and separate part, there was an additional hearing where the jury heard evidence of aggravation and mitigation—the pros and cons that would either get someone the death penalty or save them from it. In order for the defendant to get the death penalty, there had to be at least one of ten aggravating factors. Here are the ten factors:

1. The defendant had a prior conviction for a capital offense, or a history of serious felonies.
2. The capital felony was committed while the defendant was committing another capital felony.
3. The defendant created a grave risk of death to others.

4. The crime was committed for financial or other gain.
5. The victim of the murder was a judge or prosecutor executing his official duties.
6. The defendant hired a killer.
7. The crime was "outrageously or wantonly vile, horrible, or inhuman in that it involved torture, depravity of mind, or an aggravated battery of the victim."
8. The defendant killed a police officer, prison guard, or fireman in the line of duty.
9. The offense was committed while the defendant was on the run from prison.
10. The offense was committed in the course of resisting arrest.

If one of these aggravating factors was proven, the defendant was eligible for the death penalty. But it was not mandatory. The jury could consider mitigating evidence and decide whether the defendant would live or die.

The Supreme Court found that the need for at least one aggravating factor for the death penalty adequately narrowed the class of defendants eligible for the ultimate punishment. And though there was some discretion allowed to juries, they had clear guidelines on what they could consider. This meant that Georgia's death penalty scheme complied with the Furman requirements and was approved. So Gregg would face execution.

Next they considered Florida. That state's scheme differed from Georgia's in two respects. First, at the sentencing hearing (after the conviction in the first part of the trial), the jury had to determine if there were one or more aggravating factors. They then were asked specifically to weigh these aggravating factors against any mitigating evidence that was presented. This was called a weighing scheme.

Second, the jury's role was advisory. They presented their recommendation to the judge, who had the power to disregard what they said. But he had to explain his reasoning clearly if he decided to disregard the jury recommendation. And there was a clear onus on him to have very good reasons for imposing the death penalty: "The facts suggesting a sentence of death should be so clear and convincing that virtually no reasonable person could differ."

The Supreme Court found that the sentencing judge's discretion was limited in a specific way, and reviewable. Because of the inclusion of the weighing scheme it came very close to the ideal suggested in the Model Penal Code. Thus, Florida also complied with Furman, and Proffitt could be executed.

The third state they considered was Texas. They found that the Texan scheme differed widely from both the Model Penal Code and the schemes adopted by Georgia and Florida. Instead of requiring aggravating factors for a felony to be considered a capital offense, they severely limited the types of crime that could draw down the death penalty. By narrowing the definition of a capital crime, they complied with Furman in a different way.

In 1976, Texas legislated for five classes of crime which were capital felonies. They were:

1. Murder of a policeman or fireman.
2. Murder committed in the course of a kidnapping, burglary, robbery, rape, or arson.
3. Murder committed for pay (i.e. a professional hit man, or contract killing).
4. Murder committed while escaping from a prison.
5. Murder of a prison employee by a prison inmate.

If a defendant was convicted of capital murder, it was up to the prosecution to seek the death penalty. They did not have to. But when they did, the trial moved on to the second phase—a sentencing hearing. The jury had to consider "special issues."

These "special issues" were whether the murder had been deliberate or unplanned; whether the defendant constituted a danger to anyone, including fellow prisoners; and whether, if there had been any provocation leading to the murder, the response of the defendant had been unreasonable.

If the murder was deliberate, or if the condemned was a danger to others, or if they had massively overreacted to a minor provocation, they would face execution. But if none of those factors was proven, the sentence would automatically be life imprisonment.

The Supreme Court ruled that Texas's narrow legal definition of capital murder served the same purpose as the aggravating factors used by Georgia and Florida, and thus complied with the Furman decision. The "special issues" consideration allowed mitigating evidence to be presented. The Texan scheme was found to be constitutional. Jurek could be executed.

In the end, he wasn't. His sentence was commuted to life imprisonment. But Texas went on to execute more people than all the other states put together since the moratorium on executions was lifted in 1974.

Two states found that their schemes fell short of the requirements that followed the Furman decision.

The North Carolina General Assembly, like the Texas Legislature, narrowed the definition of first-degree murder to "murder perpetrated by means of poison, lying in wait, imprisonment, starving, torture, or by any other kind of willful, deliberate, and premeditated killing, or which shall be committed in the perpetration or attempt to perpetrate any arson, rape, robbery, kidnapping, burglary, or other felony."

North Carolina also made first-degree rape a capital offense.

There was no discretion in the application of the death penalty. If convicted of a capital offense, you would get an automatic death sentence. This meant that North Carolina had failed to comply with the Furman requirements and so the Supreme Court rejected their scheme. Woodson succeeded in his challenge and would not be executed.

Finally, the Supreme Court rejected the scheme proposed by Louisiana. The State Legislature, just like North Carolina, narrowly defined capital murder. It was first-degree murder, a capital offense, if the defendant deliberately killed during the commission of a kidnapping, rape, or armed robbery; if the defendant deliberately killed a fireman or police officer in the line of duty; if the defendant deliberately killed and had a prior conviction for murder in any degree; if the defendant killed more than one person, or tried to kill more than one; or if the defendant had been paid to kill.

Aggravated rape and aggravated kidnapping and treason were also capital offenses. But because there was no discretion in sentencing and no consideration of mitigating factors, the North Carolina scheme was shot down by the Supreme Court. So Roberts would not face execution.

In all, five cases had been considered, representing five states' responses to the Furman decision. The Supreme Court found that three of those states now had schemes in place that made executions constitutional, while two did not. But now states knew what was required if they wanted to resume executing prisoners. The way was open for the lifting of the death penalty ban.

As for the five prisoners, Roberts and Woodson succeeded in having their death penalties overturned. Jurek failed, but Texan authorities in 1982 commuted his sentence to life imprisonment. Proffitt was executed. But Gregg, the man whose name is still remembered in connection with the landmark decision, avoided his fate.

Gregg was due to be executed on July 29, 1980. The day before his execution he succeeded in escaping from the maximum security prison at Reidsville, Georgia. Along with three other convicted murderers on death row, he sawed through the bars of his cell. The four men then dressed in homemade prison officer uniforms—complete with fake badges. They walked calmly through the prison and entered the prison visitor's car park. The aunt of one of the four had left a car with the key in the ignition. The four convicts got into the car and drove off. They drove to North Carolina, where a biker acquaintance of theirs, William "Chains" Flamount, put them up in a rented house that he owned.

That night, they hit a bar to celebrate their release. During the course of a wild night, a bar fight broke out and Gregg was beaten to death by a local man, James "Butch" Horne. His body was dumped in a nearby river. The other three were quickly recaptured.

The *North Carolina Star News* reported: "Atlanta—Three escapees from Georgia's death row headed back to Georgia Friday after deciding not to fight extradition. Meanwhile a Charlotte man was charged with accessory after the fact in the death of a fourth Georgia escapee."

The three who had escaped with Gregg were named as Timothy McCorquodale, twenty-seven; Johnny Johnson, twenty-six; and David Jarrell, twenty-five.

"The four convicted murderers disguised themselves as guards and strolled out of the maximum security prison at Reidsville, Ga., but three of the men were recaptured about forty-eight hours later near Charlotte," reported the *North Carolina Star News*, "Shortly before police flushed the three unarmed convicts out of a house with tear gas, authorities fished Gregg's beaten body out of a nearby lake."

James Horne was charged with second-degree murder, and former bike gang member William Flamount was charged with accessory after the fact of murder. He had provided accommodation for the escaped prisoners. The *North Carolina Star News* went on:

> Authorities said the three won't be charged in Gregg's death. James Fuller, a civil-rights attorney who represented the Georgia inmates for the NAACP Legal Defense Fund, released a note in which the three men said they feared for their lives.
>
> 'First that we will be shot while supposedly trying to escape on the return trip to Georgia,' the note said. 'And secondly, that we might be beaten to death once back at Reidsville in retaliation for the embarrassment caused to the state of Georgia because of the escape.'

This fear proved unfounded. The men were returned safely to Georgia, where they had to face the remainder of their sentences. Timothy McCorquodale was executed in the electric chair on October 21, 1987. Johnson and Jarrell had their sentences commuted to life imprisonment.

12

BACK WITH A BANG

The Furman decision highlighted deficiencies in death penalty legislation, resulting in a ten-year hiatus during which no one was put to death. The Gregg decision showed that states could eliminate those deficiencies and resume capital punishment. This, many of them did. The first man to face execution after the moratorium was Gary Gilmore.

Gary Mark Gilmore was born in McCamey, Texas, in 1940. He believed that he was the illegitimate grandson of famous magician Harry Houdini, but this was almost certainly not true. His father was physically abusive and emotionally distant, and the family relocated a lot during his childhood. By his teens, Gary had drifted into petty crime. It began with him setting up a car theft ring at the tender age of fourteen. By twenty-two, he had progressed to armed robbery and assault and was jailed for eight years in 1964. From then on he was in and out of prison.

On the evening of July 19, 1976, he carried out another armed robbery, this time of a gas station in Orem, Utah. The following evening he robbed a motel manager in Provo. In both cases he ordered the employees to do as he said, but despite their compliance, he shot and killed both men—Max Jensen and Bennie Bushnell. After shooting Bushnell, Gilmore tried to dispose of the pistol but accidentally shot himself in the hand, leaving a trail of blood for investigators to follow. He was also seen throwing the gun into bushes near the service garage where his truck was parked. It did not take long for authorities to track him down.

Gilmore was charged with just one murder, that of Bushnell. He was convicted on October 7, 1976. The jury then sat again to consider sentencing and recommended the death penalty due to the special circumstances of the murder. This was all carried out in compliance with the Furman requirements set out by the Supreme Court. Gilmore was given the choice of being hanged or facing a firing squad, the two methods of execution available in Utah. He chose the firing squad, afraid that the hanging might be botched. Execution was scheduled for November 15th of that year. Gilmore announced publicly that he would not be appealing, but there were still inevitable appeals on his behalf, none of which he supported. The execution was put back and he tried to kill himself. Against his wishes, there were a number of stays of execution through the efforts of the American Civil Liberties Union (ACLU). But the final stay was overturned at seven thirty in the morning on January 17, and he was due to face the firing squad later that morning.

Gilmore had made his feelings plain at a Board of Pardons hearing in November 1976, saying of the ACLU, "They always want to get in on the act. I don't think they have ever really done anything effective in their lives. I would like them all—including that group of reverends and rabbis from Salt Lake City—to butt out. This is my life and this is my death. It's been sanctioned by the courts that I die and I accept that."

The night before the execution, Gilmore had requested an all-night gathering of friends and family at the prison mess hall. That evening he was served the traditional last meal of steak and potatoes but was only able to face a glass of milk and a mug of coffee. But Gilmore's uncle had smuggled three miniature bottles of Jack Daniel's whiskey into the prison, which Gilmore did knock back.

The next morning, once news was received that the stay of execution was overturned, Gilmore was led to an abandoned cannery behind the prison, which served as the death chamber. He sat on a chair and

Dr. Alfred P. Southwick, the dentist who advocated the electric chair, and who decided it would be a chair rather than a couch or bath.

Thomas Edison, the inventor who advocated alternating current for the electric chair.

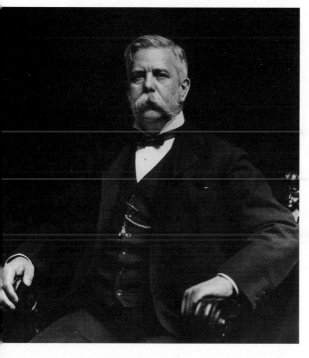

George Westinghouse, the industrialist who opposed the development of the electric chair to preserve the reputation of his alternating current.

A horse is electrocuted in an early experiment by Harold Brown.

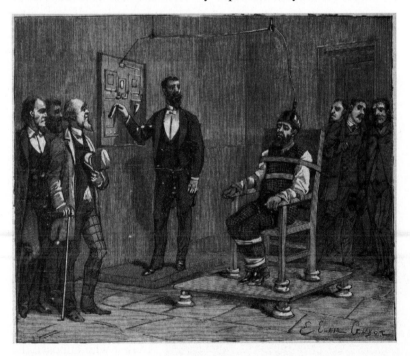

William Kemmler, the first victim of Old Sparky.

The electric chair in
Sing Sing, New York.

The electric chair in Arkansas, used until 1948.

Topsy the Elephant was the biggest victim of execution by electricity. Although Thomas Edison filmed the execution, he had nothing else to do with it.

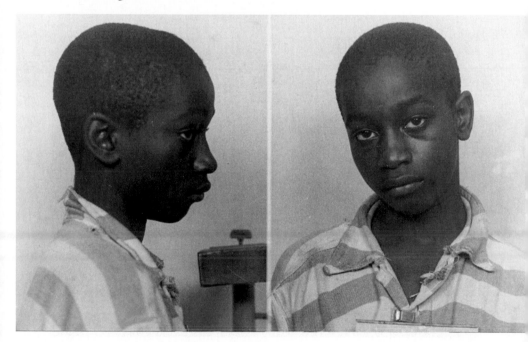

George Stinney, aged 14, was the youngest child sent to the chair. Accused by the State of South Carolina, he was later found to be innocent.

Ruth Snyder.

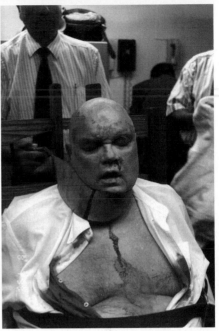

Allen Lee Davis was so obese that Florida had to make a new chair to accomodate him. The execution went badly wrong.

Ruth Snyder, photographed in her death throes with a hidden camera by Tom Howard of the New York *Daily News*.

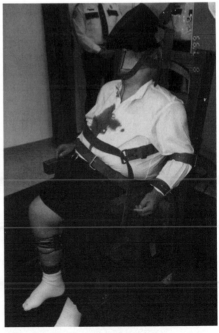

Davis bled badly during the botched execution, leading to a temporary moratorium on electrocutions in Florida.

Charles Lindbergh and the prosecutor Norman Schwarzkopf during a break in the trial.

Bruno Richard Hauptmann, convicted of the kidnapping and murder of the baby son of aviation hero Charles Lindbergh.

Charles Lindbergh gives evidence at the trial of the century.

Mob hitman Abe Reles turned state witness, and brought down Murder Inc.

Louis Buchalter, mob hitman brought down by Abe Reles.

Louis Capone and Emaneul Weiss, executed together at Sing Sing.

Ethel and Julius Rosenberg, the couple who went to the electric chair for selling atomic bomb secrets to the Russians.

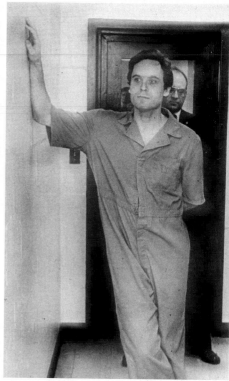

Charming serial killer Ted Bundy relaxing in court.

The original "rebel without a cause," Charles Starkweather with his girlfriend Caril Fugate.

Robert Gleeson, who died shouting "Kiss my ass!" was the last man to die in Old Sparky.

was strapped to it. Behind the chair, a wall of sandbags had been set up to catch any stray bullets. He could not see the firing squad. They were behind a black curtain with five small holes in it. The five marksmen, all local police officers, would shoot through the holes. Gilmore was asked had he any final words, to which he replied, "Let's do it."

The local Catholic chaplain administered the last rites, the order was given, and five bullets thudded into the convict's chest, killing him instantly. He was an organ donor, and after his execution his corneas were donated to two people. His body was then cremated.

Gary Gilmore had shown the world that execution was back on in America. His death was immortalized by British punk band, The Adverts, in their song "Gary Gilmore's Eyes" in 1977, and then by an inevitable television Movie of the Week, *The Executioner's Song*, in 1982. This starred Tommy Lee Jones and was based on a popular factual book by Norman Mailer.

13

TOP TEN—THE MOST NOTORIOUS VICTIMS OF OLD SPARKY

In over a hundred years of use, well over a thousand people met their deaths on the electric chair. They ranged from a fourteen-year-old boy to hardened mafioso who had survived a lifetime of crime. Rapists, serial killers, hit men, traitors, and incorrigible repeat offenders all ended up frying for their crimes. It is impossible to outline every victim of the chair without turning this volume into an encyclopedia but some cases stand out.

They stand out because of the national interest they generated, or because of the depravity of the murderers, or the fame of their victims. Below, in no particular order, are the most notorious victims of Old Sparky.

JULIUS AND ETHEL ROSENBERG
THE RED SCARE

The story of the Rosenbergs had everything for a country on the cusp of the space age. It had the red menace of a communist plot, the glamour of espionage, atomic bomb secrets, and a grisly execution of a husband and wife. The fact that they both looked two decades older than their given ages and looked like they would have been more comfortable in the 1850s than the 1950s didn't take from the story of Old Sparky's most famous victims.

The decision to fry the couple on June 19, 1953, has always been controversial. Were they guilty, or just innocent patsies in the Great Game that has always been played between competing superpowers? They became a cause célèbre for liberal opponents of the death penalty, as well as those who wanted greater cooperation between America and the Soviet Union.

Four decades after their execution, new research seems to indicate that Julius was spying at a low level for the Russians, while his wife Ethel was convicted in the wrong. Neither gave away the secret of the Bomb.

But the story begins far earlier than 1953.

Julius Rosenberg was born in New York in the dying months of World War I. His parents were Jewish immigrants from Europe and worked in a local shop. Julius attended the Seward Park High School before going on to pursue a degree in electrical engineering at the City College of New York. He was politicized at an early age, becoming a leader in the Young Communist League while in college.

Ethel Greenglass was three years older and from a similar Jewish background. In her teens she wanted to become an actress and singer but eventually took a secretarial job at a shipping company. While working there she became involved in labor disputes and joined the Young Communist League. In 1936 she met Julius at one of the meetings. She was instantly drawn to the serious young man. When he graduated in 1939, the couple married.

They settled in New Jersey and Julius got a job at the Army Signal Corps engineering lab at Fort Monmouth. The lab carried out important research on electronics, radar, and missile guidance systems throughout the war, and Rosenberg was an engineer-inspector. In 1942 the former Young Communist was approached secretly by Bernard Schuster, a high-ranking member of the American Communist Party, who introduced him to Soviet spymaster Semyon Semenov. Rosenberg began secretly passing over secrets, including a complete set of designs for the Lockheed P-80 Shooting Star, the very first jet plane used by the US Air Force.

Rosenberg also let his handlers know that his brother-in-law, David Greenglass, was working on the top secret Manhattan Project, which eventually produced the atomic bombs that ended the war. He helped recruit Greenglass to his spy ring. But near the end of the war, the army found out about Rosenberg's membership of the Young Communist League, and he was fired.

After the war there was an uneasy balance of power between the Americans and the Soviets, but the Americans had the Bomb. However, by the end of that decade the Soviets had developed an atomic bomb of their own. Stunned at the startling speed at which they had caught up, the United States began an investigation and discovered that a German refugee physicist, Klaus Fuchs, had been passing along secrets. As the conspiracy unraveled, Greenglass was implicated. From this it was only a short step to his sister Ethel and her husband Julius.

Greenglass did his best to shield his sister for a while but eventually claimed that she knew all about Julius's work as a spy and had actively participated, typing out reports for him to pass on. The Rosenbergs were arrested in early August. They weren't even given time to allow Ethel to make arrangements for the care of their two young children. Another associate of theirs, Morton Sobell, attempted to flee to Mexico, where he was holidaying at the time, but he was apprehended by Mexican authorities and handed over to the United States for trial.

Sobell and the Rosenbergs came before a grand jury in August 1950, and Sobell's wife did her best to blacken the Rosenbergs in order to paint Sobell in a better light. She testified: "Julius proceeded to tell me that he knew that David was working on the atomic bomb, that he felt there was not a direct exchange of scientific information among the Allies, and that it would only be fair for Russia to have the information too. He asked me if I would relate this to David. His wife said that I should at least relay the message, that she felt that David might be interested. She felt that even if I was against it, I should at least discuss it with him and hear what he had to say."

Her testimony badly damaged the Rosenbergs but did not get Sobell off the hook. All three were indicted, along with Anatoli Yakovlev, General Counsel of the Soviet Delegation in New York. Bail was posted so high that the Rosenbergs had no possibility of getting out, and their two children were shunted among unwilling relatives before being finally placed in the Jewish Children's Home in the Bronx. Ethel cried herself to sleep at night under the stress. But Julius didn't break; no confession was forthcoming.

Believing that Julius was the linchpin, top government officials decided to go for the death penalty. They believed that if he was facing the chair, he would cut a deal and give up the other members of his spy ring. To racket up the pressure, they also went after the death penalty for Ethel, even though the evidence against her was very slim.

"It looks as though Rosenberg is the kingpin of a very large ring, and if there is any way of breaking him by having the shadow of a death penalty over him, we want to do it," said Gordon Dean, chairman of the Atomic Energy Commission.

Just ten days before the trial was due to begin, the Greenglasses were persuaded to change their original stories, strengthening the case against Ethel Rosenberg. They claimed that secret information was passed to Julius in front of Ethel and that she knew all about it. She even typed out the information for him to pass on. This new version of events got Sobell a reduction in his charges and got his wife off the hook entirely.

The trial opened on March 6, 1951. Sobell was tried alongside the Rosenbergs, before Judge Irving Kaufmann. The prosecution's primary witness was now David Greenglass, and his evidence was damning. He told of handing over a drawing of the mechanism of the Nagasaki bomb to Julius and of seeing his sister type up notes of the secrets.

Throughout the trial Julius and Ethel did not crack. Not only did they refuse to divulge names—names that might have saved their lives—they refused to testify or answer questions, repeatedly asserting their Fifth Amendment rights not to incriminate themselves when asked about the Young Communist League and their membership of the Communist Party.

On March 29, the Rosenbergs were convicted of espionage, and on April 5, Judge Kaufman sentenced them both to death. With their fate decided, the couple continued to maintain their innocence, denying passing on the vital atomic bomb secrets. But the judge had no sympathy, saying, "I consider your crime worse than murder. I believe your conduct in putting into the hands of the Russians the A-bomb years before our best scientists predicted Russia would perfect the bomb, has already caused the Communist aggression in Korea, with the resultant casualties exceeding fifty thousand, and who knows but that millions more of innocent people may pay the price of your treason."

Julius Rosenberg, a committed communist to the end, saw the death sentence as an inevitable result of a political frame-up and conspiracy, saying, "This death sentence is not surprising. It had to be. There had to be a Rosenberg case because there had to be an intensification of the hysteria in America to make the Korean War acceptable to the American people. And there had to be a dagger thrust in the heart of the left to tell them that you are no longer gonna get five years for a Smith Act prosecution [a prosecution for urging the overthrow of the government], or one year for contempt of court, but we're gonna kill ya!"

There was scant public sympathy for this view at the time, but many people were concerned that there was little real evidence against the couple, particularly Ethel, and the sentence did seem very harsh. Morton Sobell, also convicted, had been sentenced to thirty years (he served seventeen) rather than the chair. Between the trial and the executions there were widespread protests and claims of anti-Semitism. But the mainstream Jewish organizations and the American Civil Liberties Union did not get behind the campaign. It received more sympathy abroad than at home.

Among those opposing the executions were Jean-Paul Sartre, Albert Einstein, Jean Cocteau, writers Bertolt Brecht and Dashiell Hammett, and artist Frida Kahlo. Pablo Picasso wrote, "The hours count. The minutes count. Do not let this crime against humanity take place." Even the Pope voiced his concerns, but in February 1953 President Dwight D. Eisenhower rejected all appeals. The international outcry was to no avail.

The date was set for June 18, and the Rosenbergs were transferred to Sing Sing Correctional Facility in Ossining where the New
York State Executioner, Joseph Francel, was waiting. From Cairo, on
the edge of the Catskills, he had been executioner since 1939, and this
would be one of his final times on the switch. During his tenure he
oversaw 137 executions.

There was a glimmer of hope for Julius and Ethel on June 17, when
a Supreme Court justice granted a temporary stay of execution. But the
new legal objection was dealt with quickly—the full court sitting the
following day to ensure that this did not drag on for weeks or months.
After a tense few hours, the Court, at noon on Friday, June 19, ordered
the execution to go ahead. The new time was set for eleven o'clock that
evening.

This immediately set the lawyers into a frenzy. The late hour—
the normal time for executions in Sing Sing—brought the procedure
into the Jewish Sabbath, and the Rosenbergs were Jewish. Desperately
playing for time, their lawyer, Emmanuel Hirsh Bloch, argued that this
offended their faith. His plan backfired; instead of postponing the execution, the court decided to bring it forward three hours. The Sabbath
begins at sunset on Friday evening, so the execution was rescheduled
for eight o'clock in the evening, two hours before sunset.

The execution of Julius Rosenberg went without a hitch. The protocol was for three jolts of electricity to be used in succession. From eyewitness testimony, Julius died immediately, making the final two jolts
unnecessary. Then it was Ethel's turn. Looking nervous but defiant, she
was strapped into the chair and the electrodes secured in place. Her
body jerked as the jolts ran through her. Then the door to the execution
chamber opened, and a doctor examined the slumped body. Her heart
was still beating. Another powerful jolt was discharged through her,
then a fifth. Her head began to smoke as the final charge ran through
her, and the small room reeked of burning flesh. But the doctor was able
to confirm that she was finally dead.

Julius and Ethel Rosenberg were buried at Wellwood Cemetery in
Pinelawn, New York.

So, were they guilty? Opinion is divided. Soviet leader Nikita Khrushchev said he had been told that they helped Russia enormously. But Boris Brokhovich, one of the leaders of the Soviet nuclear program, was dismissive in a *New York Times* interview: "You sat the Rosenbergs in the electric chair for nothing. We got nothing from the Rosenbergs."

It seems clear now that Julius Rosenberg was a spy for the Russians and did pass on valuable secrets, especially on US electronic systems and jet plane development. But he did not compromise the atomic bomb program.

The chief witness against the Rosenbergs, Ethel's brother David Greenglass, was also prosecuted for espionage. Because of his cooperation with the authorities he received a fifteen-year sentence, of which he served nine. On his release he recanted his statement, saying he testified against his sister and brother-in-law in order to save his wife from prosecution.

The two children of the Rosenbergs, Michael and Robert, were rejected by their relatives but were eventually adopted by a high school teacher and his wife. They continued to protest their parents' innocence, only finally acknowledging, in 2008, that their father had been a Soviet spy. They consider their mother an innocent woman, set up by the government. In the light of what is now known, it is difficult to dispute this view.

TED BUNDY
THE BANAL FACE OF EVIL

Ted Bundy is the ultimate boogey man. We think of serial killers as loners—weirdos who cannot meet our eye. We think we can spot them easily. But no one spotted Ted Bundy. He was a friendly, engaging, and handsome young man, who had no difficulty getting a date. In fact, he was the sort of man any young woman would be happy to bring home to her mother.

Yet he stalked and hunted women as a hobby, killing at least thirty and maybe up to a hundred. His smiling face showed that evil can wear a mask of banal ordinariness. As he chillingly said of himself: "I am the most cold-hearted son of a bitch you'll ever meet."

But monster though he was, he cried like a baby on the eve of his execution and could not face his final meal.

Theodore Robert Cowell was born on November 24, 1946 to Eleanor Louise Cowell at the Elizabeth Lund Home for Unwed Mothers at Burlington, Vermont. His father is unknown—but might have been Eleanor's abusive father. Eleanor's parents raised Ted as their own son, to avoid the stigma of admitting that their daughter had produced a bastard. It was many years before Ted realized his true parentage.

Samuel Cowell, whom Ted thought was his father, was a tyrannical bully who injured animals and beat his family members regularly, once throwing one of his daughters down the stairs. He was a racist and bigot, a perfect role model for a future serial killer. From an early age Ted showed signs of abnormality. One family member recalled waking up from a nap to find herself surrounded by knives, while three-year-old Ted smiled down at her.

When Ted was five, his real mother married Johnny Bundy. But Ted and his adoptive father failed to bond, despite Johnny's best efforts. Ted was a bit of a loner in high school but did not noticeably stand out. He was caught a few times for burglary and enjoyed peeping into uncurtained bedrooms. He was developing an obsession with dead and mutilated bodies.

After a year at the University of Puget Sound, Bundy transferred to the University of Washington where he studied Chinese. But he dropped out in 1968. He seemed immature and unambitious, and an early girlfriend dumped him for this reason. In 1969 he began a relationship with divorcée Elizabeth Kloepfer from Utah, who worked as a secretary at the University of Washington School of Medicine. He re-enrolled in college, this time as a psychology major. He even worked on a suicide help hotline. Ann Rule, a writer who knew him at the time, said he was "kind, solicitous, and empathetic."

He switched to studying law and seemed to be getting his life on track. Along with his relationship with Ms. Kloepfer, he began to date the woman who had rejected him a few years previously. He juggled the two relationships without either woman realizing she was not the only one in his life. Then he ditched the woman who had ditched him, just to prove to himself that he could do it. In 1974, he began to skip classes. And women began to disappear. Ted Bundy had found his true calling.

According to his own testimony, Bundy had attempted his first kidnapping in 1969 and his first murder a few years later. But his accounts varied. He told one investigator he killed two women in Atlantic City in 1969, while another investigator was told he waited until 1971 in Seattle. No one knows for sure, and investigators suspect he may have begun killing in his teens. Eight-year-old Ann Marie Burr of Tacoma disappeared when Ted was fourteen and living in that town.

It is known that he began a kidnapping and killing spree early in 1974. It began when he broke into the basement apartment of eighteen-year-old Karen Sparks and beat her unconscious before raping her. She survived, but with permanent brain damage. From then on, female college students began disappearing at the rate of roughly one a month. The only thing they had in common was that they were young, white, and had their hair parted in the middle.

As authorities grew increasingly concerned, Bundy began to work at the Washington State Department of Emergency Services in Olympia, the government agency involved in tracing the missing women and tracking him down. He began to date Carole Ann Boone, a twice-divorced mother of two, as fear grew in the local community.

The Pacific Northwest murders climaxed on Sunday, July 14, when two women were abducted in broad daylight at a crowded beach at Lake Sammamish State Park, twenty miles from Seattle. A good-looking young man in tennis whites, with his arm in a sling, had introduced himself to the women as Ted, and asked for their help to unhitch a boat from his car. He approached many women that day and most refused to go back to his car. But two did. The two women were abducted four hours apart. He kept the first woman alive and forced her to watch as he murdered the second. He then killed the first.

It had been a risky thing to do, and many witnesses at the beach gave detailed descriptions, both of the man and his Volkswagen car.

A number of people came forward to identify the subsequent police mug shot as Ted Bundy, but investigators did not believe the clean-cut and well-adjusted young law student could be their killer, so he was not detained.

In August 1974 Bundy moved to the University of Utah Law School, relocating to Salt Lake City and leaving his divorced girlfriend in Seattle. He remained in touch but dated many other women as well. The only fly in the ointment was that he was struggling with his course work, finding the intricacies of the law baffling. However, he had his hobbies . . .

A string of unexplained murders began in September, with women disappearing every three or four weeks. The murders were never linked to Bundy—until he confessed to them on the eve of his execution.

However, there were suspicions. Elizabeth Kloepfer, the girlfriend he had left behind in Seattle, phoned police to remind them that she had identified him as a suspect in the earlier Pacific North West murders. This time she was interviewed in detail, as Bundy began to rise in the list of suspects. But there was nothing beyond suspicion to link him to the disappearances and murders.

In 1975 Bundy began to concentrate on Colorado and women began to disappear in that state. He refined his MO, using crutches and pretending to be injured to present a less threatening face to potential victims.

Meanwhile cops in Washington had hit a dead end in their investigation of the string of disappearances, which had ended as suddenly as they began. So they tried an innovative new method. They commandeered the King County payroll computer and inputted the many data lists they had compiled—lists of acquaintances of the victims, Volkswagen owners, sex offenders, and so on. Out of the thousands of names, twenty-six showed up on four separate lists. One of the twenty-six was Ted Bundy. Detectives also manually compiled a list of their hundred hot suspects—and Bundy featured there as well.

But before they could make their move, Bundy was stopped at a routine checkpoint in Utah. The Highway Patrol officer noticed the front seat of Bundy's Volkswagen was missing, so he searched the car and found handcuffs, ski masks, trash bags, and a full burglary kit. Bundy's apartment was also tossed, but the investigators overlooked a stash of Polaroids Bundy had taken of his victims. They did not have enough to hold him, but the net was closing. Bundy was placed under twenty-four hour surveillance as Washington cops flew in to interview Kloepfer once more.

Eventually a forensic examination of Bundy's car uncovered hairs that matched with some of his victims. There was still too little evidence for a murder charge, but on February 23, 1976, Bundy went on trial for the attempted abduction of Carol DaRonch, a victim who had managed to escape his clutches. He was sentenced to one to fifteen years in Utah State Prison. He immediately began to plan his escape but was transferred to Colorado to face a murder charge before he got his opportunity.

But on June 7, 1977, his chance came. As he was representing himself on the murder charge, he was not handcuffed in court. During a preliminary hearing at Pitkin County Courthouse in Aspen, he went to the law library during a recess and jumped through a second-story window. He sprained an ankle but got away. Six days later he was recaptured. But the trial was going his way; he was winning the pretrial motions, and the scant evidence was being thrown out as inadmissible. The prosecutors were getting worried. Bundy stood a good chance of acquittal if he could just remain calm and let the process grind to a conclusion. Instead, he made another break for freedom.

After months of sawing with a smuggled hacksaw blade, he cut a hole in the roof of his cell and wriggled into the crawlspace in the ceiling. Now he had his escape route. He waited until a few days after Christmas, when most of the staff were on holiday, then disappeared through the crawlspace. He dropped through the ceiling of the apartment of the chief jailer—who was out with his wife that evening—stole a set of clothes, and walked out the front door. By the time his escape was discovered, he was in Chicago.

He stole a car and arrived in Tallahassee, Florida, and on January 8, rented a room at a boarding house near Florida State University. It took him only a week to return to his psychopathic ways. He bludgeoned and sexually assaulted four young women in a fifteen-minute orgy of violence that horrified the community. Two survived; two died. And in early February he killed again. A few days after that he fled Tallahassee, but three days later he was stopped in a stolen car. After a brief struggle he was arrested. The arresting officer had no idea he had captured one of the FBI's Most Wanted.

The trial was back on, with the two Florida murders substituted for the Colorado indictments. This time Bundy was not going to get off the hook so easily. The eyes of the world were on him now—250 reporters from five continents were in attendance, and it was the first trial to be televised nationally. Once more, Bundy chose to handle his own defense. But he had a strange notion of what a criminal defense involved. He focused on grandiose gestures and bluster, rejecting a more low-key and sensible approach. He was offered a deal: plead guilty to three homicides and get a seventy-five year sentence. The death penalty was off the table. But Bundy couldn't bring himself to take the deal. It would mean pleading guilty before the whole world. So he fought the charges instead. The prosecution case was weak, but stronger than it had been in Colorado.

The jury took only seven hours to convict Bundy on two counts of murder, three of attempted murder, and two of burglary. He was sentenced to death on the murder charges. Six months later he was convicted of another murder, picking up a third death sentence.

In medieval and early modern times the gap between sentence and execution could be as short as a few hours. It still is in China. But in the United States the gap can be several years, as a lengthy appeals process is gone through. Bundy had several years to contemplate what he had done. During this time he began to open up to various interviewers, and a frightening picture emerged. He loved the idea of possession—especially of possessing things he should not have. So he shoplifted compulsively and enjoyed stealing cars. Rape was an act of possession, and he said that he began killing women as a matter of expediency—leave no witnesses. But then he discovered he enjoyed killing women.

"The ultimate possession was the taking of a life. And then the physical possession of the remains," he told Stephen Michaud and

Hugh Aynesworth (*Ted Bundy: Conversations with a Killer*). He also revealed that he enjoyed using the decomposing bodies of his victims as sexual toys, often visiting the remote disposal sites days or weeks after the murder. He also hacked off the heads and kept them as souvenirs.

The execution was set for March 4, 1986, but then put back to July 2. However, fifteen hours before sentence was to be carried out, it was postponed indefinitely as the full case was reassessed. One question that was being considered was whether Bundy had the mental capacity to be tried. Eventually the sentence was put back more than three years, being rescheduled for January 24, 1989. This might seem slow, but in terms of the normal appeals process and the legal minefield surrounding it, it was actually very fast. Facing the end of the road, Bundy began to talk more freely to investigators, admitting to the Pacific North West murders and a number of other ones he had not been connected with. He also confessed to murders in Idaho, Utah, and Colorado. Some of his confessions may have been fabricated to buy more time, but it became obvious that he had killed at least thirty women. The total may well be over a hundred. There was a move to get the families of potential victims to petition for a stay of execution to allow Bundy to reveal more details of his crimes, but the families refused to cooperate. There would be no further stays.

Bundy thought of one last ploy; suicide would deny prosecutors the satisfaction of seeing him fry. He spoke of it the night before his execution. But death row prisoners are monitored carefully to prevent them taking their own lives. He had no option but to face the chair. He was somber and depressed. Fred Lawrence, a Methodist minister from Gainesville, spent the night with Bundy, and the two men prayed together. Outside the gates of the prison a large crowd had gathered. This is common. Executions are no longer public events, but they generate huge public interest. Normally the crowd holds a candlelit vigil protesting what they see as state-sanctioned murder. Not this time. Five hundred people had gathered to celebrate the death of the man they regarded as a monster.

On the morning of January 24, 1989, Bundy was woken early and offered a last meal of his choice. But he turned this down. Instead the prison kitchen prepared the traditional fare given to condemned men with no special requests. He was presented with a medium-rare steak, eggs over easy, hash browns, and toast with butter and jelly. This was washed down with milk, coffee, and juice. But Bundy had lost his bravado. He couldn't face the meal and didn't eat any of it.

A little before seven o'clock in the morning, two guards led the ashen-faced prisoner into the death chamber. They strapped his chest and limbs to the shiny wooden chair. Bundy scanned the window to the witness room, looking for familiar faces. There were forty-two people crowded into the room and very few friendly faces. He recognized some of his prosecutors and gave a small nod in their direction. He appeared to be mumbling, and then he bowed his head. His head, shaven for the electrodes, glistened with the gel that had been applied to conduct the current.

Superintendent Tom Barton bent down and asked Bundy if he had any last words. The killer hesitated for a moment, and when he spoke his voice wavered. Looking at one of his lawyers, Jim Coleman, and at the Methodist minister who had spent the previous night with him, he said, "Jim and Fred, I'd like you to give my love to my family and friends."

The two men nodded. Then the final strap was secured across Bundy's mouth and chin and the metal skullcap was bolted into place. The black veil fell across the front of Bundy's face, and Barton signaled that it was time. An unnamed officer pushed the button, and 2,000 volts coursed through Bundy's body. Through the window, the witnesses saw his body tense and his hands clench on the arms of the chair. A small puff of smoke rose from his right leg, where the second electrode was located.

After a minute the current was switched off, and Bundy's body immediately relaxed and went limp. A paramedic walked up and pulled open his shirt, listening for a heartbeat. A second shone a light into his eyes. Both men nodded. The job was done.

It didn't take long for word to get out, and at the gates of the prison a cheer welled up, as some in the crowd began to chant: "Burn, burn, burn!" Others sang and hugged and banged on pans and pots.

"I wish I could have been the one flipping the switch," said Florida police officer David Hoar. Police chief Jim Sewell was more reflective: "Regardless of what Bundy did, he was still a human being."

A number of hours later, a white hearse bearing Bundy's remains left the prison, and those who were still outside the gates cheered once more. Bundy was cremated in Gainesville, and his remains were scattered at an undisclosed location on the Cascade Mountains of Washington State as he had requested.

The Boogey Man had been banished.

ANNA MARIA HAHN
THE BLONDE BORGIA

Often dubbed angels of mercy, there is a breed of serial killer who preys on the elderly and vulnerable, often posing as a friend or caregiver of their victim. Some are motivated by the desire to be at the center of drama or have a God complex, while others are motivated by nothing but greed. They see the elderly as easy sources of income.

Anna Marie Hahn was the latter. She had a gambling problem and murder gave her the bucks to pay her bills. A German-American, she became notorious as the Blonde Borgia and Arsenic Anna. She showed no mercy for her elderly victims but begged for mercy before the switch was thrown at her execution.

Anna Filser, the youngest of twelve children, was born in Bavaria in 1906, but the family sent her to America in disgrace when she gave birth to an illegitimate son at the age of twenty-three. Anna stayed with relatives in Cincinnati and quickly married fellow German immigrant Philip Hahn. She found a job at a telephone exchange alongside him but soon grew bored of the hours and quit. The couple opened two delicatessens, but she grew bored of these too. There were three mysterious fires, resulting in three successful insurance claims. Anna was beginning to find ways of making money the easy way.

She desperately needed more though and hit on the ingenious method of taking out a large insurance policy on her husband. He fought

her on this—perhaps remembering the mysterious fires—but was suddenly struck ill and rushed to the hospital. Doctors barely managed to
save his life, which denied Anna her payout. It is not known whether the
incident aroused the suspicions of Philip Hahn, but when he got out of
hospital he also got out of the marriage.

It was the middle of the Depression, money was tight, and Anna
had to support herself and feed her son. She also had a severe gambling
problem. In an effort to make more money she began betting on the
racetracks, but was not successful. She needed a way of making money
and decided that she would take care of elderly men as a paid companion and live-in aide.

She chose her prey from within the tight German-American community. She began by befriending Ernest Kohler. She became indispens-
able to the elderly neighbor. Like all those who knew him, she seemed
devastated when he died suddenly on May 6, 1933. But her grief was
assuaged somewhat when he left her a house in his will. Life was looking up; when you have funds you don't have a gambling problem, you
just have a gambling habit.

Soon she began to look after another elderly man, seventy-two-
year-old Albert Parker. Sadly he too passed away shortly after she
began to look after him. He had loaned her $1,000 prior to his death,
and she had given him an IOU. But that document mysteriously disappeared and she kept the money. In the summer of 1937, Jacob Wagner,
seventy-eight, died and generously left his caring friend $17,000 in his
will. She moved on to George Gsellman, who lasted a month and left
her $15,000.

There was a rare survivor. George Heiss grew suspicious after Anna
gave him a mug of beer. A few flies landed on the beer and promptly
died. He asked Anna to take a sip, and when she refused, he swished
it down the drain and ordered her from the house. But he didn't go to
the police about his suspicions, so Anna was free to continue her grisly
business.

The deaths were becoming more frequent. Less than a month after
Gsellman's death, Georg Obendoerfer took a trip with Anna and her son
to Colorado and got sick en route. He passed away in agony, and initially

she tried to claim that she did not know the man. When it became clear that she had traveled with him, police began to look at her affairs and noticed a suspicious bank transfer from the dead man to her account. An autopsy was ordered. When the medical report indicated high levels of arsenic in Obendoerfer's body, two previous victims of the Blonde Borgia were exhumed. They were found to have died of arsenic poisoning too. It was too much of a coincidence: Anna was arrested and charged with multiple murders.

Justice moved swiftly in those days. She had escalated her killing spree to one a month in mid-1937; by November of that year her trial was underway. It was a sensation, reported in the press all over the country. It lasted four weeks and Anna tried to claim that she was carrying out mercy killings, saving her beloved charges from long, lingering deaths. But at the end there was no hesitation on the part of the jury. Eleven women and one man found Anna guilty and refused to recommend mercy. This meant an automatic death sentence. It would be the first time a woman would be executed in Ohio.

There was little public sympathy for Hahn. She had killed at least five elderly men, but the number was suspected to be as high as thirteen. She had tried to poison her husband, and the relatives she stayed with in Cincinnati when she came from Germany had also died suddenly, leaving her their home. There was a pattern, and it was a disturbing one. The execution was set for March 10, 1938.

That date passed in the inevitable appeals morass but eventually all avenues were closed. On Tuesday, December 6, Ohio Governor Martin Davey said he would not offer a last minute reprieve and the execution was scheduled for eight o'clock the following evening.

On hearing final confirmation that she was to face the chair, Hahn was allowed to meet a number of newspapermen the day prior to the execution. During the meeting she maintained her poise and still claimed to be nothing more than an angel of mercy. She also gave a letter to her attorneys in which she confessed to a number of the killings.

That evening guards came to her cell and cut one of her blue pajama legs to permit the attachment of the electrodes, and a spot on the back of her head was shaved in preparation.

The following day, she was in hysterics as the enormity of what was to come hit her. She was an emotional wreck, pleading for one last sight of her son Oscar. He saw her for a while, about three hours before the execution. He tried to be brave but could not stop himself from crying. After the visit Hahn needed to be supported by two female guards on her walk to the death chamber. As they walked along death row, there were eleven condemned men whom they passed. Each man stood as the women led Hahn along the corridor, and as she passed they called out: "God bless you."

Then they approached the death chamber.

"Oh heavenly father! Oh God! I can't go!" she screamed.

"There was stark terror in her eyes as she looked from side to side, with the attendants half-dragging and half-carrying her across the floor," the *Pittsburgh Press* reported.

She passed out and collapsed on the floor and had to be revived with an ammonia capsule then dragged into the chair, where she was secured with leather straps. The *Pittsburgh Press* went on:

> The final minutes of her life were spent pleading for a last sight of her twelve-year-old son Oscar, who tried vainly all day to see Governor Martin Davey and make a last plea for her life.
>
> She writhed as the guards adjusted straps to her legs. Warden James C. Woodard and a guard held her in the chair until she sank with a moan and did not move again until the shock of electricity hit her.

As the horrified witnesses looked on, she screamed, "Don't do this to me. Oh no, no, no no. Warden Woodard, don't let them do this to me. Please don't. Oh, my boy. Think of my boy! Won't someone, anyone, come and do something for me? Is there anybody to help me? Is nobody going to help me?"

Despite her crimes, the warden was moved to tears, but he said, "I am sorry, Mrs. Hahn. There is nothing I can do."

As the black mask was lowered over her face, Catholic priest Father John Sullivan, the prison chaplain, approached Hahn and the two began to recite the Lord's Prayer. He held her hand for a moment, but she said, "You might be killed too, Father," and he let go.

Here is the *Pittsburgh Press* account of her final seconds:

Father Sullivan began slowly saying the Lord's Prayer, phrase by phrase, as the straps were buckled on her legs, and as the electrode, clamped over a shaved spot on her head, was adjusted to the electric wires.

The woman repeated after him—'Our Father, who are in Heaven—'

There was a sharp catch in her voice as she intoned the words. Phrase by phrase, while a hushed silence fell over the chamber, she said the prayer.

The attendants tied down the black mask. From its depth came her final words—'But deliver us—'

A red light over the chair flashed on. The current raced through her body as she jerked convulsively once, and then was still. The current cut off the final few words of the prayer.

For one minute the red light glowed, and then went out. Dr. Keil pressed a stethoscope against her heart. He listened for several seconds, then put the stethoscope in his pocket and turned and faced the crowd in the chamber.

'Sufficient current has passed through the body of Anna Hahn to cause her death,' he said, and glanced at his watch. 'At 8.13 and a half.'

It had taken the State less than two minutes to claim the life of Mrs. Hahn.

She was buried in non-sanctified ground at the Holy Cross Catholic Cemetery in Columbus, Ohio.

The *Cincinnati Enquirer* bought her last confession, promising to fund Oscar's education as payment. What became of Oscar is not known, though he was fostered in the Midwest and served in the navy in the dying days of World War II, before returning home to complete his education. The newspaper kept their side of the deal.

MURDER, INC.
THE MEN OF THE MAFIA KILLING MACHINE

Everyone thinks of serial killers as the most depraved and evil people on the planet. They are not. They are damaged people who kill out of compulsion, unable to control their impulses. But far more chilling are the cadre of professional hit men who thrive in the world of organized crime. These monsters kill for a living and place the value of human life at $500, or $50,000, or whatever the fee is at that time and that place. They show no compassion—killing women and children if the price is paid. They will even turn on colleagues and friends if the bucks are right. And they are quite willing to make the victim suffer—if that is what the client requests.

For a while the hit men even became organized, with top mafioso hiring out jobs to the sociopaths who ran and staffed Murder Incorporated. One of the hit men clocked up one hundred kills while on a retainer from Murder Incorporated during the 1930s. He was on a wage and got a bonus for each kill carried out.

It was one of the most lawless periods in American history until the FBI, with the aid of Old Sparky, began to crack down on the crime families.

It all began with an idea of Johnny Torrio, a Brooklyn gangster who had moved to Chicago and risen high in the ranks during the profitable prohibition years. In the late 1920s he conceived the idea that the five main Mafia families of New York and the various crime syndicates throughout the rest of the country should get together and work for the common good. A meeting was convened in Atlantic City in May 1929, attended by leading underworld figures such as Lucky Luciano, Al Capone, Meyer Lansky, Bugsy Siegel, Frank Costello, Dutch Schultz, Louis Buchalter, and Albert "Mad Hatter" Anastasia. What emerged from the three-day conference was a loose confederation of mainly Italian and Jewish organized-crime groups nationwide. The National Crime Syndicate (a name given to the loose body by the press) would act as a mediator among different factions, deciding on matters such as territories and resolving disputes. Gang wars such as the one in Chicago that culminated in the St. Valentine's Day Massacre were bad for business. The Syndicate would provide an alternative that was more cost efficient. The group needed to enforce its rulings, so an enforcement wing was established, dubbed by the press as Murder Incorporated, or Murder, Inc. Essentially, this was a group of gunmen, leg breakers, and hit men embedded in the Brooklyn Mafia, who were on call throughout the country. The members, from the Brooklyn neighborhoods of Brownsville, East New York, and Ocean Hill, were paid a retainer each week and were given bonuses for jobs carried out. The group was initially headed by Louise "Lepke" Buchalter, and later by Albert "Mad Hatter" Anastasia.

They were active throughout the 1930s and were responsible for between four hundred and one thousand murders—many unsolved to this day.

Murder, Inc. consisted of two factions. The Jewish Brownsville Boys were headed by Abe "Kid Twist" Reles, reporting to Louis Buchalter and Jacob Shapiro. The Italian Ocean Hill Hooligans were led by Harry Maione, reporting to Albert Anastasia. But there was close cooperation between both groups.

One of their most feared killers was Abe Reles, a psychopathic product of the slums of Brownsville. He had no conscience, killing on the least provocation. Stories of his savagery abound. Despite his small size, he was fearless. His favorite method of killing was with a narrow ice pick, which he would ram through his victim's ear, right into the brain. In the days of less sophisticated forensic pathology, these deaths were sometimes put down to natural cerebral hemorrhage. It is not known how many hits he carried out for Murder, Inc., but he killed frequently. Several of his kills had nothing to do with business. According to the legends that grew around him, he once killed a car-wash worker for leaving a smudge on his fender. On another occasion, he killed a parking lot attendant for failing to fetch his car fast enough. Once he brought a guest to his mother-in-law's home for supper. When she left after the meal, Reles and another gang member murdered the guest and removed the body. He was never worried about being caught; who would cross him?

But in 1940 he was arrested and charged with a string of murders. Knowing he faced the electric chair when convicted, he decided to break the Mafia's code of Omertà (code of silence) and snitch on his colleagues. It was the break the authorities needed and the end of Murder, Inc.

Reles's testimony brought seven hit men to a comfortable seat on Old Sparky. The Department of Justice's electricity bill rose sharply as the gangsters fried. It would take several books to outline the life and crimes of the men Reles snitched on, but here are the highlights.

Louis Buchalter was a labor racketeer and one of the bosses of Murder, Inc. His idea was that those ordering a kill could not be connected with the kill afterward because it would not have been carried out by one of their gang. Instead, they would contact Anastasia, who would pass the contract to Buchalter. Buchalter would then pick one of his Brownsville thugs and pass the assignment along. That meant that the killer had no idea who he was working for and the man who hired him had no idea who had carried out the hit, making subsequent investigations difficult.

Buchalter rarely took part in the murders. He was the facilitator and paymaster. But under the law, a party organizing a killing is guilty of murder. He was also heavily involved in other crimes and was indicted and convicted in 1936 on a charge of violating Federal antitrust laws. The trial took place in his absence, as he was on the run at the time. Convictions on drugs charges swiftly followed. He remained on the run until 1939.

In 1941 he went on trial for the murder of candy store owner Joseph Rosen. Reles testified that he had overheard Buchalter ordering the hit and the mobster was convicted, along with two lieutenants (Louis Capone and Mendy Weiss), and sentenced to death. The three men went to the chair in Sing Sing on March 4, 1944.

Harry Maione—nicknamed "Happy" because of his perpetual scowl—led the Ocean Hill Hooligans and was a leading Murder, Inc. hit man. He was implicated in several murders. His right-hand man was Frank Abbandando, a handsome man who liked fancy clothes, fast cars, and women. Abbandando was a sexual predator who favored rape over conventional dating and committed thirty killings around Brooklyn—at a fee of $500 per hit. His favorite method was to drive an ice pick through his victim's chest.

In 1937 Louis Buchalter was worried that prosecutors were moving in on the group, so he ordered several people killed whom he feared were potential witnesses against him. One was a petty loan shark, George Rudnick. A three-man hit squad took him out in 1937. Maione and Abbandando were joined by Harry Strauss for the job.

The three men cornered the loan shark in a garage and beat him to death, crushing his head during the attack. At least they thought they did. When they opened the trunk of their car to put the body in, Rudnick began to cough and tried to sit up. So Maione picked up a meat cleaver and began hacking at his head, while Strauss took out his trusty ice pick and stabbed at their victim's chest. He became frenzied, inflicting sixty-three stab wounds.

This was the crime for which Maione and Abbandando went on trial in 1941, and Reles's evidence sent them to the chair on February 19, 1942.

Reles even testified against one of his closest friends, Martin "Bugsy" Goldstein. This thug had grown up in East New York, Brooklyn, and worked closely with Reles for many years. Reles testified that he had been one of the killers of Irving Feinstein. Feinstein was small fish, a gambler and loan racketeer, who had crossed a local crime boss and moved into territory that he should not have. Murder, Inc. took him out as a favor to the crime boss.

A three-man team arrived at Feinstein's home on East 91st Street—Reles, Goldstein, and Harry Strauss. Reles and Goldstein subdued the gambler, while Strauss got out his ice pick. But the man struggled and managed to bite a chunk out of Strauss's finger. This infuriated the hit man, who decided that Feinstein had earned a harder death. So the three men tied him up with a loop of rope around his neck and the end secured to his feet so that as he struggled he would slowly strangle himself. Then they stood back and laughed as he slowly and painfully expired. But Strauss was still unsatisfied, so they took the body to a vacant parking lot and set it on fire. Resisting the urge to roast marshmallows over the fire—they did consider this—the three men instead retired to a fish restaurant nearby to celebrate the successful hit.

This was the crime for which Reles's testimony sent his friend Goldstein and also Harry Strauss to the chair. Both men were electrocuted on June 12, 1941. Asked if he had anything to say after being convicted, Goldstein, ever the joker, said, "Judge, I would like to pee on your leg."

Strauss had been involved in a few of the murders Reles had testified about, and that is no surprise. Of the seven men sent to the chair by the informant, he was by far the worst. He was responsible for more than a hundred hits at a conservative estimate. That makes Ted Bundy look like an amateur in comparison.

Harry "Pittsburgh Phil" Strauss was born in Brooklyn and never did visit Pittsburgh. He just liked the nickname. His associates called him "Pep." He developed a taste for killing at an early age and saw violence as a way of getting noticed. He believed that if it was known how good he was at the job, he would eventually move into crime's big league. The call to work for Murder, Inc. was the big league for the young thug.

Once established in the group, he quickly earned a name as the most prolific of them all. His total kills exceeded the combined total of his nearest rivals, Abe Reles, Frank Maione, and Frank Abbandando. He didn't wait to be asked, often volunteering to carry out jobs, and he was the mobster of choice for out-of-state hits. He packed simply for these hits—a clean shirt, a gun, and an ice pick. When not working he never carried a weapon, and often he would use impromptu weapons to carry out kills. That way he could not be caught with something incriminating on him.

His favorite methods included shooting, stabbing with an ice pick, and drowning. But he used a variety of murder methods, including strangulation, beating, and live burial. Some historians believe he may have killed as many as five hundred people (a figure that seems too high), but during all the years that he was active, he was arrested just eighteen times and never convicted of anything. He took care to leave no clues.

However, the testimony of Reles finally proved the undoing of the pint-sized killer. He went on trial with Goldstein for the killing of Irving Feinstein.

Knowing that the mood of the jury would be against him, and the testimony of Reles would be very damaging, Strauss decided upon a risky trial strategy. A dapper dresser always, he abandoned his good clothes and began wearing T-shirts. He stopped washing and grew his hair and beard out—not grooming either. He pleaded insanity and played it up to-the-full in the court, often babbling incoherently. Frequently he grabbed the briefcase of his lawyer and chewed on it. Finally it got too much for the court, and his hair was cut and his beard forcibly trimmed. It didn't fool the jury either, and he was convicted of murder and sentenced to the electric chair.

He maintained his insanity pose through the entire appeals process, but shortly before his death he realized it was hopeless. He asked for a shave and a haircut and resumed his dapper dress. He would go out as himself, the Beau Brummell of organized crime. One of his last visitors was long-time girlfriend Evelyn Mittleman. He looked his best for her. He had always put forth an effort for the Brooklyn beauty; to win her affections in the first place he had murdered her previous boyfriend.

He had one last ploy. He offered to turn informant but on one condition. He had to be allowed a one-on-one interview with Abe Reles. The authorities declined this kind offer. They were right; he admitted shortly before his execution that he planned on attacking Reles and biting through his jugular.

"I didn't worry about the chair, if I could just tear his throat out first," he said.

He never got the chance, going to the chair moments after his accomplice Martin Goldstein.

As for the second most prolific killer of Murder, Inc., Abe Reles, he escaped the law, but he could not escape justice.

After his testimony had put away seven contract killers and broken Murder, Inc. forever, Reles was getting ready to give evidence against yet another mobster, Albert Anastasia. He was a big fish—like Buchalter, one of the bosses, rather than a foot soldier. Reles was prepared to testify that the gangster had been involved in the killing of union longshoreman Pete Panto. This had serious implications, because Anastasia was not just a leading figure in Murder, Inc. He was also a major player in the National Crime Syndicate. He would be by far the most senior figure brought down by Reles. He was also the figure with the most powerful influence.

The trial was set for November 12, 1941, with Reles as the only prosecution witness. The prosecution knew that their star witness had to be guarded diligently. So they had six police detectives constantly protecting him as he was holed up in the Half Moon Hotel on Coney Island. Three other mob informants were also in the hotel with their guards. So the place was crawling with police. Crime boss Frank Costello—an even more senior figure in the organization than Anastasia—raised up to $100,000, which he used to bribe three of Reles's guards to kill the informant. One of the men he bribed had allegedly been involved in the disappearance of Judge Joseph Force Carter in 1930, so he had chosen well.

From here on the story becomes speculative. On the evening of November 11, Reles's wife, Rose, visited the sixth floor room where her husband was being kept. The couple argued, and then she left for the night. The following morning the assistant manager of the hotel reported hearing a loud thud. He ran and discovered the body of the gangster on the concrete roof of an extension to the hotel, which lay four stories below Reles's window. The body lay twenty feet from the wall of the hotel.

The *New York Times* carried the official account of the "accident:"

> Sometime after daylight yesterday, Abe Reles . . . climbed out on a window edge of the sixth floor of the Half Moon Hotel, fully dressed but hatless. Strong wind from the gray sea tugged at his long, crisp black hair and tore at his gray suit.
>
> Behind him, in his room, lights still burned. The little radio that had played all night, still blared and babbled . . . Reles let the two bed sheets down the hotel's east wall, two windows north of the hotel's Boardwalk front. Around one end of the upper bed sheet he had twisted a four-foot length of radio lead-in wire. He had wound the free end of the wire on a radio valve under the window.

He let himself down on the sheets to the fifth floor. One hand desperately clung to the sheet. With the other, Reles tugged at the screen and at the window of the vacant fifth-floor room. He worked them up six inches. He tugged again with his full 160 pound weight.

The strain was too much for the amateur wire knot on the valve. Little by little, it came undone. Reles tried to save himself. He kicked towards the fifth-floor window ledge with his left foot, but merely brushed the shoe leather from toe to heel. He plunged to the hotel's concrete kitchen roof forty-two feet below. He landed on his back, breaking his spine.

It is a nice story, but the problem is that Reles landed on the roof well away from the wall of the hotel. Had he tried to escape—unlikely, given that he was the star witness, and avoiding prosecution for his efforts—he would have plunged straight down. Far more likely is that two or more of his guards picked up the violent killer and swung him vigorously through the open window, setting up the sheets afterward as a cover story.

His killers were never caught. The trial collapsed, and Anastasia went on to serve with distinction in World War II before returning to a life of crime. He was assassinated in 1957.

Although Abe Reles escaped the electric chair, no one can deny that justice of a sort was served that cold, misty morning on Coney Island.

ALBERT FISH
THE BOOGEY MAN

"It will be the supreme thrill of my life," sadistic sexual predator, child killer, and cannibal Albert Fish said, when hearing that he was going to die in the electric chair. He went to his death with a smile, unrepentant about the trail of death and misery he had left in his wake.

Hamilton Howard—known as Albert—Fish was born in 1870 and was one of the first known serial killers in the United States. He was known as The Gray Man, the Werewolf of Wysteria, the Brooklyn

Vampire, the Moon Maniac, and simply as The Boogey Man. He boasted of killing children in every state, claiming a total of around one hundred. More likely his number was far smaller. He was an unreliable witness who loved to boast and shock. But whatever the final figure, Fish was a true monster.

A native of Washington, DC, his father was seventy-five when he was born, and the family had a history of mental illness. An uncle suffered dementia, a brother was confined to a state mental hospital, and his sister had a "mental affliction." His mother heard voices and suffered hallucinations, and three other relatives had undisclosed problems. On his father's death, his mother put Fish in an orphanage and the child discovered he enjoyed the physical punishment that was the norm in those institutions. "I was there till I was nearly nine, and that's where I got started wrong. We were unmercifully whipped. I saw boys doing many things they should not have done," he told investigators later.

At twelve, now home with his mother, Fish had his first homosexual experiences with a local telegraph boy. He was also introduced to deviant practices such as eating feces and drinking urine. In his late teens Fish became a rent boy and also began raping young boys. He was a deviant who enjoyed an unorthodox and destructive lifestyle. But at the age of twenty-eight his mother arranged a marriage for him and he settled down, having six children with his young wife. He was working as a house painter, often traveling extensively for jobs, but did not put his old ways completely behind him. He continued to molest young boys, generally under the age of six. In his thirties he began to fantasize about sexual mutilation, but it took a long time before fantasy merged into reality. He waited until he was aged forty-one before his assaults escalated. He was staying in St. Louis at the time and he began sexually molesting an intellectually disabled young man. He tied the nineteen-year-old up and tried to slice his penis with scissors. But he panicked when he saw the look of fear on his victim's face. Leaving the youth ten dollars to cover his medical bills, Fish fled the city and returned to his home in New York. But the incident had turned a switch in Fish's mind, and now he began going to brothels frequently, often engaging in sado-masochistic practices with others of similar inclinations. But this period of his life was cut short when he was convicted of larceny and sent to Sing Sing. This also brought on the end of his marriage. When he got out of prison his wife had abandoned him, leaving him the children to raise on his own. Around this time he began to hear voices in his head, as his mind began its degeneration. He began experimenting with self-harm, often embedding needles into his groin, pelvis, and abdomen for sexual gratification. He tried flagellation and also put wads of burning cotton up his anus. He stopped cooking his meat, as his obsession with cannibalism grew.

Fish chose victims who were powerless—handicapped, poor African-Americans, and children. He claimed to have attacked a man in Delaware in 1910 but no record exists of the assault. A few years later he stabbed a mentally handicapped boy in Washington. He was beginning to get a taste for torturing, mutilating, and murdering young children with his meat cleaver, butcher's knife, and handsaw. He was prevented a number of times from attempting to abduct children but may well have succeeded as well. Records are scanty, and he claimed himself to have been killing regularly.

In May 1928 Fish saw a classified ad in the *New York World* from a young man looking for work in the country. Fish thought it would be fun to offer the guy a job, tie him up, mutilate him, and leave him to bleed to death. But when he made contact with Edward Budd, eighteen, he spotted Budd's ten-year-old sister Grace and decided on a new victim. Telling the family that he was on the way to his niece's birthday party, he asked whether the young girl would like to accompany him. He said he would have her back by nine. The girl's mother, Delia, was reluctant, but her father said, "Let the poor kid go. She don't see much good times." It was a decision that would haunt him for the rest of his life.

That evening there was no sign of the young girl and no word from the kindly man who had taken her away. After a sleepless night, they contacted the police, who quickly established that the name given by the man was false, and the address where he said his niece's birthday was being held was bogus. Beyond that, they had nothing to add.

Several years passed for the confused and grieving family. A sixty-six-year-old suspect was arrested but found not guilty of the abduction.

No one had any idea what had happened to the smiling girl. Then, in 1934, the family was horrified to receive an anonymous letter with graphic descriptions of cannibalism. The letter had come from Fish and recounted the experiences of a friend of his who had been stranded in China.

"At that time there was famine in China. So great was the suffering among the very poor that all children under twelve were sold for food in order to keep others from starving. A boy or girl under fourteen was not safe in the street. You could go in any shop and . . . part of the naked body of a boy or girl would be brought out and just what you wanted cut from it. A boy or girl's behind, which is the sweetest part of the body and sold as veal cutlet, brought the highest price."

The letter went on to recount how his "friend" developed a taste for human meat, and when he returned to America, he kidnapped, fattened, and ate children:

He told me so often how good human flesh was I made up my mind to taste it. On Sunday June the 3, 1928 I called on you at 406 W 15 St. Brought you pot cheese—strawberries. We had lunch. Grace sat in my lap and kissed me. I made up my mind to eat her. On the pretense of taking her to a party. You said, yes, she could go. I took her to an empty house in Westchester I had already picked out. When we got there, I told her to remain outside. She picked wildflowers. I went upstairs and stripped all my clothes off. I knew if I did not I would get her blood on them. When all was ready I went to the window and called her. Then I hid in a closet until she was in the room. When she saw me all naked, she began to cry and tried to run down the stairs. I grabbed her and she said she would tell her mamma. First I stripped her naked. How she did kick—bite and scratch. I choked her to death, then cut her in small pieces so I could take my meat to my rooms. Cook and eat it. How sweet and tender her little ass was roasted in the oven. It took me 9 days to eat her entire body.

Whether it was to soften the impact on the family or increase their sense of horror, he concluded: "I did not fuck her, though I could of had I wished. She died a virgin."

Writing a letter to the family of a victim might seem like an unnecessary risk, but serial killers often have a need to insert themselves into an investigation. They get a vicarious thrill from closeness to the case. And sometimes they just like to torture the family. This was almost certainly an element of what Fish was doing.

He made one mistake, however. Although he did not sign the letter, he put it in an envelope with a small hexagonal emblem emblazoned with the letters NYPCBA—the New York Private Chauffeur's Benevolent Association. A janitor at the company admitted stealing some stationery, but he left it at a boarding house at 200 East Street when he moved out. The next tenant in the boarding house was Fish. The cops finally had a suspect.

Fish initially agreed to be interviewed and then brandished a razor blade. He was swiftly disarmed, and the arresting officer, Detective William King, knew he had his breakthrough. Fish didn't even attempt to deny the murder of the little girl. He admitted that her older brother was his initial target, and then he had switched. He said that it had not occurred to him to rape the girl, but he disturbingly admitted that he had ejaculated while strangling her.

Two more grisly murders were laid at the feet of Fish. On July 14, 1924, eight-year-old Francis McDonnell disappeared from Staten Island. After a search he was found hanging from a tree in a nearby wooded area. He had been strangled and sexually assaulted, and he had suffered extensive cuts. His left hamstring had been stripped of all the flesh. Fish claimed he had been trying to castrate the boy, but more likely he had taken the flesh to eat. Descriptions of an elderly man with a gray mustache seen in the area at the time matched Fish. There was no doubt of his guilt. After being convicted of Grace Budd's killing, Fish admitted the McDonnell one.

The third monstrous killing he was definitely responsible for was that of Billy Gaffney. The four-year-old had been playing with friends in February 1927 when he and another child disappeared. When the other, three-year-old Billy Beaton, was found he told searchers that the Boogey Man had taken his friend. Gaffney's body was never recovered. A man seen lurking nearby matched Fish's description.

Fish was glad to admit his guilt, saying, "I took the boy. Stripped him naked and tied his hands and feet and gagged him with a piece of dirty rag I picked from the dump. Then I burned his clothes. Next day, about 2:00 p.m., I took tools, a good heavy cat-of-nine-tails. Home made, short handle . . . I whipped his bare behind until the blood ran down his legs. I cut off his ears, nose—slit his mouth from ear to ear. Gouged out his eyes. He was dead then. I stuck the knife in his belly and held my mouth to his body and drank his blood."

He then took some choice cuts to eat and disposed of the rest of the body. He gave shocked investigators a detailed account of the recipe he used to cook the boy, gravy, onions and all.

On March 11, Fish went on trial for the murder of Grace Budd. He pleaded insanity, saying that he heard God in his head telling him to kill children. Several experts testified to his weird sexual fetishes, which included sadism, masochism, and more. His lawyer said that Fish was a "psychiatric phenomenon," unique in the range of his sexual abnormalities.

Unbelievably, the former manager of the Bellevue Psychiatric Hospital, where Fish had been treated during his second incarceration (for sending obscene letters), said that Fish was abnormal but sane. Menas Gregory said that urophilia (love of urine), coprophilia (a fetish for feces), and pedophilia were "socially perfectly alright," and Fish was "no different from millions of other people."

The twelve jurors looked at one another and shook their heads.

They had no doubt that Fish was insane—but as one explained to the press, they felt he should be executed anyway. Such evil could not walk the world.

After his conviction, Fish admitted to two more killings (McDonnell and Gaffney). Six other children, aged between four and seventeen, were almost certainly killed by the Gray Man. As to all the others he claimed, there is considerable doubt. For one thing, his confessions were imprecise and it was often not clear whether he was talking about molesting a child, killing a child, or eating a child. And the murder descriptions were not linked to actual missing children. It is probable that he killed less than ten, but raped and molested hundreds. That would be common with very active pedophiles.

A few days before his death, Fish requested pen and paper and wrote several pages, his final statement. This he handed over to his lawyer, James Dempsey, to distribute after his death. But on reading it, the lawyer immediately decided to suppress it. He told reporters, "I will never show it to anyone. It was the most filthy string of obscenities that I have ever read."

Fish went to the death chamber in Sing Sing on January 16, 1936. He was eager for the experience and looked forward to the sensations that would follow once the current began to flow. It was the ultimate buzz for a masochist.

He entered the chamber at 11:06 p.m. and helped the guard position the electrode on his leg—unusual behavior for a condemned man. Then he sat back and allowed them to fit the skullcap with the other electrode. As the death mask was lowered over his head, he muttered, "I don't even know why I am here."

One concern the prison authorities had was that Fish had a large number of metal pins in his leg, which he had inserted over the years as part of his spectrum of sexual fetishes. Would these affect how the electrocution went? It was an unfounded fear. Within three minutes of entering the death chamber, Fish was pronounced dead. The electrocution had gone perfectly. Fish had found the perfect climax to his life of depravity.

BRUNO RICHARD HAUPTMANN
THE CRIME OF THE CENTURY

In the days before fame became debased by fifteen-minute wannabes, reality television stars, and pop-idol winners, Charles Lindbergh was the real deal. A dashing airman in the early days of flight, he achieved worldwide fame overnight—but he earned it.

At the age of twenty-five the US Air Mail pilot and Air Corps reservist won the Orteig Prize for flying solo nonstop from America to Europe. He took off from the Roosevelt Field in Garden City, Long Island, on May 20, 1927, and landed in Paris, France, the following day. This was the first solo crossing of the Atlantic, a breakthrough in the new and glamorous field of aviation. Lindbergh was front page news on both sides of the Atlantic.

He had been interested in machines for as long as he could remember and had dropped out of college to learn to fly. For two years he had supported himself as a barnstormer, performing in flying circuses all over the country. He did it all—stunts, wing walking—every crazy thing you could do in the air. Then he had done a year of training with the fledgling Army Air Service. On completion he was a second Lieutenant in the Air Service Reserve Corps. By then he was one of the most experienced fliers in the country and picked up a job as one of the first Air Mail pilots.

He also applied to be one of the fliers on Admiral Richard Byrd/ Donald McMillan's North Pole expedition of 1925, but the team was already chosen.

Life in the Air Mail was exciting. Twice he had to bail out and parachute to land, but both times he managed to locate his wrecked plane and ensure that the mail was delivered—not on time but at least safely. Early in 1927 he went on leave, to oversee the building of his transatlantic plane, *Spirit of St. Louis*. Financing the project with a loan, a donation from his employers, and his personal savings, Lindbergh was not considered a serious contender for the prize for the first solo crossing.

When he made it, the world sat up and took notice. In Paris the American flag was flown above the Foreign Office, the first time that honor had been accorded a non-president. He was awarded the Lêgion d'Honneur, the highest award the French goverment gives. Back home he got a ticker-tape parade in his honor and was awarded the nation's highest military decoration, the Medal of Honor, for his historic exploit. He was a hero. The Jazz Age valued its heroes, and he was feted everywhere.

He married well two years later and had six children. He settled in a large mansion in rural East Amwell, New Jersey, near the town of Hopewell. Life seemed idyllic.

Until it all came crashing down on March 1, 1932, when his life intersected with that of a man from a completely different background, with a completely different destiny.

Bruno Richard Hauptmann was just three years older than Lindbergh but born a world away, in the old German empire, in the village of Kamenz, not far from Poland. He had a normal enough childhood, attending school to fourteen and participating in the local scout movement. He trained as a carpenter for a year, and then switched to machine building. But in 1917, his father died and two brothers were killed in the war. Bruno was conscripted the same year. He ended up on the Western Front, where he was gassed, and then hit on the helmet with flying shrapnel during a shelling. The blow knocked him out and he was left for dead by his comrades. When he finally came to, he managed to crawl to safety—but was sent back up the line only hours later.

Many soldiers were traumatized by the war and found settling into civilian life difficult. Hauptmann turned to crime, perhaps looking for the excitement of action. He robbed two women, and then burgled a house, earning himself three years in prison. On his release he continued breaking into houses and was rearrested. To escape a further prison term he stowed away on a liner and entered the United States illegally. He landed in New York in September 1923 and disappeared into the German community in the city. He worked as a carpenter and married a waitress in 1925.

But the economy crashed in 1929, plunging America into the Great Depression. Hauptmann had a wife to support and began to look for easy money. Crime seemed the answer. This time he decided on the big score, a crime so audacious and profitable that if he pulled it off, he could retire on the proceeds. He began to look for a suitable target. One man was in the news all the time. Fame and glamour—he must have money to go with it. And he lived in an isolated rural spot. Lindbergh was the perfect victim.

On March 1, 1932, the family nurse tucked twenty-month-old Charles Lindbergh Junior into his crib. She wrapped him in a blanket and pinned it to the sheets to prevent him moving during his sleep. Charles Senior was often away on business, but that evening he was at home. At nine thirty at night he heard a noise which he assumed came from the kitchen but thought nothing more of it. Half an hour later the nurse discovered that the crib was empty. She ran to check if the baby was with his mother but Anne Morrow Lindbergh did not have him. During the subsequent search of the house, Charles Lindbergh found a white envelope on the windowsill above a radiator. Grabbing a gun, he went around the house looking for intruders, while his wife phoned the police. They arrived twenty minutes later—followed swiftly by the newspapermen and by Lindbergh's lawyer.

There were clues. Tire prints were found, and a three-piece ladder hidden in a nearby bush. But no sign of the baby. The envelope that Lindbergh had found in the nursery confirmed their worse suspicions. This was a kidnapping. They were ordered to pay a ransom of $50,000; delivery instructions would follow. That was all.

It was, as newspaperman H. L. Mencken described it, "the biggest story since the Resurrection." Immediately, the full force of the American justice system was mobilized. Even President Herbert Hoover got involved, ordering the Bureau of Investigation (the forerunner of the FBI), the Coast Guard, Customs Service, and Immigration Service, to join the hunt for the missing toddler. Leading underworld figures such as Al Capone offered to help, though their motives were far from pure. Capone suggested that he be released from prison to liaise with the kidnappers—an offer that was rejected as soon as it was made.

This flurry of activity showed how highly Lindbergh was regarded; the president did not make it a habit to involve himself in kidnapping incidents, which were seen as matters for the local police.

A few days later, with no sign of the missing child, the first of a number of ransom notes arrived. The notes appeared to be written by someone whose first language was German. A Brooklyn teacher, John Condon, became the agreed-upon intermediary between the kidnappers and the Lindberghs.

In early March, Condon had his first meeting with the man sending the ransom notes, who said he was a Scandinavian sailor and that the child was on a boat, safe. But, worryingly, he asked if he would "burn" if "the package were dead."

On April 2, $50,000 was handed over to a cab driver, who gave Condon a note explaining that the child was with two women, who had no involvement in the kidnapping. But nothing came of that—the child was not returned and the agony for the Lindberghs continued. Then, on May 12, a delivery truck driver pulled to the side of the road about four and a half miles from the Lindberghs' home to relieve himself. He disappeared into a grove of trees and was horrified to find the body of a tiny child. Charles Lindbergh had been found.

An autopsy revealed that his skull had been badly fractured. It was probable that he had been killed within a very short time of his abduction. He may have been killed straight away or he may have struck his head during the abduction, possibly falling down the ladder and dying accidentally. Whatever actually happened, during the entire ransom process the child was already dead.

The news shocked Congress into passing legislation that made kidnapping a federal offense, allowing the Bureau of Investigation a freer hand in the case. The investigation became heavy-handed as they searched for an inside man in the Lindbergh household. Their focus fell on Violet Sharp, a British servant. They questioned her so vigorously that she took her own life—ingesting silverware polish that contained potassium cyanide. Subsequently it became apparent that she had no involvement.

The press dubbed the kidnapping "the Crime of the Century." Unfortunately it was not the investigation of the century. Thirty months dragged on with no fresh leads. The investigators focused on tracking the notes in the ransom drop; they had recorded the serial numbers. They used a map to record where the bills showed up and a pattern began to emerge. The notes were being passed along the rouge of the Lexington Avenue subway, right through the German-Austrian neighborhood of Yorkville.

The ransom had also included gold certificates. These had been used as a sort of alternative currency in the United States up until 1933. One of the gold certificates from the ransom had been used by Richard Hauptmann—a German with a criminal record. When Hauptmann was arrested, a search of his home uncovered over $14,000 of the ransom money.

Under a vigorous interrogation—which included physical beat-ings—Hauptmann stuck to his story. He had been left the money by a friend and former business partner who had returned to Germany and conveniently died.

But equally damaging was the discovery of a drawing of the ladder used in the kidnapping and also that Hauptmann had the address and phone number of John Condon, the intermediary with the Lindberghs. It was too much of a coincidence. He was charged with kidnapping and murder.

The trial was a sensation. Reporters swarmed the town of Fleming-ton, New Jersey, and every hotel room was occupied. One paper, the *Daily Mirror*, paid for Hauptmann's defense—in return for rights to publish Hauptmann's story.

The evidence against him was solid. In addition to having the ran-som money in his possession, his handwriting was suspiciously similar to that of the kidnapper's. Wood from his home matched the wood used in the ladder that was found at the Lindbergh home. There was too much evidence against him, and the jury had no difficulty convicting. Hauptmann was sentenced to death.

The inevitable appeals followed and were rejected. The execution would go ahead. Near the end, intense pressure came on Hauptmann to confess. A newspaper offered him a large sum for his story, but he turned it down. Even the prosecution got in on the action. An offer was made that the death sentence would be commuted to one of life impris-onment if Hauptmann confessed and gave the Lindberghs closure. He refused. He maintained his innocence right up to the end.

Shortly before facing "Old Smokey," as the electric chair at New Jersey State Prison in Trenton was called, Hauptmann wrote his final statement:

I am writing this literally within the shadow of the electric chair. For upward to fourteen months I have been confined in the cell nearest to the execution chamber in the New Jersey penitentiary. The courts have now said that I shall die on the night of April 3, and that I shall die in the chair that is just beyond the door that faces me and has faced me every waking hour of my life these past fourteen months. The courts have said that on the night of April 3, I shall be prepared to leave the cell which has been my home; walk through the door which has been facing me these weary months; tread the few steps that lead from that door to the electric chair; that on that night I shall be led out on a walk from which I shall never return.

When I rise to join in that last deathly procession, I shall walk as any man walks, striding along one foot ahead of the other. I shall breathe the air my guards are breathing. I shall hear things that are being said, with ears that are as the ears of other men. I shall say with a voice that is the same as voices of other men that a tragedy is being enacted, that a life is being wantonly taken, that I am innocent of the crime of which I have been convicted, as innocent as any one in the world; and then, if the decision of the court is carried out, I shall be strapped into the chair, and in a few fleeting seconds this body that is mortal will be no longer living and breathing but just a mass of clay.

And I ask, WHY? Why must this thing be? Why should this thing happen? Why should the State of New Jersey take from me that which is most precious to all men—life? Why should they widow my loyal wife and orphan my lovely baby? Every hour, every day, since the Flemington jury rendered their verdict, I have asked myself that question. I am as innocent of the crime of killing the Lindbergh baby or even the slightest participation in that or any crime like it, as any one who reads this.

. . . unexpected like a lightning bolt or earthquake, came my arrest for the murder of Charles Augustus Lindbergh, Jr. It is impossible to describe how I felt when I realized that I was being charged with that most dastardly crime of all times. It must all be a joke, it must all be a farce, all some horrible mistake! I knew nothing about the Lindbergh baby. I knew nothing about the ransom money. I knew nothing about that

crime or any crimes in connection with it, and I confidently
expected that within a day or two I would be returned to my
home, my wife, and my baby.

That didn't happen.

And so I sit, ten feet removed from the electric chair, and
unless something can be done to aid me, unless something can
be done to make some one tell the truth, or unless some one
does tell it, I shall at eight o'clock Friday evening, in response
to the call from my keepers, raise myself from my cot for the
last time and shall walk that 'last mile.' I suppose there will be
in that chamber some of those who have had part in the preparation of my case for the prosecution. It is my belief that their
suffering, their agony, will be greater than mine. Mine will be
over in a moment. Theirs will last as long as life itself lasts.

On the afternoon of April 3, 1936, Hauptmann had a last visit from
his wife and baby son. Then he enjoyed his final meal. Unlike many who
refuse the meal or opt for the standard one, Hauptmann chose some of
his favorites. He had a salmon salad, corn fritters, sliced cheese, olives,
and celery, followed by a fruit salad and cake. He washed it all down
with milk and finished with a coffee. His spiritual adviser, Reverend
James Matthiesen, remained in the cell with him. A few minutes before
the guards came to take him to the death chamber, he reverted to his
native German, saying, "Ich bin absolut unschuldig an den Verbrechen,
die man mir zur last legt." ("I am absolutely innocent of the crime with
which I am convicted.")

When the guards arrived he walked with quiet dignity to the
chamber and sat calmly in the chair. He said nothing and made no gestures to the fifty-two witnesses.

"He sat down just like he was going to eat dinner at his table at home,"
said one of the reporters present. "He certainly did die a brave man."

The execution was flawless. The time from when he entered the
chamber at 8:40 p.m. to the official pronouncement of his death was

just seven and a half minutes—perhaps helped by his calmness. He was cremated and his ashes scattered in his native Germany by his widow. In the years that have passed there has been considerable controversy about his conviction and about the heavy-handed methods used by the police. But however they got the result, there is little doubt that Hauptmann was the Lindbergh kidnapper.

SACCO AND VANZETTI
ANARCHISTS CONVICTED IN THE WRONG

Nicola Sacco and Bartolomeo Vanzetti were dangerous armed anarchists who believed in the violent overthrow of the American government. They were labor agitators and strike organizers who were members of a group that bombed and killed to further their political aims. When they went to the electric chair in August 1927, twenty thousand people gathered on Boston Common. But they were there to protest the execution. They knew that the man who went to the electric chair a few minutes before the two anarchists did was probably the real guilty party and that Sacco and Vanzetti were innocent scapegoats.

It was a massive miscarriage of justice that is controversial to this day.

Both anarchists were Italians. Vanzetti was a fishmonger, born in the Piemonte region of northern Italy in 1888. Sacco was a cobbler from the poorer far south of the country, born three years later. They did not meet until they had both moved to America. Their paths first crossed at a strike in 1917. By that stage they were both involved in an anarchist group inspired by Luigi Galleani, an Italian anarchist who advocated revolutionary violence and published a periodical, *Subversive Chronicle*, to further these aims. He also published a practical guide to bomb making. At the time Italian anarchists were regarded almost as we regard Al Qaeda cells today. The group was suspected of several bombings and assassination attempts, including one attempted mass poisoning. Two years later Galleani was deported.

But the cells remained active, with up to sixty anarchists waging a campaign against politicians and judges. A friend of Sacco and Vanzetti's was killed when the bomb he was planting to kill Attorney General Mitchell Palmer went off prematurely. But such political activity requires funds, and, like all terrorist groups, the anarchists were also involved in robberies and conventional crime.

On the afternoon of April 15, 1920, two men were bringing the payroll to the Slater-Morrill Shoe Company factory in Braintree, Massachusetts. The cash was in two steel boxes when the guards were approached by two men. One guard attempted to draw his pistol but was shot and killed. The raiders also killed an unarmed paymaster, shooting him in the back as he attempted to flee. The robbers jumped into a dark blue Buick and drove off, shooting randomly into the crowd of workers as they escaped.

This was the second factory robbery in a few months. In December, a shoe factory in Bridgewater had been targeted, but no one was killed in that attempted robbery. Police immediately suspected local anarchists of being behind the two robberies. Sacco and Vanzetti were known agitators, and despite having no criminal records they were in the frame from the start. During a roundup of local activists, the police found a car that they thought might have been a second getaway vehicle and they impounded it for examination. They waited to see who would turn up to reclaim the car. Four men showed up, including Sacco and Vanzetti. But the men smelled a rat and escaped before the cops could capture them. However Sacco and Vanzetti were identified and were soon in custody.

When questioned they both denied owning guns—a denial that rang hollow when they were searched and the guns taken from them. Not only were they carrying, the guns were loaded. The bullets taken from Sacco matched those at the crime scene, and the gun taken from Vanzetti was identical to the one stolen from the guard who had been murdered during the robbery. It was enough; both men were charged with murder.

Immediately the anarchists began a campaign of retaliation. Two days after their arrest, the Wall Street bombing occurred. Dynamite was used in a horse-drawn cart. The huge bomb was loaded with shrapnel to maximize the damage. Thirty-eight people were killed, and 134 wounded. The group also began worldwide embassy bombings.

Vanzetti was tried for the attempted robbery and attempted murder in Bridgewater. The robbery had happened on Christmas Eve, 1919. There was not enough evidence to charge Sacco or any of the other anarchists. Several witnesses put Vanzetti at the scene of the robbery, but their descriptions varied. Some said he had a big bushy mustache, others said it was smaller, or more shaped. "Man with a mustache" was the only thing the descriptions had in common. But there was also physical evidence, including a shotgun shell retrieved at the scene which matched several shells found on Vanzetti when he was arrested.

To counteract this, the defense paraded sixteen separate witnesses, all of whom testified that they had purchased eels from Vanzetti during the period that the prosecution alleged he was carrying out the robbery. Eels were a traditional festival food for some sections of the Italian community. But not all the witnesses spoke good English, and the succession of people talking about foreign traditions did not go down well with the jury. The prosecution found it easy to make the witnesses appear confused and inaccurate.

Though he was losing the case, Vanzetti chose not to testify on his own behalf. His team felt that he would not come across well under cross-examination, being a committed anarchist and enemy of the state. He was convicted and was sentenced to twelve to fifteen years in prison. Strike one for the state.

This trial was followed by a second one—for the Braintree robbery. This time Sacco was also on trial and the charge was murder. It was a tense time; fearing a bomb attack on the courthouse, the courtroom was fitted with cast-iron shutters and heavy sliding doors. Police ringed the building, and Sacco and Vanzetti had an armed escort at all times.

The evidence was ambiguous at best. Sacco had been absent from work on the day of the robbery and the two defendants had been seen in the vicinity on that morning. One witness did say that he had seen Sacco shoot the paymaster, Berardelli, as he was trying to escape. Another

testified that as the getaway car was driving off, Sacco had leaned out
the window and waved a gun at him.

If the prosecution relied heavily on ever-unreliable eyewitnesses,
so did the defense. Both men provided alibis, backed up by witnesses.
But were the witnesses fellow anarchists? This was what the prosecution alleged.

The actual physical evidence was inconclusive. Experts agreed that
one of the fatal bullets could have come from Sacco's gun. But the
prosecution could not say for certain, even after firing test shots and
comparing them to the recovered bullet. The defense said that the bullet
did not match the gun. That should have been a score for Sacco.

The case against Vanzetti was that he had been present during a
felony murder, so he was as guilty as the man who pulled the trigger.
There was no suggestion that he had fired on the day. But he had been
seen, according to witnesses, in the vicinity, and one put him in the
getaway car.

In a theatrical gesture near the end of the trial, the district attorney produced a flop-eared cap which had been left at the crime scene.
Many people had said it was similar to a hat Sacco once owned. He
threw the hat at Sacco and told him to put it on. Despite the fact
that it was clearly several sizes too small for the Italian shoemaker,
District Attorney Frederick Katzmann continued to refer to the cap
as his.

The evidence was very poor, but Sacco and Vanzetti had made
a negative impression on the jurors. No one liked radical anarchists.
The jury retired for three hours, ordered dinner, and then returned with
guilty verdicts.

The death sentence was automatic. So were the protests that followed around the world. There were demonstrations in sixty Italian cities alone. Leading left-wing intellectuals, artists, and writers jumped
on the bandwagon. There was doubt about the guilt of the two men and
even more questions over the conduct of the trials, which had been slip-
shod. A number of motions for a retrial were made and denied. Unless
there was some dramatic new development, they were going to the
chair.

Then there was a sensation; a man came forward and claimed it was he who had killed the guard and the paymaster.

Celestino Madeiros was a career criminal awaiting trial for murder. The case against him was strong and he knew he was facing the chair. He told the police that he had been part of a criminal gang drawn from the Italian community in Providence, Rhode Island. The group was led by Joe Morelli and had a history of attacking shoe factories. They also used a car similar to that seen in the vicinity of the Braintree robbery. They ticked all the boxes.

This new version of what happened also explained one troubling thing: why so many witnesses had put Sacco at the scene. The leader of the gang, Joe Morelli, could have been Sacco's twin. The resemblance was uncanny. But the latest motion for a retrial based on this new evidence was turned down. The judge felt that Madeiros was not a credible witness. Public reaction was shocked, but the judiciary was unmoved. Now, nothing short of a pardon could save Sacco and Vanzetti.

Many petitioned. Those adding their names to the campaign for clemency included John Dos Passos, Dorothy Parker, Albert Einstein, George Bernard Shaw, H. G. Wells, and even Benito Mussolini. Ordinary workers got involved as well. In August 1927 the Industrial Workers of the World, a trade union, called for a three-day nationwide walkout to protest the executions. In the Walsenburg coal district of Colorado, 1,132 of 1,167 miners left their posts, sparking the Colorado coal strike.

Sacco and Vanzetti remained defiant while in prison, calling on their supporters for revenge on the powers of the state that they blamed for their incarceration. They wrote dozens of letters protesting their innocence. Their demeanor convinced many of their innocence. But innocent or not, an aura of violence hung around them. On August 15, just a week before the scheduled execution, a bomb destroyed the home of one of the jurors who convicted them.

The day before the execution twenty thousand people thronged Boston Common, calling for a last minute reprieve. In their cells at Charlestown State Prison, both men refused to see a priest on their last day. Although they were Italian Catholics, they had chosen a different

path and stuck to their principles to the end. Vanzetti, through his lawyer, asserted the pair's innocence one last time and asked that no violence should follow their deaths.

That evening the death chamber was busy. The man in charge was
Robert Greene Elliott, who held the title of State Electrician for the
State of New York. He also worked for the neighboring states, including
New Jersey, Pennsylvania, Vermont, and Massachusetts. He had been
appointed in 1926 and would hold the post until 1939.

A devout Methodist, his parents had hoped he might enter the min-
istry. But as a child he had read about the electric chair and began to
wonder what it would be like to throw the switch. A qualified electrician, he joined the prison service. At the time the state electrician
was Edwin Davis, who passed the torch to John Hulbert in 1913. Hulbert was a nervous man who became depressed over the work he was
expected to do. He oversaw 140 executions, and only the fee of $150
per job kept him at it. But he finally suffered a nervous breakdown in
1926 and retired. "I got tired of killing people," he said. Three years
later Hulbert, still brooding over the 140 executions he had carried out,
put a gun to his head and took his own life.

Elliott applied for the vacant job and got it. He had assisted both
Davis and Hulbert and was ready for the responsibility.

Elliott had a detached attitude to the job and tried his best to perfect the method. He began with 2,000 volts for three seconds, and then
lowered the charge to 500 volts for the rest of a full minute. This cycle
was repeated until the process ended with one more high voltage jolt.
The first high voltage charge was designed to render the victim immediately unconscious so that he would not suffer during the process. The
lower voltage would heat the vital organs, cooking them to the point
where life was extinguished, without causing too much bodily burning.
A higher voltage would have caused burning, leaving terrible smells,
smoke, and other unpleasant side effects (for the watcher—not the
victim!). The oscillating cycle of shocks would also cause the heart to
go into arrest, bringing death quickly.

During the time he was state electrician, Elliott also ran an electrical contracting business on the side. The night he executed Sacco

and Vanzetti he collected a fat fee of $450—roughly $6,000 in today's terms—for his grisly work. But this was not his busiest night. Though he was opposed to the death penalty himself, he executed 387 people during his career. Once (January 6, 1927), he carried out six executions in two different states in a single evening.

On August 22, 1927, he knew he had to get everything right because of the high profile of the case. In his memoir, *Agent of Death*, he wrote: "I knew that the eyes of the world were on Boston that night, that the least thing out of the ordinary or the slightest mishap in the death chamber would be inflated into a sensation that might result in serious repercussions."

The first to enter Elliott's chamber was Madeiros, who still maintained that he was guilty of the crime for which Sacco and Vanzetti would later meet their deaths. His electrocution, at eleven o'clock at night, was carried out flawlessly, and the chair was readied for its next victim. Sacco walked calmly to the chair and sat down, waiting patiently as the electrodes were strapped in place. Then he said, "Farewell, Mother." A few minutes later, he shouted, "Long live anarchy!" They were his final words; he died on the first attempt, at eleven thirty.

The final man to enter the chamber at midnight that night was Vanzetti. He was as calm as Sacco had been. A bookish man, he quietly shook hands with the guards and thanked them for their kind treatment of him in his final days and hours. In a controlled voice, he said, "I wish to forgive some people for what they are now doing to me."

Sacco and Vanzetti, wrongly convicted and executed, became poster boys for anarchists and communists worldwide. There were violent demonstrations in many cities throughout Europe and Asia, and wildcat strikes closed factories worldwide. Three died in demonstrations in Germany and ten thousand people turned out for the funerals of the two men in Boston.

"It was one of the most tremendous funerals of modern times," reported the *Boston Globe*.

Controversy reigned for decades and opinion is still divided. Were the killings carried out by Madeiros and his gang or by Sacco with

Vanzetti present? We will never know, but there is enough doubt to make their conviction unsafe. This was the view of Massachusetts Governor Michael Dukakis, who asked for a review in 1977 on the fiftieth anniversary of the executions. Based on that review, he took the bold decision to declare that both men had been unfairly tried and convicted, and that "any disgrace should be forever removed from their names."

He did not issue a pardon, because that would imply they were guilty. But significantly he did not assert their innocence. That is a question that may never be answered.

CHARLES STARKWEATHER
REBEL WITHOUT A CLUE

The teen culture did not emerge until the fifties, with the arrival of Elvis Presley, Bill Haley, and James Dean, the original rebel without a cause. But James Dean did not invent the moody teenager kicking against authority. He just reflected what was already out there—a youth culture growing up on postwar austerity who felt alienated and out of touch with their parents' generation. The old certainties were gone and kids felt they did not fit in. So they sought their own music, their own clothing, and their own way of belonging.

And some just never fit in.

If you are looking for the ultimate teen idol, he is not James Dean but Charles Starkweather, the Rebel Without a Clue.

Starkweather decided to impress his young girlfriend by shooting her father; then the two lovers went on a road trip across the Badlands of Nebraska, leaving a trail of dead bodies in their wake. And like Dean, Starkweather came to a violent end. He was sentenced to die in the electric chair, guilty of eleven murders.

The story was immortalized in the movie *Badlands*, starring Martin Sheen and Sissy Spacek.

Charles Raymond Starkweather was born in 1938 in Lincoln, Nebraska. He came from a good working-class family and was raised well. But he had a medical condition which left him slightly bowlegged and he had a speech impediment. So his school years were marred by bullying and misery. But in his teens he grew physically strong and began to hit back at his tormentors. In a matter of months he went from well-behaved child to troubled and troublesome teenager. He developed a James Dean obsession and styled his hair to match the pint-sized actor. But though he had the look and the swagger, he did not have the confidence. He was a misfit and a loner, prone to violent outbursts.

As an eighteen-year-old dropout, he was introduced to thirteen-year-old Caril Ann Fugate. Her older sister was dating one of Starkweather's few friends. Caril was the ideal girlfriend for Charles. So many years his junior, she looked up to him and fed his ego. She was impressed by his looks, his car, and the fact that he seemed to have endless money to spend on her. The fact that he stole the money and the gifts he gave her was not immediately apparent. He worked minimum wage as a garbageman, but she only saw the James Dean look-alike. He, in turn, felt that Caril gave him a reason to live.

But it was not all roses. Starkweather's father threw him out, forcing the young man to fend for himself. He felt depressed, believing that his life would amount to nothing. The only solution to his difficulties seemed to be crime.

On November 30, 1957, Starkweather went into a service station and tried to buy a stuffed dog for Caril. He had no money and was refused credit. Furious, he returned later on that bitterly cold night with a shotgun and robbed the store. He took the attendant, Richard Jensen, away in his car, stopping in a remote area. The attendant struggled and in the scuffle the gun went off, hitting the attendant in the knee. As Starkweather stood over the injured man, he decided this was the moment his destiny changed. For once he was the one in charge. He shot Robert Colvert in the head. Afterward, he claimed that he felt he left his former self behind that night and was now a new man, facing a new future.

He told Caril Ann Fugate about the shooting but said that an accomplice had actually pulled the trigger. She wasn't fooled, but like her boyfriend she seemed to exult in the violence. He had killed without remorse, and he felt powerful and euphoric. He had money in his pocket. He was not one of the suspects and their secret seemed to bind the couple more closely together. All was good.

Good, apart from the fact that he was fired as a garbageman and thrown out of his apartment for falling behind on the rent. All was about as bad as it could get. On top of that, he knew that Caril's parents did not like him and were against the relationship. But the relationship was the only thing that gave his life meaning. He was nuts about his girl and felt he could win over her parents. In late January 1958, he called on them while Caril was still at school. He had a rifle with him, and he said he had been planning on inviting Caril's stepfather, Marion Bartlett, out hunting. But Marion and Velda (Caril's mother) immediately began arguing with him, telling him firmly to leave their daughter alone. He was thrown out of the house. He returned some time later for his gun and was thrown out again.

When Caril returned from school she was shocked at the way her boyfriend had been treated. She went in and argued with her parents. Starkweather followed her in, and the argument became physical. Velda struck Starkweather, and then Marion came at him with a hammer. Starkweather shot him in the face and then turned his rifle on Velda, shooting her too. In his rage he turned the gun around and battered her head with its butt. Her two-year-old child, Betty Jean, began to cry and Starkweather turned, driving the butt of the gun into the child's head.

Starkweather later claimed that Velda had tried to attack him with a knife. He went on, "I picked up that knife that the old lady had . . . started to walk in the bedroom . . . and the little girl kept yelling, and I told her to shut up, and I started to walk again, and just turned around and threw the kitchen knife I had at her. They said it hit her in the throat, but I thought it hit her in the chest. I went on into the bedroom. Mr. Bartlett was moving around, so I tried to stab him in the throat, but the knife wouldn't go in, and I just hit the top part of it with my hand, and it went in."

The teenage lovers cleaned up as best they could. They stuffed Velda's body into the toilet in the outhouse. Marion was dragged into the chicken coup. And the dead baby, Caril's sister, was put in a cardboard box and left in the outhouse with her mother. Caril and Charles spent the next six days living in the house as if nothing had happened, telling callers that they could not come in because of an outbreak of flu. But they fled hours before the police, their suspicions aroused, raided the house.

Starkweather and Fugate were now on the run. They drove to the remote farmhouse of seventy-year-old August Meyer, a friend of Starkweather's parents. They shot the old man and stole his car, but they crashed and had to abandon the vehicle. Two teenagers picked them up and were killed for their troubles. The body count now stood at seven and would grow over the coming hours.

They drove back to Lincoln, breaking into a house in one of the wealthier sections of town. They killed the owners of the house and their maid, stole their jewelry and money, and made off in their car. It was time to leave Nebraska.

With a manhunt in full swing in their home state, they drove into Wyoming. They needed a new car, one whose plates were not known to the cops, so they stopped outside the small town of Douglas, where they had spotted a salesman asleep in his car. They shot him where he slept in the passenger seat. Two days, seven kills. Caril got into the rear and Starkweather got behind the wheel, and they tried to drive. But the car had an emergency brake, unusual in those days, and Starkweather was unable to get it started. A motorist stopped to help, but when Starkweather pointed the gun at him, he knew he was in trouble. He grabbed the barrel and struggled with the teen killer.

Just then, Deputy Sheriff William Romer drove by and stopped to check out the commotion. At that point Caril Fugate could see the writing on the wall. Their car would not start, the cops were here, and Starkweather could not wrestle the gun from the motorist who had stopped to help. So she decided to abandon her lover and jump to the side of the angels. She ran from the car, shouting, "He killed a man," as if she was completely innocent of the murder spree.

Starkweather let go of the gun and ran from the stolen car, getting back into his first car. He turned the key and took off at a high speed. Immediately Romer set off in pursuit, calling for reinforcements as he gave chase. Douglas Police Chief Robert Ainslie and Sheriff Earl Heflin of Converse County, Wyoming, were in a car together and joined the chase. As Starkweather zoomed by at over 100 miles per hour, they got in behind him, their lights flashing. As Ainslie drove, Heflin leaned out the window and took careful aim, shooting out the back window of Starkweather's car. As the window exploded in a cloud of glass shards, the fleeing car suddenly came to a dead stop in the middle of the road. The flying glass had cut Starkweather's ear and he believed he had been shot. He thought he was going to bleed out.

He kept the James Dean swagger to the end. As the cops covered him with their guns, he got out of the car. They ordered him to put up his hands, but he ignored them. They shot at the ground and ordered him to lie down. He ignored them. Then he put his hands behind his back. Thinking he was about to pull a gun, they fired another warning shot at his feet. Finally he got the message and brought his hands back into view. All he had been trying to do was to tuck in his shirt so that he would look right for the arrest.

The mug shot would be an iconic teen image. Starkweather was bloodied and in chains; stubble was on his chin and a cigarette dangled nonchalantly from his lips. He wore a black leather biker's jacket and tight jeans with pointy-toed cowboy boots.

Right to the end Starkweather continued to show the poor judgment that had characterized his short life. He had the choice of being tried in Wyoming or Nebraska. The difference was that in Wyoming he would go to the gas chamber, while in Nebraska he would face the electric chair. He chose the chair. Had he elected to be tried in Wyoming he would have received a life sentence, as the governor was vehemently opposed to the death penalty. The governor of Nebraska had no such qualms.

Fugate claimed that she was an unwilling captive, forced to go along with Starkweather because he had threatened to kill her family. This defense had a flaw; she had been there when her family had been killed, right at the start of the killing spree, and she had helped clean up after the event. But once Starkweather realized his beloved Caril was abandoning him, he began the same game. He claimed that she had been the most trigger-happy person he had ever met and was the chief killer.

Both were convicted. They were only tried for one killing, that of Richard Jensen, the teenager they had killed at the start of the two day spree. Starkweather received the death penalty. Because of her age (at fifteen she was the youngest female ever tried for first-degree murder), Fugate was sentenced to life. She was paroled in 1976, making a new life for herself. In 2013 she was seriously injured in a traffic accident which killed her husband. She is still recovering from those critical injuries.

Starkweather went to the chair at Nebraska State Penitentiary in Lincoln at 12:04 a.m. on June 25, 1959. To the end he was defiant. When asked to donate his eyes after his death, he said, "Nobody ever did anything for me when I was alive. Why should I help anybody when I'm dead?"

The day before his execution he gave a brief interview, in which he said, "I don't know why I killed folks. I don't have an answer for that. The people were just there and I killed them and I don't know why."

Asked had he any regrets, or would he do anything differently, he said, "Not really, 'cos my life has been a failure and if I could go back in time I am sure I would do the same thing all over. I know I am crazy. I know I am a monster. People laugh at me and tell me how ugly I am, all of my life. I just got mad. All that anger inside of me, all my life it has been building in me. I just despise people and I hate people because they just laugh at me and call me ugly names. I just had to kill them. If I could go back into time I would kill as many more people as I could because I hate people. I know they are going to kill me in the electric chair and I don't really care, because I am going to be famous for all time just like my idol James Dean. I am looking forward to dying so that I can go to heaven and meet my idol James Dean."

Minutes before the execution, the doctor who was meant to pronounce death suffered a fatal heart attack. But that did not delay proceedings. The execution went ahead as scheduled. Afterward, Starkweather got his final wish. With six films and a television miniseries inspired by his story, he did become famous for all time.

LEON CZOLGOSZ
ANARCHY IN THE USA

William McKinley was a popular president. The twenty-fifth man to hold that honor, he was a veteran of the Civil War and successful lawyer before entering politics for the Republican Party. A native of Ohio, he did well in Congress but lost his seat in the Democratic landslide of 1890. The following year he changed direction, being elected governor of Ohio. He gained a reputation for fairness and moderation, appealing to both the laboring classes and the moneyed classes. This proved a springboard for a presidential bid in 1896.

The country was in the depths of an economic depression. He campaigned on a commitment to retaining the gold standard and promised protective tariffs against foreign competition which would support business and restore prosperity.

He won the election and his policies slowly saw a return to prosperity. He also won the Spanish-American War of 1898 decisively, gaining the territories of Puerto Rico, Guam, and the Philippines. The United States also annexed the independent Republic of Hawai'i. With those achievements behind him and being a popular figure, he had no difficulty winning a second term in the Oval Office in the 1900 election. He looked forward to continuing his economic policies and his overseas expansion.

Like all politicians, he had to keep an eye on the future. He listened carefully to public opinion, and often his policies were formed on that basis. A man of the people, he liked to mingle and press the flesh at every opportunity. He was not a difficult man to approach.

Following his inauguration in March, McKinley went on a tour of the nation, traveling by train with his wife and team of advisers. The trip would end in Buffalo, New York, at the massive Pan-American Exposition. It was a great success. No president had ever officially toured the west and he was rapturously received. But he canceled the last leg of the tour when his wife became ill and returned to Washington. After taking care of some state business he retired to Canton, Ohio, to prepare for an important public speech he would still give in Buffalo.

Now the visit was not the end of his nationwide tour, but part of a ten-day trip which included a visit to Cleveland to visit an army camp.

On Thursday, September 5, he arrived in Buffalo and was paraded through the fair. The plan was to deliver a major speech that day, and then the following day he would visit the Niagara Falls before returning to the fair for a meet and greet at the Temple of Music in the Exposition. His security people were unhappy with the meet and greet, feeling it would be difficult to guarantee his safety.

"No one would wish to hurt me," he assured them.

The gates of the fair were opened at six o'clock on the morning of Thursday, September 5, and the crowd began to gather early, eager for a glimpse of the popular president. Of the 116,000 who passed through the gates that day, at least 50,000 of them filled the space in front of the esplanade to see the president deliver his address. After a brief introduction and a call for silence, he began to speak.

Not everyone in the crowd was a supporter of President McKinley. That is the nature of politics. The audience had a fair sprinkling of Democrats, a few socialists, and an occasional anarchists. One of the anarchists was there with a purpose.

Leon Czolgosz was a native of Ohio, like McKinley. But he had not been born into privilege. Born in 1873, he was the son of a poor Polish Catholic emigrant who had arrived in the United States a decade previously. When he was five, the family moved to Detroit, and by fourteen he was working in a glass factory in Pennsylvania. At seventeen he switched employment, joining the Cleveland Rolling Mill Company, but during the economic crash of 1893 the workers went on strike and Czolgosz found himself out of work. At times of great stress, people often fall back on their ethnic community but Czolgosz found no comfort among the Polish Catholics. Instead he began to associate with members of the labor movement, joining a workingman's socialist club. But they were not radical enough for him, so he moved on to the Sila organization, where he was introduced to anarchism. Anarchism was always more popular in Europe than America. They advocated overthrowing the existing government, often by violent means, and returning power to the people. In the United States, the anarchist movement was dominated by people of recent European descent. There is no doubt that Czolgosz held radical views, but he was also an awkward man trying to fit in. This often led to him appearing desperate, which aroused the suspicion of the secretive anarchists.

Czolgosz attended a number of strikes, showing his support for the workers. But he developed a respiratory problem and had to curtail his activities. He retreated to the farm in Ohio that his father had purchased. But his new beliefs often clashed with the more traditional Catholic views of his family, and the time he spent on the farm was a tense one. He became reclusive, burying himself in his socialist books. In 1901, the radical heroine of the anarchist movement, Emma Goldman, delivered a speech in Cleveland. Czolgosz was in the audience and approached Ms. Goldman afterward, speaking to her briefly. She introduced him to some local socialists.

But his social awkwardness, his shifty ways, and his indiscreet inquiries about the movement aroused the suspicion of some. In fact, an Anarchist newspaper, *Free Society*, issued a warning about him: "The attention of the comrades is called to another spy. He is well-dressed, of medium height, rather narrow shoulders, blond and about 25 years of age. His demeanor is of the usual sort, pretending to be greatly interested in the cause, asking for names or soliciting aid for acts of contemplated violence. If this same individual makes his appearance elsewhere the comrades are warned in advance, and can act accordingly."

Czolgosz did not fit in, even among the marginalized. But he wanted to be taken seriously by the anarchist movement. He had to make a big statement.

By the summer of 1901, he was living in Buffalo and when he heard the president was visiting, he knew this was his opportunity. On September 3, he went to Walbridge's Hardware Store on Main Street and bought a small 32 caliber Iver Johnson revolver for $4.50. Two days later he was waiting when the presidential train pulled into the station. As the locomotive slowed, a canon was fired in salute but the canon was so close to the track that it blew in the windows of the train. Luckily no one was hurt. At the station the crowds were too big to allow Czolgosz any sort of shot, so he abandoned that plan. But not the idea as a whole. As he later stated to police, "It was in my heart. There was no escape for me. I could not have conquered it had my life been at stake. There were thousands of people in town on Tuesday. All those people seemed to be bowing to the great ruler. I made up my mind to kill that ruler."

Later that day the president gave a speech before thousands as scheduled. Czolgosz tried to elbow his way to the front of the crowd where he could get a clear shot, but he never got close enough. There was no point in firing randomly towards the stage; he wanted to hit his target. After the presidential speech McKinley went backstage and Czolgosz tried to follow him but was blocked by security guards. He had to go back to his boarding room that night with the job undone.

The following morning, Friday, September 6, he was at the fair early, but McKinley boarded a train for a tour of the nearby Niagara Falls. The assassin waited impatiently as the hours passed before the presidential party returned. Finally, McKinley was back in the grounds of the fair—but could Czolgosz get close enough this time?

At three thirty in the afternoon, McKinley stopped for refreshments before proceeding to the Temple of Music, where he was to do a meet and greet, shaking hands with as many people as he could in the brief time allocated. He could shake fifty hands a minute and was scheduled to be there for ten minutes, so five hundred people in the crowd would get to press the presidential flesh. Czolgosz stood in line, his hand wrapped in a handkerchief as if it were injured. Unknown to the security detail, the bandage actually concealed his revolver.

Security was tight. Police were at the doors and detectives lined the aisles. A dozen soldiers in full dress uniform were not there for decoration. McKinley took his place at the top of the aisle that had been blocked off for the reception and the crowd began to stream by as the organ belted out "The Star-Spangled Banner." After five minutes the doors of the room were closed to cut off the crowd, and the remaining people streamed in a line past the president, most getting just a few seconds and a radiant smile. One twelve-year-old girl, Myrtle Ledger, asked for the president's red carnation, which he cheerfully handed over. The Secret Service watched carefully as a tall, scowling man approached, but he shook hands grimly and moved on. At 4:07 p.m. Czolgosz reached the top of the line. Seeing his injured hand, McKinley instinctively reached out his left hand to shake, to spare the man pain. But Czolgosz violently struck away the proffered hand and drew up his bandaged hand to reveal the revolver.

Before anyone could react, he fired off two rounds, striking the president twice in the torso.

As McKinley staggered back Czolgosz prepared to take a third shot. But an African-American man next in line, James Parker, bravely rushed forward and slammed into the assassin, making a grab for the gun. Two of the security detail rushed in as the men struggled and soon Czolgosz disappeared beneath a pile of men, many of whom were getting in blows with fists and rifle butts. As the beaten man muttered, "I have done my duty," the swarm of people were infuriated and the beating increased.

McKinley had staggered but was caught and guided to a nearby chair. Believing he was not seriously injured, the president immediately assumed control of the situation, calling for a halt to the beating that was going on a few feet from him. But as Czolgosz was being led away, an agent struck him to the ground with a single punch. Blood was running high.

As the panicked crowd attempted to flee the Temple of Music the president was put on a stretcher and taken out back to where an ambulance was waiting. He was rushed to the hospital. On the way, he loosened his suit and a bullet fell out. It had been deflected by a button and had only grazed him. Unfortunately, the other bullet had entered his abdomen, causing considerable damage.

Today McKinley would have been on his feet in a matter of weeks. The wound was serious but not life threatening. The bullet had torn through his stomach and lodged in the muscles of his back. But the big problem was infection. In the days before penicillin an abdominal wound generally meant a lingering death from gangrene. An operation was performed which closed the holes in McKinley's stomach, but the surgeon was unable to locate and remove the bullet, in part due to McKinley's obesity. For a day or two it appeared McKinley was recovering. His strength returned and he was able to sit up and chat with visitors. Despite being nearly sixty and overweight, he had a very strong constitution. But gangrene was creeping slowly along the path of the wound, infecting his stomach and other organs. It was only a matter of time.

Within a few days McKinley was eating lightly but suffering terrible indigestion. This was the effect of the infection on his stomach. A day after this he was drifting in and out of consciousness, and at 2:15 a.m. on Saturday, September 14, he passed away. Theodore (Teddy) Roosevelt was sworn in as the twenty-sixth president of the United States. He said, "When compared with the suppression of anarchy, every other question sinks into insignificance."

The whole country was horrified. Czolgosz was transferred to Auburn State Prison to await trial. Justice moved swiftly; on September 16, the grand jury indicted him on a count of first-degree murder. The only thing of note about the indictment was that Czolgosz refused to talk to the lawyers appointed to defend him—sticking to his anarchist principles of refusing to recognize the court and its officers. When it came to trial—just nine days after President McKinley succumbed to his injuries—Czolgosz pleaded guilty and then ignored the court. The judge, Truman White, did not accept the guilty plea and entered a plea of not guilty on the assassin's behalf.

Even if he had spoken to his defense team, nine days was hardly sufficient time to prepare an adequate defense. In the absence of any communication from their client, his lawyers were left with no option but to plead insanity. They presented no witnesses and Czolgosz said nothing on his own behalf. This left the field open for the prosecutor to play up the anarchist angle.

The insanity plea did not wash and the jury took just an hour to convict, returning their verdict on September 24, 1901. From fatal shot, to death of the president, to trial and conviction had taken less than three weeks, unseemly haste by modern standards. Two days later, the jury was asked to consider punishment and recommended the death penalty. Asked if he had anything to say, Czolgosz still would not speak, just shaking his head.

The execution was scheduled for October 29—just forty-five days after his victim's death. There were no last-minute appeals and no postponements. He entered the death chamber between two guards calmly and unafraid. The time was seven o'clock in the morning.

Witness Charles R. Huntley told the *Buffalo Commercial*:

Czolgosz did not show any signs of fear and he did not tremble or turn pale; he walked into the death room between two men, and walked with a firm step. He stumbled as he came into the room but did not fall, nor did his knees weaken. I was quite surprised at his demeanor, as was everyone else, I should say. He was perfectly strong and calm. He just slid himself into the chair exactly as a man might who expected to enjoy a half hour's repose. The fact that in a moment a death current was to be forced through him did not seem to perturb him in the least.

He spoke very plainly and in a voice which did not waver in the slightest degree. He said first that he was not sorry for having killed the President, and, as the straps which bound his jaws were put in place, he said that he was sorry he could not see his father. It was a general surprise to hear his voice after the men had begun to affix the electrodes. The witnesses were somewhat startled and were amazed at the man's calmness. But the men at work beside him and in front of him did not pause. They kept on affixing the appliances. There was no spirit of bravado manifest at all. He said a few things just as if he felt it his duty to say them . . .

The majesty of the law was perfectly sustained. There wasn't a hitch anywhere and not an incident which could merit the faintest criticism. Czolgosz was sentenced to die in the electric chair, and his death was effected quickly and certainly. It was but an incredibly short time after the murderer walked into the death chamber when the doctors in attendance pronounced him dead. There had been no scene; no one had fainted or grown excited. Everyone conducted himself with remarkable sang-froid. The attendants were busy right up to the moment of turning on the current, and had but stepped back when the body of the assassin was in the grasp of the powerful current. As I have said, not a thing marred the formality. Everything went off smoothly.

Sheriff Samuel Caldwell agreed, saying:

> I was impressed with the idea that the assassin was a man of great nerve. Although guards had hold of his arms, the prisoner could have walked unaided to the chair. Aside from the prisoner's last words, there was not a sound in the death chamber, and the prisoner himself gave no evidence of fear.
>
> As soon as he had been seated in the chair and his face covered so that his nose and month were alone exposed, Warden Mead raised his hand and Electrician Davis turned on the current which snuffed out the prisoner's life as with a snap of the finger. The electrician then felt the prisoner's jugular vein. Dr. MacDonald did the same, and was followed by Prison Physician Gerin. The doctors then stepped back, and Warden Mead again raised his hand. Again the current was applied and was continued about 50 seconds.
>
> When the electricity was again shut off, the physicians examined the body by the usual means, and at the end pronounced that the man was dead. The prisoner's nerve was evidenced by his conduct from the moment he entered the death chamber. No groan escaped him, and his lips did not even move except when he was making his final statement to the effect that he did not repent his crime. When the electricity entered the assassin's body it stiffened with successive jerks, but death was so quick that he did not have time to groan.

Czolgosz's last words were an expression of regret that he would not meet his father again and a defiant declaration, "I killed the President because he was the enemy of the good people—the good working people. I am not sorry for my crime."

After the execution the prison authorities refused to release the body to the family. Instead it was placed in a plain wooden coffin, which was then filled with sulfuric acid. The remains were dissolved within hours. There would be no body for the anarchist movement to create a martyr.

THE CHAIR TRAVELS
OLD SPARKY IN THE PHILIPPINES

Execution methods become associated with different countries and different cultures. The guillotine is as French as a beret or a burgundy, the garrote as Spanish as paella. Stoning is indelibly associated with the Middle East, and the electric chair with the United States. In fact, the electric chair, despite seeming to be a high tech and modern solution to the execution problem, has been taken up by no other countries.

Every single country in the world decided the chair was not for them. The closest it came to traveling was during the war when British Prime Minister Winston Churchill suggested that once Hitler was captured and tried, he would be executed on an electric chair in Trafalgar Square, London. He may well have been joking.

The Philippines were the only country outside of the United States that decided to give the chair a try, and the only reason they did was that they were under American control at the time. A while after the United States pulled out, they unplugged the chair.

Capital punishment has been a controversial topic in the Philippines, a predominantly Roman Catholic country. Many oppose it. The country was ruled by the Spanish until 1898. Under colonial rule, firing squad, garrote, and hanging were the methods of choice. This remained the case in the early years of American rule. But in 1926, the US authorities introduced the electric chair. It was used for a number of years but when the government changed to a commonwealth in 1935 executions were suspended.

In 1946 the Philippines became a sovereign independent state and executions resumed. Rape, murder, and treason were capital offenses. Political assassinations were common and many of the executions were political. Fifty-one people were electrocuted in fifteen years. Once President Ferdinand Marcos came to power, the number of electrocutions rose sharply. Ironically Marcos had been sentenced to death himself in 1938, but was acquitted on appeal.

The electric chair was used until 1976, when it was replaced by firing squad. In 1986, the Philippines introduced a new constitution which made it the first Asian country to drop capital punishment. It was briefly reintroduced in the nineties, but on April 15, 2006, the sentences of 1,230 death row prisoners were commuted to life imprisonment. The death penalty is no longer part of the Philippines justice system.

During the years of the electric chair, the most famous case was the trial of three men accused of the brutal gang rape of a popular actress. Maggie dela Riva was born in 1942 and appeared in over thirty films. She still works in television. She graduated high school at sixteen and trained as a secretary, but then she began getting work as an actress. In addition to her movies, she also became a regular feature on ABS-CBN, the main commercial radio and television station in the Philippines. This work made her a household name and by the time she was twenty-five, everyone in the country knew her face. It was 1967 and she was on every television screen. A group of rich kids used to prowl the posh hotels in Pasay City, a suburb of Manila. Pasay is a well-off section of the capital, famous for its entertainment and its restaurants. The nightlife there is second to none and it is a tourist magnet. The group used to prowl the streets and the hotels, drinking and looking for women. Some of the members —a sort of Philippine Rat Pack—were well known, including Jaime Jose Y Gomez. He came from a wealthy and politically well-connected family and was well known in his own right as a band leader.

In the small hours of June 26, 1967, Maggie dela Riva was on her way home from the television studio. She was accompanied by her maid, Helen Calderon. They drove down 12th Street in the Quezon district and were very close to home. Just then, four men in a convertible drove up behind them and came abreast of dela Riva's car. They tried to bump her from the side and she had to break sharply to avoid a collision, and then she hit the gas and tried to pull to the left to evade them.

She was right outside her own house. The other car tried to bump her again, and dela Riva swore at the driver. Then he got out and rushed towards her. In panic, she began blaring the horn of her car. He grabbed her and pulled her from the car. His three companions each reached out and pulled her by the legs and neck into the convertible, and then they took off, leaving the maid behind.

The four men in the convertible were Jose Y Gomez, Basilio Pineda Jr., Eduardo Aquino Y Payumo, and Rogelio Canal Y Sevilla. They swiftly drove to the Swanky Hotel in Pasay. The hotel staff knew what was going on and turned a blind eye as the terrified woman was dragged in.

The men led dela Riva up to the second floor where they had a room. Dela Riva was forced to sit on the bed, surrounded by Jose and Canal. Aquino and Pineda stood in front of her. Pineda ordered her to do a striptease for them. Once the actress was completely naked, Jose stripped and pushed her backwards onto the bed. He then raped her. She struggled violently and he struck her several times to subdue her. After that, the others took their turns. Twice during the rape she passed out, which took from their enjoyment. So they paused to throw water over her face and slapped her to revive her. During the ordeal, they also threatened to shoot her and to throw acid in her face. They also threatened to seek her out and disfigure her if she spoke to police afterward.

At six o'clock in the morning, after an hour of rape and torture, they were finished with her. They took her out onto the street and put her in a taxi, then walked away, laughing.

When she got home, the shocked actress was confronted by a large crowd, including police officers and reporters. Her maid had raised the alarm. She fell into her mother's arms and sobbed, "Mommy, mommy, I have been raped. All four of them raped me."

The trial took place at the end of September, and dela Riva bravely stood on the witness stand to deliver her damning testimony. Pineda pleaded guilty. The other three denied the rape. But all were found guilty on October 2, and were sentenced to death. Four hotel employees who aided the rapists were given lesser sentences.

Canal did not live long enough to face the electric chair. While on death row he overdosed on drugs and passed away in 1970. The other three were electrocuted in 1972. Because of the celebrity status of the victim, it was one of the most notorious trials in Philippine history and attracted huge interest. President Marcos ordered that the executions be televised.

The three men went to the chair on May 17, 1972. The *Manila Times* wrote that the three men were given a mild sedative to help them through the final day. Then they were transferred from the prison hospital to the anteroom of the death chamber at midnight. Weeping relatives were allowed spend the final few hours with the men.

At seven o'clock in the morning, the official death sentence was read out, and then the men got their final breakfast: fried chicken, bread, and coffee. Lunch was their last meal and consisted of chicken, lobsters, and ice cream, along with side dishes. Pineda and Aquino ate. But Jose could not, even when his sister tried to spoon feed him.

At three o'clock that afternoon, silence descended on the prison. The paper noted: "A pale and dazed Jose was the first to walk the final steps to the execution chamber. He had just recovered from shock and had to be placed under sedation. His eyes stared blankly and unseeing as he walked between two priests with lips repeating their prayers."

The execution did not go well. Witness Basil Caranting wrote: "Three guards pulled down three switches, of which only one is the live switch. Everybody in that chamber witnessed how a human body contorts when 2,000 volts of electricity is coursed through it. There was a smell of burning flesh. When the initial shock was over, the duty doctor approached the chair and examined the body. He shook his head and in a loud voice proclaimed: 'Sir, the condemned man is still alive.'"

A second jolt was needed.

Then it was Pineda's turn.

The *Manila Times* wrote: "Pineda came next. He had a minor hassle with prison guards when, owing to a slight confusion, they started to lead Aquino to the death chamber ahead of him. He was strapped into the chair at 3:40 p.m., and pronounced dead at 3:55 p.m. Aquino came last. He died at 4:10 p.m. While he was in the death chamber, his mother, who had been keeping him company since morning, fainted into the arms of her eight other children."

The very public nature of the executions made a deep impression across the country. Dean Jorge Bocobo, a Filipino journalist, wrote: "As a young man my family lived just blocks away from the Swanky Hotel in Pasay City where the incident took place. I remember vividly the newspaper pictures of those men with shaven heads just before they were fried from brain to balls in the electric chair. For many of my generation, that seared in our young minds forever this message: Rape is Evil! The victory of justice in this case was self-evident in the grace, bravery and enduring humanity that lives in Maggie dela Riva."

14

REFINING THE DEATH PENALTY

Once the Furman objections had been overcome by the Gregg decision in 1976, the majority of states reintroduced the death penalty. The execution of Gary Gilmore opened the floodgates and many more executions were scheduled. Death row began to fill up in many prisons. But in the wake of the Gregg decision, several other landmark cases were heard which limited and defined how America would practice the death penalty. In this chapter we will look at the main decisions and how they affected capital punishment.

At one time, several crimes were punishable by death, including rape, aggravated larceny, treason, kidnapping, and, of course, murder. But as standards of decency evolved, it became difficult to justify the death penalty in all such cases. Over the years since 1976, America has evolved its thinking on capital punishment in several important aspects so that now only certain classes of murder draw down the ultimate sanction.

IS RAPE A DEATH PENALTY OFFENSE?

In 1977, just a year after the reintroduction of the death penalty, the Supreme Court decided that it was against the Eighth Amendment to execute people for rape. The landmark decision was handed down in *Coker v. Georgia.*

Ehrlich Anthony Coker was bad to the bone. He was a career criminal with a propensity for extreme violence and ended up serving a lengthy sentence for rape, kidnapping, aggravated assault, and first-degree murder. This had not resulted in the death sentence because his case was heard during the moratorium. Instead he got three life sentences, two twenty-year sentences, and an eight-year sentence. He had raped and killed a sixteen-year-old, and raped and badly injured another sixteen-year-old. But eighteen months into his sentence, he managed to escape from Wade Correctional Institute in Georgia. While he was on the run, he broke into the home of newlyweds, Allen and Elnita Carver, near Waycross, Georgia. He tied Allen up in the bathroom and then raped sixteen-year-old Elnita before bundling her into the couple's car, which he then stole. He was arrested in the stolen car with his terrified victim tied up beside him. Rape was a capital offense and after his conviction the jury sentenced him to die in the electric chair during the sentencing portion of the hearing. They did this because of the presence of aggravating factors. He had previous convictions for a capital offense (first-degree murder), and the rape was committed during the course of another capital felony—an armed robbery. The Georgia Supreme Court upheld the sentence. Then the defense attorneys brought their appeal to the US Supreme Court.

In the plurality opinion (a sort of average opinion handed down by a divided court) written by Justice Byron White, he noted that rape in itself does not cause serious injury, writing: "Although it may be accompanied by another crime, rape by definition does not include the death of or even the serious injury to another person."

The court also considered legal practice at the time. In 1925 only eighteen states had allowed the death penalty for rape, and by 1971 this number had dropped to sixteen—less than half of the states that allowed executions. But post-Furman, only one state retained rape of an adult woman as a capital offense—Georgia. Of the sixty-three rape cases in Georgia considered by the Supreme Court, they found only six of those involved a death sentence, and only five of those death sentences were upheld by the Georgia Supreme Court. So the US Supreme Court concluded that death sentences were rare in rape cases—an unusual punishment.

They acknowledged the seriousness of rape, but added, "In terms of moral depravity and of the injury to the person and to the public, it does not compare with murder, which does involve the unjustified taking of human life." For that reason, the Court concluded that the electric chair was excessive punishment for "the rapist who, as such, does not take human life." The aggravating factors considered by the jury did not change this. The death sentences against Coker and four other rapists sentenced to the chair (John Hooks, John Eberheart, Donald Boyer, and William Hughes) were commuted to life imprisonment.

The death penalty for the rape of an adult was no longer constitutional. However two states—Mississippi and Florida—retained the death penalty for the rape of a child. The main consequence of the Coker decision was that the death penalty was largely restricted to crimes in which someone had been killed.

As for Ehrlich Coker, he is still behind bars at the Philips State Prison in Georgia, after serving the first thirty-seven years of multiple life terms. Interestingly, his son Eric Lee Coker is also doing time in North Carolina. He was sentenced to a minimum of twenty-one years for repeatedly molesting a fourteen-year-old relative and for trying to hire a hit man to take out his wife.

In later years, the Supreme Court revisited the question of rape when the case of *Kennedy v. Louisiana* came before it. Patrick O'Neal Kennedy, from greater New Orleans, was a huge 300 pound man who violently raped his eight-year-old stepdaughter, causing her extensive internal injuries. He was offered a deal to plead guilty and avoid the death penalty in 2003, but refused. On conviction he was sentenced to death, a decision upheld by the Louisiana Supreme Court.

The US Supreme Court ruled, in 2008, that the death penalty was not constitutional for the rape of a minor. Thus the death penalty is now unconstitutional in all cases that do not involve murder or crimes against the state (espionage and treason).

FELONY MURDER

Felony murder is a special class of murder. If a defendant accidentally kills someone in the course of a felony, he can be charged with murder. Or if he is involved with others in a felony and someone else in the criminal enterprise commits murder then all those involved can be charged with murder, even if they had nothing to do with the killing and did not approve it. So, if you are the lookout in an armed robbery and someone gets killed inside while you are outside and well away from the crime, you are still guilty of murder. Not every state recognizes felony murder, but in those that do, it can be a capital offense. This has been upheld by the Supreme Court in two key rulings. The decision in *Enmund v. Florida* was that the death penalty could not be imposed on someone who did not kill, attempt to kill, or intend to kill. But in *Tison v. Arizona*, the court decided that the death penalty could be imposed on someone who was a major participant in a felony and acted with reckless indifference to human life.

In other words, executing someone for felony murder is constitutional, but each case has to be carefully considered on its merits.

Earl Enmund was a getaway driver in an armed robbery of a couple in rural Florida. His accomplices, Sampson and Jeanette Armstrong, rang the doorbell of the farmhouse of Thomas and Eunice Kersey. When Thomas opened the door, they held him at gunpoint, but Eunice came out with a gun and wounded Jeanette. Then Sampson shot back, killing the couple. Both Armstrongs were sentenced to death and so was their getaway driver, Enmund. While the sentences of the Armstrongs were upheld, that of Enmund was commuted to life imprisonment after the Supreme Court ruled that he had not participated in the killing and had not agreed to the killing taking place.

Raymond and Ricky Tison were not so lucky when their case came before the Supreme Court. Their troubles all began with a prison break in 1978. Their father, Gary, had been doing life at the Arizona State Prison in Florence for killing a prison guard. Ricky, Raymond, and their brother Donald visited him for an informal picnic—a practice allowed by the prison. But instead of food and beverages in their cooler box, they had sawn-off shotguns and revolvers. They sprang their father and his cellmate, Randy Greenawalt, and drove towards California. But their car broke down near the border. A Good Samaritan stopped to help. For his troubles, he, his wife, his twenty-two-month-old son, and his fifteen-year-old niece were killed. They were all killed by Gary Tison. A few days later, Tison and Greenawalt killed a honeymooning couple. It is not known which of them did the actual killing, but they had acted together. They were finally captured after a shoot-out, during which Donald Tison was killed. The others escaped into the desert where Gary Tison died of dehydration and heat exhaustion. Raymond and Ricky Tison were quickly recaptured, as was Greenawalt. All three were sentenced to death for four murders and numerous other crimes. Although Greenawalt and Gary Tison had been the shooters, the two young brothers were sentenced to death for felony murder. They appealed, and the Supreme Court ruled that they could be executed. Unlike Enmund, they had willingly been part of a felony which resulted in many deaths. They had shown reckless disregard for human life and could be executed.

Greenawalt was executed by lethal injection, but the two brothers eventually had their sentences commuted to life in prison because they were in their teens at the time of their father's prison break.

The Enmund and Tison decisions determined how felony murders are handled in capital cases to this day.

CAN WE EXECUTE THE MENTALLY HANDICAPPED? ATKINS V. VIRGINIA

John Paul Penry, born in 1956, is an intellectually disabled man who raped and killed Pamela Moseley, the twenty-two-year-old sister of American football star Mark Moseley, shortly after being released from prison in Texas in 1979 for a prior rape. His attorney argued that he had the reasoning capacity of a seven-year-old. While this was an exaggeration, he was seriously mentally subnormal. Whether his problems were enough to classify him as disabled is open to debate. Despite this, in 1980 he was sentenced to death for the murder. The Supreme Court considered his case twice—both times ruling that his intellectual disability did not constitute grounds for mercy.

Though a grown man, Penry now fills his time drawing in coloring books and he still believes in Santa Claus. After being tried and retried three times, he is no longer on death row but is serving life for the murder of the young woman he raped. However, the Supreme Court, in *Penry v. Lynaugh* (1989), decided that it was not against his Eighth Amendment rights and was not a cruel and unusual punishment to execute a mentally impaired man.

This is the background to *Aikens v. Virginia.*

On the night of August 16, 1996, Daryl Atkins and William Jones abducted an airman from Langley Air Force Base at a late-night convenience store. They robbed him, forced him at gunpoint to withdraw money from an ATM and then shot him eight times. Aikens was most likely the shooter. Jones gave evidence against Aikens in return for a life sentence. Aikens was convicted of first-degree murder, and the trial moved on to the sentencing phase. The jury heard that Aikens had an IQ of 59, making him mildly "mentally retarded," as the phrase was in those days. Despite this, he was sentenced to death.

The Supreme Court of Virginia upheld the sentence, basing their decision on *Penry v. Lynaugh*. But when the case came before the US Supreme Court, the justices felt that the prohibition against cruel and unusual punishments needed to be interpreted in the light of "evolving standards of decency that mark the progress of a maturing society." They noted that twenty-one states had enacted legislation banning the execution of the intellectually disabled, leaving only ten death penalty states without this ban. That was a clear consensus.

Atkins would not face the executioner.

However, they did leave a degree of discretion to individual states: each state was entitled to define what they considered to be intellectual disability.

Some years later, in July 2005, a jury in Virginia reconsidered the Atkins case. They found that his years of contact with his lawyers—and his years of incarceration away from drugs and alcohol—had improved his IQ and that he was therefore eligible for execution. He was given an execution date of December 2, 2005, but this was later stayed. Three years later, due to misconduct on the part of the prosecution, Atkins's sentence was once again commuted to life imprisonment.

Following the Atkins decision, three criteria were used to determine if someone was mentally eligible for execution. If they had sub-average intelligence (low IQ), a lack of fundamental social and practical skills, and had both conditions from a young age, they were considered mentally disabled and ineligible for execution. The cutoff point for low IQ was set at seventy. In 2014, in *Hall v. Florida*, this was altered slightly. Those with a borderline low IQ (70 to 75) could still claim mental disability if they could show other symptoms.

The execution of those with intellectual disabilities remains one of the most controversial aspects of the death penalty.

CAN WE EXECUTE JUVENILES?
ROPER V. SIMMONS

Religions and legal systems vary as to what age we become legally and morally responsible for our actions. At times it was as young as seven and children that age were hanged in England for minor crimes throughout the seventeenth and eighteenth century. The United States sent a fourteen-year-old child, George Stinney, to the electric chair in South Carolina in 1944. Since the death penalty came back into force in 1976, America has executed twenty-two men who committed their crimes while aged under eighteen. One of them was sixteen at the time of the triple murder he was convicted of, while the rest were seventeen. Three went to the chair: James Terry Roach in South Carolina on January 10, 1986; Dalton Prejean on May 18, 1990 in Louisiana; and Christopher Burger in Georgia on December 7, 1993. The rest were executed by lethal injection.

Several landmark decisions now govern how capital punishment applies to juveniles. The first was in 1988—*Thompson v. Oklahoma*. William Wayne Thompson, with others, beat to death his abusive brother-in-law. He was fifteen at the time and was tried as an adult and sentenced to death. The decision of the Supreme Court was that in the light of evolving standards of decency in society, it was not constitutional to execute someone so young. His sentence was commuted to life in prison.

So how young is too young? The Supreme Court attempted to answer this in *Stanford v. Kentucky* a year later. Kevin Stanford, a repeat offender, was just seventeen when he carried out an armed robbery at a gas station in Jefferson County, Kentucky. He raped the attendant and then shot her twice in the head, killing her. He was convicted and sentenced to death. When the Supreme Court considered the case they upheld the sentence. Justice Antonin Scalia wrote, "We discern neither a historical nor a modern societal consensus forbidding the imposition of capital punishment on any person who murders at sixteen or seventeen years of age. Accordingly, we conclude that such punishment does not offend the Eight Amendment's prohibition against cruel and unusual punishment."

Now the age limit was set at sixteen. That result would hold until 2005, when the Supreme Court considered the case of *Roper v. Simmons*.

Christopher Simmons was a troubled young man from Missouri. At the age of seventeen he decided to rob and murder someone, just for the experience. He believed that as a juvenile he would get away with it. With some young companions, he broke into a neighbor's home and tied her up before driving to a state park where he threw her off a bridge to her death. She was alive and conscious when he threw her into the river, hog-tied and gagged. She died of drowning.

Describing the crime as "heinous," the prosecutor sought and got the death penalty. As the case worked its way through the appeal process, the Missouri Supreme Court rejected the death penalty as Simmons was of low mental capacity. The State appealed this, and the case was considered by the US Supreme Court (*Roper v. Simmons*; Donald Roper being the superintendent of the correctional facility where Simmons was waiting on death row).

At this hearing the court ruled that it was cruel and unusual punishment to execute a person under the age of eighteen at the time of the murder, and the reason was that society had moved on and punishments had to keep pace with evolving standards of decency. There was a wealth of research to show that juveniles lack maturity and a sense of responsibility and are capable of more reckless behavior than adults. Most states barred people under the age of eighteen from voting, serving on juries, or marrying without parental consent. So how could they be eligible for execution?

The court also noted that only seven other countries permitted the execution of juveniles in the decade prior to the case—Iran, Pakistan, Saudi Arabia, Yemen, Nigeria, the Democratic Republic of the Congo, and China. All seven had since removed or restricted the practice. That left the United States as the only country in the world which executed juveniles. With the Simmons decision, the Supreme Court changed that.

Immediately the death sentences of seventy-two death row inmates were commuted to life in prison. Texas was the state affected most: there were twenty-nine juvenile offenders awaiting execution. In Alabama there were fourteen. No other state had more than five.

MITIGATING FACTORS MUST BE CONSIDERED
LOCKETT V. OHIO

Sandra Lockett was a getaway driver for a gang who robbed a pawn-shop and killed the owner. Under Ohio law, she was guilty of aggravated murder and the death penalty was mandatory unless the victim had started the incident in which he had been killed, the killing had been carried out under duress, or the killing had been the result of mental deficiencies. None of these mitigating factors applied in the Lockett case, so she was sentenced to die.

Other mitigating factors could not be considered under the rules in Ohio. They were not part of the process. The Supreme Court was asked to consider whether this ban on considering other mitigating factors was constitutional. By a seven to one vote the Supreme Court upheld Lockett's appeal and ruled that all mitigating factors must be considered in a death penalty case, not just a selection of listed mitigating factors.

THE "I DIDN'T DO IT" DEFENSE
HOLMES V. SOUTH CAROLINA

Bobby Lee Holmes was convicted of raping, beating, and robbing forty dollars from an eighty-six-year-old retired school teacher Mary Stewart in her home in South Carolina in 1989. She died a year later from the injuries she received in the horrific attack, and Holmes was convicted of her murder. He appealed and was granted a retrial, where he was convicted once more.

During the retrial he tried to argue that another man, Jimmy McCaw White, a known felon, was also in the vicinity at the time and was the actual killer. But he was prevented from making this case because the court considered the forensic evidence against him so strong that he would not be able to raise an inference of innocence. The Supreme Court was eventually asked to consider whether this decision of the lower court was constitutional.

The final ruling was unanimous. The South Carolina court did not have the right to exclude evidence on the grounds that the prosecution case was so strong that new evidence could not provide an indication of possible innocence. It was not the job of the court to decide whether evidence not heard was too weak to be put to the jury. The original court had denied Holmes "a meaningful opportunity to present a complete defense." Even if his story seemed preposterous, he had a right to tell it. His conviction was overturned. There would have to be a retrial.

For Holmes it was immaterial because his story of a third party carrying out the rape and murder was a fabrication. In 2007, he finally confessed to the murder in court and received a life sentence without the possibility of parole. And he didn't even get to enjoy the intervening period out of prison. In 1992, while incarcerated and awaiting the original trial, he had assaulted a fellow inmate, beating him with an iron bar and breaking both his arms. For this he had received a twenty-year sentence. So the Supreme Court win made no material difference to his situation.

WHAT CONSTITUTES A HEINOUS CRIME?

In many states one of the aggravating factors which could draw down a death penalty is that the crime is vile and heinous. But what exactly constitutes a heinous murder? Several Supreme Court decisions have tried to put some precision into a vague aggravating factor.

Robert Godfrey was a Georgia man who became unhinged when his marriage broke up. He tried to reconcile with his wife but she rejected this effort. So he came to the trailer where she was staying with her mother and fired a shot through the window, killing his mother-in-law instantly. He then broke through the door of the trailer. As his young daughter tried to run out, he struck her on the head with the shotgun. Then he shot and killed his wife before calling state troopers and calmly waiting for them to arrive.

He was convicted of two first-degree murders and under the rules in Georgia at the time, he was sentenced to death. However the Supreme Court in *Godfrey v. Georgia* (1980) held that a death sentence could not be handed down when the only aggravating factor was that the murder was "outrageously or wantonly vile." The justices made the point that if that was the only criterion, then it became a subjective matter as to what was a vile or heinous crime and thus opened the door to the sort of arbitrary and capricious application of the death sentence that had resulted in the original moratorium during the early seventies.

Though it could not be the only aggravating factor, the heinous-ness of a murder did remain a consideration and further Supreme Court appeals narrowed down what it meant in practice.

One of the cases considered was that of Jeffrey Walton, from Arizona. On March 2, 1986, he walked into a bar in Tucson with two companions. They planned on abducting and robbing someone in the bar and then dumping him in the desert while they made their getaway. The man they chose was an off-duty marine—Thomas Powell. They robbed him at gunpoint and forced him to drive out into the desert, where

Walton shot him once in the head. Walton then gleefully boasted to his companions that he had "never seen a man pee in his pants before."

A week later Walton was arrested and immediately admitted his involvement, leading detectives to the spot where he had shot the unarmed and defenseless man. They got a shock—the bullet had not immediately killed the marine. He had been blinded and disabled by the head wound and had died only hours before they got there of shock, dehydration, and other complications.

The jury convicted Walton of first-degree murder, and then the judge moved on to the second part of the trial—sentencing. In Arizona this was not a function of the jury. The judge sentenced Walton to death, finding that the crime was "heinous, cruel, or depraved," and had been carried out for gain. During the inevitable appeals process the Supreme Court was asked to consider two questions: was it constitutional for the judge to handle the sentencing section without the help of the jury; and was the crime committed in an "especially heinous, cruel, or depraved manner."

The Supreme Court ruled that the jury need not be involved in assessing the facts during the sentencing phase of a capital murder trial, as the mitigating and aggravating factors do not necessarily relate to the facts of the murder itself. For instance, a prior record has no bearing on whether the defendant is innocent or guilty, only on how the court might sentence him. So it was not a matter the jury need consider. The Supreme Court later changed its mind on this question, though. (*Ring v. Arizona*, 2002)

On the question of the heinousness of the crime, the Supreme Court decided that the definition of heinousness was not constitutionally vague. This was a reversal of the *Godfrey v. Georgia* ruling. They based the decision on the fact that in Arizona a judge, rather than a jury, decided if a crime was especially vile or heinous, and a judge would presumably be well versed in the law and would make the correct decision. The Court was showing remarkable faith in frail humanity.

In *Ring v. Arizona*, the Supreme Court changed its mind and ruled that juries must be involved in assessing aggravating and mitigating factors in death penalty cases.

Timothy Ring was an armed robber who held up an armored car at the Arrowhead Mall in Glendale, Arizona, on November 28, 1994, and shot the driver in the head. Although he had a minimal criminal record prior to the murder, he was sentenced to die. When the case came before the Supreme Court, the justices by a narrow margin ruled that Arizona's sentencing scheme, with no jury involvement, was unconstitutional. This immediately cast doubt on the sentences of 168 death row inmates who had also been sentenced by judges in the absence of juries. Ring is currently serving a life sentence in Arizona.

SUMMARY

The Supreme Court has considered many capital cases since 1976, and as a result they have defined very precisely how the death penalty may be applied and what factors must be considered in imposing it.

Some of their key decisions are that juveniles (under eighteen at the time of the murder) can no longer be executed; mentally handicapped people, so long as they qualify by reason of the degree of their handicap, cannot be executed; the death penalty cannot apply for rape or robbery, just first-degree murder; it can be imposed for felony murder, but is not automatic; mitigating factors must be considered, as well as aggravating factors; the defendant has a right to make a full defense, however unlikely his story; and the jury must be involved in imposing the death penalty.

That left one question to be answered—and perhaps the most controversial of all. Given that one in twenty-five on death row is innocent of the crime for which they have been convicted, is it constitutional to execute an innocent person? That is a question we will come back to in a later chapter.

15

THE RISE OF LETHAL INJECTION

When the moratorium on executions came in 1967, the vast majority of death penalty states were either exclusively using the electric chair or using it in conjunction with a second execution method. In close to a century of use it had become the most popular execution method in the United States. But despite its popularity, it had not advanced. The procedure and equipment were still the same as those used during the Kemmler execution that began it all.

Every other electronic device had progressed with the times. Radios had replaced valves with transistors; the wax cylinders of the phonograph had been replaced with the magnetic strips of cassettes. The world had moved on. But not Old Sparky.

Once seen as a symbol of modern progress, by the seventies it was a relic of the barbarous past, suitable for exhibit in horror shows and wax museums. So when the moratorium was lifted nine years later, in 1976, it gave many states a chance to reassess how they would bring about the deaths of convicted murderers. The chief objection to electrocution was that it was most certainly not humane nor painless. There had been too many instances of prisoners surviving the first jolt and still being conscious. Several had been in obvious pain and some had even caught fire. Even when it went smoothly, it was a terrible sight for witnesses to behold. Could technology once more come to the rescue?

One idea had been around almost as long as the electric chair itself. Lethal injection had first been proposed back in 1888, the year the New York Commission had opted for electrocution. The idea came from Dr. Julius Mount Bleyer, a New York physician, in a sixteen-page pamphlet entitled "Scientific Methods of Capital Punishment." He believed that the injection of massive overdoses of opiates would result in unconsciousness, followed swiftly by death. It would be cheaper and more humane than hanging. His idea was ignored.

But in Nazi Germany the idea was taken up. As the Nazis experimented with ways of ridding the Master Race of the impurities of those "lives unworthy of life," they experimented with the idea. Hitler authorized certain doctors to find ways of ending the lives of those suffering from incurable genetic conditions or mental problems. During the two years that the Action T4 Program ran, 70,273 people were put to death in innovative ways. It began in 1939 with the secret killing of children born with birth defects. The method used was often an injection of phenol, an anesthetic. Soon the practice spread to Jewish children and juvenile delinquents. But when the program moved to the elimination of adults, shooting or the gas chamber were the preferred methods.

After the war, Britain revisited the question of the death penalty. A Royal Commission on Capital Punishment met for four years between 1949 and 1953. Despite the fact that former Prime Minister Winston Churchill had previously suggested building an electric chair in Trafalgar Square, London, to execute Hitler, the commission dismissed electrocution, saying, "Neither electrocution nor the gas chamber has, on balance, any advantage over hanging."

They recommended that if hanging were to be replaced, only two alternatives were possible. Lethal gas, applied through a mask, or lethal injection. Both methods were rejected because the commission felt that the prisoner would struggle, making them difficult to administer.

"Furthermore, the British Medical Association vigorously protested against any member performing this service or instructing lay persons in the techniques," they noted. Britain continued to use hanging until the death penalty itself was abolished in 1965.

When the moratorium on executions was lifted in 1976, the United States had a chance to consider alternatives to electrocution. There had been nearly a decade with no executions and the public had lost the stomach for Old Sparky. Utah saw the first post-Furman execution, when Gary Gilmore opted for firing squad. Utah was one of the few states that had not switched to the electric chair. For many years they allowed the choice of hanging, beheading, or firing squad. No one opted for beheading, so it was removed from the books. Most went for firing squad. In 1955 they had voted to allow electrocution, but they never built a chair so it never became an option.

The next execution after Gilmore did not take place until 1979, when small-time crook John Spenkelink was executed in Florida for killing a fellow crook. They used the electric chair but already moves were afoot to replace Old Sparky in several jurisdictions.

In 1977, Oklahoma had to make a decision on how they would carry out future executions. After a decade lying idle, their electric chair was no longer in safe working order, so they had a stark choice: spend money renovating it or spend that money coming up with a better execution method. They decided on the latter. State Senator Bill Dawson put out a call for ideas, and Dr. Stanley Deutsch, the chair of the Anesthesiology Department of Oklahoma University Medical School, responded. He said that drugs could be administered through an intravenous drip that would cause a quick and painless death. That year Oklahoma legislated to allow the new method be used. It was called the Chapman Protocol, after State Medical Examiner Jay Chapman: "An intravenous saline drip shall be started in the prisoner's arm, into which shall be introduced a lethal injection consisting of an ultra short-acting barbiturate in combination with a chemical paralytic."

The same year, Texas introduced similar legislation to replace their chair with lethal injection. Over the coming decades, thirty-seven of the thirty-eight states using capital punishment switched to lethal injection.

The first convict to face the needle was Charles Brooks Jr. on December 7, 1982. He was the first man to be executed in Texas since 1964 and the first African-American to be executed anywhere following the Gregg decision which began the moratorium. He had stolen a car and shot the mechanic from the used car lot, on December 14, 1976.

After a last meal of T-bone steak, fries, and biscuits, followed by peach cobbler and washed down by iced tea, he was strapped to the gurney and wheeled into the death chamber at Huntsville, Texas. A vein was found and the saline drip was inserted in his arm. The guards were having difficulty doing this, so the medical observer, who was only there to certify death, stepped in and inserted the needle. Then Brooks was asked if he had any last statement. He had converted to Islam in prison and he said a brief prayer. After that, the warden took over. Instead of injecting the three drugs separately, he mixed the three together. They began to react with one another, producing a gloopy mess. But he managed to inject it into the saline solution. Brooks clenched his fist, raised his head defiantly and then fell back on the gurney unconscious. It took only a few minutes, and Brooks's death appeared smooth and peaceful.

After a number of trials the execution procedure is now fairly stand-ardized. The condemned is strapped onto a medical gurney and two IV drips are inserted, one in each arm. Only one is used for the execution. The second is a backup in case of mishaps. Sterilized needles are used. This might seem unnecessary; what are the chances of infection if the prisoner is going to die within minutes anyway? But it is necessary for the attendants more than for the prisoner. And on one occasion, a prisoner was hooked to the IV, with the saline solution already in his bloodstream, when a temporary stay was phoned in. The authorities had to ensure that James Autry (convicted of shooting a priest during a robbery) was in good health later, for his eventual execution.

Once the IV is in place, the saline solution begins to feed into the veins. Then the three-drug cocktail is administered. It begins with sodium thiopental or pentobarbital, an ultra short-acting barbiturate. This is a powerful anesthetic which will render the prisoner uncon-scious in well under a minute. It is often used for medically induced comas. One of the side effects is a depression of respiratory activity. This alone would eventually cause death. But there are two more shots to come.

The second injection contains pancuronium bromide, a muscle relaxant. It causes complete, fast paralysis of the muscles of the body, including the diaphragm which controls breathing. This injection would lead to death by asphyxiation within a number of minutes. If the patient was conscious, this would be an extremely painful and frightening death—though that would not be obvious to onlookers. The victim would struggle to breathe, fighting desperately, but unable to even flicker an eyelid. To onlookers he would just look glassy-eyed and still.

The final drug is potassium chloride, which stops the heart, causing death by cardiac arrest.

All three drugs on their own are fatal. The third, which causes burning of the skin, would be extremely painful if administered to a conscious patient. The prisoner is always hooked up to a heart monitor, which will let the attending physician pronounce the time of death. This usually occurs well under ten minutes.

The IV line runs from the gurney to a room next door to the death chamber, divided by a curtain. The technicians can inject the poisons out of sight of the prisoner and monitor his progress.

If all goes right, lethal injection is a simple and painless way of slipping into the beyond. But nothing in life is guaranteed to run according to plan. Sometimes there are difficulties finding a suitable vein. Many prisoners are drug abusers, so their veins would not be in the same condition as those of the healthier non-prison population. Veins can collapse, requiring the attending technicians to try again repeatedly. Occasionally prisoners are obese, with the veins well concealed. One execution took so long that the prisoner was unstrapped from the gurney midway through for a toilet break!

The other problem is consciousness. Anesthesiology is a well-established branch of medicine, but even the best can get dosages wrong. In general surgery, one to two in a thousand experience some degree of anesthesia awareness. This can range from being mildly aware of sensations, to full-blown consciousness and the experience of all the pain during an operation. But because of the effects of the anesthesia, they cannot communicate that something has gone wrong.

Autopsies of prisoners who have died by lethal injection show clearly that the amount of the first drug used is typically borderline and many would not have been deeply unconscious when the second and third drugs were administered. This means that what looks like a peaceful death from the comfort of the witness room might in fact have been a terrifying ordeal, where the prisoner died screaming on the inside. This is not a common situation, but prisoners are no different biologically than the general population, so we know it has happened on a number of occasions.

In recent years some prisons have experimented with an even simpler system than the three-drug sequence. It began in Ohio on December 8, 2009, with the execution of rapist and murderer Kenneth Biros. After saying that he was being paroled to heaven and was going to spend his holidays with Jesus, he was injected with sodium thiopental. Nine minutes later he was pronounced dead. The powerful anesthetic had taken a little longer than the traditional cocktail. But it was used because of concerns that the earlier method could cause severe pain in a small number of cases. The one-drug protocol was identical to the way animals are put to sleep.

Since then, thirteen states have either switched to the single drug method or announced their intentions to switch. The dose of sodium thiopental used in executions is typically 5 grams. This is more than three times the amount used for assisted suicide in countries that allow that. It is also a far higher dosage than was used in the early days of lethal injection.

Aside from the problem of finding a suitable vein in some prisoners, lethal injection would appear to be a very efficient execution method. Of course, it is never that simple. Opponents have argued that it is not actually painless as practiced currently in the United States. The barbiturate used can wear off quickly, leading to anesthesia awareness and a very uncomfortable death. Normally sodium thiopental is used to induce unconsciousness, but a different drug is used in surgery to maintain unconsciousness. What happens if a prisoner wakes before he dies? After all, the drug is administered by a prison employee, not by a highly trained anesthetist.

Jay Chapman, the Oklahoma Medical Examiner who introduced lethal injection, told the *New York Times* in 2007: "It never occurred to me when we set this up that we'd have complete idiots administering the drugs."

Typical of this was the execution of Angel Diaz on December 13, 2006, in Starke, Florida. The technicians punctured the veins in Diaz's arms when inserting the intravenous catheters, so the drugs were injected into soft tissue instead of into the bloodstream. Because of this, the first drug failed to anesthetize him, and he was grimacing and moaning for the first twenty-six minutes of a procedure that should have taken less than seven. He suffered chemical burns, nearly a foot long, on both arms and was almost certainly conscious and in great pain for most of the lengthy and botched execution. He took thirty-four minutes to die. Following the public outcry, Governor Jeb Bush put a ban on all executions in Florida. The ban lasted two years.

The problem is not so much the lethal injection procedure itself, but who is administering it. It is a medical procedure being carried out by people with no medical training or background. A research article published in the prestigious medical journal *The Lancet* revealed the extent of the problem. In Texas and Virginia, the two states studied, the researchers found, unsurprisingly, that the executioners had no training in anesthesia, and because the execution was controlled from a room outside the death chamber, the prisoner was not being properly monitored to guarantee that the anesthesia had taken before the second and third drugs were administered. In other words, mistakes were not just possible, they were virtually inevitable.

Forty-nine autopsies were analyzed from a number of states, and they showed that in forty-three cases the level of thiopental in the bloodstream was less than that required for surgery. Shockingly, a massive 43 percent of executed prisoners had such low levels of the sedative in their system that they were most likely conscious during their execution. The authors of the report were led to the inescapable conclusion that a large number of executed inmates were aware and suffered extreme pain and distress during the five to ten minutes of their execution. Far from being a humane alternative to the barbarity of hanging, it was an escalation of the horror for many of those put to death.

"Because participation of doctors in protocol design or execution is ethically prohibited, adequate anesthesia cannot be certain. Therefore, to prevent unnecessary cruelty and suffering, cessation and public review of lethal injections is warranted."

There is another reason why lethal injection might not be the perfect replacement for the electric chair, and that reason has nothing to do with how it is administered. It has to do with outside commercial forces and public sensibilities within the European Union.

Sodium thiopental, the most important ingredient in lethal injection, was used for years in medical anesthesiology. But in recent years its use has declined and newer and better drugs have replaced it. There was just one supplier of the drug in the United States, an Illinois pharmaceutical company called Hospira. In 2009, they decided to move production to their plant near Milan, in Italy. But the Italian government demanded a guarantee from Hospira that the drug would not be used for executions, which are illegal in Italy and throughout most of Europe. As Hospira could not control what purchasers did with the drug, they decided the only solution was to suspend its production.

"We cannot take the risk that we will be held liable by the Italian authorities if the product is diverted for use in capital punishment. Exposing our employees or facilities to liability is not a risk we are prepared to take," said a spokesperson, Daniel Rosenberg.

The Italian setback was swiftly followed by more problems. The United Kingdom introduced a ban on the export of sodium thiopental in December 2010 because of the European Union Torture Regulation. A year later, the European Union extended trade restrictions to prevent the export of medicinal products that could be used for executions to the United States, stating, "The Union disapproves of capital punishment in all circumstances and works towards its universal abolition."

As supplies ran low, states began to explore other options, including pentobarbital, a drug often used for animal euthanasia. Oklahoma executed John David Duty with this as part of the cocktail in 2010, and Ohio executed Johnnie Baston with this drug alone, one year later.

In theory lethal injection provides a peaceful passage to the great beyond, and the one-drug protocol should be even gentler than the initial three-drug cocktail. How does the reality square up?

In September 2009 officials in Ohio had to abandon the execution of Romell Broom, after struggling for two hours to find a suitable vein in his arms, legs, hands, and ankles. Five years later Dennis McGuire was executed in the same state and it took more than twenty minutes for him to die. He was gasping for air and struggling to breathe for more than ten of those minutes, as the drugs began suppressing his respiratory system.

Even worse was the execution of Clayton Lockett in the Oklahoma State Penitentiary at McAlester on April 29, 2014. The thirty-eight-year-old was convicted of murder, rape, and kidnapping. Due to the lack of the traditional drugs, a new mixture of untried drugs was being tested on Lockett. The execution began badly. The prisoner was in such a state of terror that he had to be Tasered to get him onto the gurney. The officials struggled to insert the IV into his arm and then moved on to his groin, where they found a vein, and the procedure began as usual (aside from the Tasering, which was decidedly unusual). But there was one difference: Lockett did not pass out. He appeared to lose consciousness, and then he began to speak during the execution process, then he seemed to quiet down again. He was declared unconscious, and then he attempted to sit up, which proved the lie of that declaration. The execution lasted an agonizing forty-three minutes before Lockett was finally declared dead. The subsequent autopsy shocked the officials: they had not killed him with their new mixture. He had died of a heart attack under the stress of the execution. That definitely crossed the line into cruel and unusual punishment.

The biggest failing of lethal injection is that it does not work as the early pioneers envisioned. Because of the lack of medical supervision, it can be difficult to find a vein. When a vein is found, unconsciousness cannot be guaranteed, and the evidence is clear that full anesthesia is often absent. The drugs used after the initial dose cause intense pain when the condemned is conscious. Death can be a prolonged and torturous affair.

In addition, the drugs used are becoming increasingly difficult to source.

Unless doctors become executioners—very unlikely—the future of lethal injection is doubtful. Will the inevitable decline in lethal injection lead to a return to the electric chair? Again, doubtful. America may need to reevaluate the whole question of capital punishment—especially in the light of the innocence problem.

16

THE PROBLEM OF INNOCENCE

One key element of the justice system, guaranteed by the Constitution, is due process. The state must respect the legal rights of the citizen. This includes the right to appeal a conviction. Generally the appeal will be unsuccessful. If the detectives and the district attorney have done their job, they will have caught and prosecuted the right guy. But nobody is perfect, and they occasionally get it wrong. A successful appeal will release a prisoner with their reputation restored. An innocent person will return to society and begin rebuilding his or her life.

Sometimes it is not an appeal that releases an innocent person. It can be new evidence. In the past this was unlikely, but with advances in forensic science it becomes easier and easier to unearth new facts. One thing that has made a huge difference is DNA profiling. Three decades ago, blood could be grouped into A, B, AB, and O. So blood at a crime scene could be consistent with a suspect. But there was no way of telling for certain that the blood came from the actual suspect. Now we can tell exactly who the blood, semen, or saliva came from. There have been many cases of blood and semen samples being reexamined for DNA evidence, which pinpointed someone other than the person convicted. Some DNA samples remain viable for testing for decades after a crime. The most famous example of this was when a Victorian shawl from London was examined in 2014, which might prove that the unknown killer Jack the Ripper was a Polish immigrant, Aaron Kosminski.

If later evidence proves someone was not a killer or that someone else was the killer, justice can be done and the innocent person released. That is part of due process, guaranteed by the Constitution.

However this is not possible in the case of the death penalty. Once someone is executed, conclusive proof of innocence is no good to the executed individual. They are dead. Execution is irreversible.

How common is this in practice? With good detective work and well-regulated trials, wrongful convictions should be a rarity. Unfortunately, major studies of false conviction show that this faith in the legal system is badly misplaced. One in twenty-five on death row may be completely innocent of the crime for which they will eventually be executed. That is a staggering amount of wrongful judicial deaths— roughly seventy since the moratorium on executions was lifted in 1976.

In 2014, the Proceedings of the National Academy of Sciences of the United States published an article entitled "Rate of False Conviction of Criminal Defendants who are Sentenced to Death." The article, by respected researchers Samuel Gross, Barbara O'Brien, Chen Hu, and Edward Kennedy, began:

> In the past few decades a surge of hundreds of exonerations of innocent criminal defendants has drawn attention to the problem of erroneous conviction. All the same, the most basic empirical question about false convictions remains unanswered: How common are these miscarriages of justice?
>
> To actually estimate the proportion of erroneous convictions we need a well-defined group of criminal convictions within which we identify all mistaken convictions, or at least most. It is hard to imagine how that could be done for criminal convictions generally, but it might be possible for capital murder.

The rate of exonerations among death sentences in the United States is far higher than for any other category of criminal convictions. Death sentences represent less than one-tenth of 1 percent of prison sentences but they accounted for about 12 percent of known exonerations of innocent defendants from 1989 through early 2012. A major reason for this extraordinary exoneration rate is that far more attention and resources are devoted to death penalty cases than to other criminal prosecutions, before and after conviction.

The figures analyzed make frightening reading. Since the mid-seventies, 143 convicts on death row have been exonerated. Some had been on death row as long as thirty-three years before their sentence was overturned and their innocence proved. A previous study had found that 2.3 percent of all death sentences between the lifting of the moratorium and 1989 resulted in exoneration. Another study suggested that if modern DNA analysis had been available, 3.3 percent of convictions would not have happened because the DNA evidence would have cleared the suspect.

Following a detailed analysis of the more than four thousand inmates on death row, the report concluded that at least 4.1 percent of these would be exonerated if they remained on death row, adding: "We conclude that this is a conservative estimate of the proportion of false conviction among death sentences in the United States."

There are roughly 3,100 American prisoners on death row at the time of publication. Are 127 of these men and women completely innocent?

In 2001, The Center on Wrongful Convictions at the Northwestern Law School in Chicago analyzed eighty-six cases of exonerations and showed that the leading cause of wrongful conviction was false or shaky eyewitness testimony, followed closely by police and/or prosecution misconduct. Sloppy forensic science, false confessions (either as a result of mental illness or of police pressure), and information from snitches given in exchange for reduced sentences, were also contributing factors.

The Innocence Project was founded in 1992 by Barry Scheck (one of O. J. Simpson's legal team) and Peter Neufeld. It is a nonprofit organization committed to exonerating wrongly convicted people. They often use DNA testing and they are also committed to reforming the criminal justice system to prevent future wrongful convictions. In more than twenty years, they have secured the release of 318 innocent people, including eighteen from death row.

They point out that through their efforts and the efforts of others, twenty people who have been sentenced to death have been proved innocent and exonerated by DNA evidence—and in half of those cases the DNA analyses pointed to the real killers. Those twenty innocent men and women had spent an average of nearly fourteen years behind bars, proclaiming their innocence. The majority were of color. This is a concern, because one of the reasons why death sentences were suspended after the Furman decision was that the penalty was applied arbitrarily and unevenly, and black defendants were more likely to be sentenced to the chair. Now the death row population more closely resembles the general population—but are black defendants getting a raw deal still? It would seem that way if the majority of exonerations continue to be of people of color.

The problem of innocence is one that the US justice system will have to urgently tackle if the death penalty is to remain in use.

17

INNOCENCE IS NO DEFENSE—HERRERA V. COLLINS

"I am an innocent man, and something very wrong is taking place tonight," were the last words of a man who knew he was going to die because the Supreme Court had decided that imprisoning and executing an innocent man was not a violation of his civil rights.

Proof of innocence is not enough to get you off the electric chair. In support of the assertion that the law is an ass, the Supreme Court ruled in 1993 that proof of innocence was not grounds for the Supreme Court stepping in and stopping an execution. New trials can only be granted in cases of procedural screwups, not in cases of new evidence being uncovered. It was a landmark judgment that has condemned several innocent people to death.

If you polled the majority of Americans they would probably believe that the death penalty, the ultimate sanction of the law, is a very serious business, and that the authorities generally know what they are doing. They would believe that people do not go to the chair or the needle unless they are proved beyond doubt to be guilty of the murder for which they are charged. But the reality is different. The truth is that an unacceptably high number of people who face execution are innocent. Death row is full of wrongly convicted prisoners.

The most recent research was done in 2013 by Samuel Gross, Barbara O'Brien, Chen Hu, and Edward Kennedy, and was published as "Rate of False Conviction of Criminal Defendants who are Sentenced to Death," in the *Proceedings of the Natural Academy of Sciences*. The academics found that 4.1 percent of all those on death row are innocent of the crimes for which they have been convicted. One in twenty-five of those executed is killed by the state in the wrong. That is a huge figure. Extrapolating that across the twentieth century, we find that roughly 340 people were wrongly executed by US authorities in that time.

With modern advances in forensics, particularly DNA evidence collected in the past but only possible to analyze now, many convictions are coming into doubt.

If you find new evidence that proves you are innocent, you are off the hook, right? Wrong. According to the Supreme Court, proof of innocence is immaterial once you have been sentenced. The Supreme Court is quite happy for innocent people to go to the electric chair once their trial was carried out in a procedural, correct manner. Innocence or guilt doesn't come into it after that.

The Supreme Court position, which affects several hundred prisoners now on death row, was established following *Herrera v. Collins* in 1993. To understand their decision, we need to look at the murder of two Texan law enforcement officials.

Texas Department of Public Safety Officer David Rucker was working on a stretch of highway a few miles north of Brownsville in the Rio Grande Valley on the night of September 29, 1981, when he encountered a car. There are no witnesses to what happened, but a few minutes later a passerby noticed the parked patrol car at the side of the road and went to investigate. He found Rucker on the ground beside the car, dead from a gunshot to the head.

Around the same time, a car was spotted speeding along the stretch of highway, away from the scene where Rucker had met his death. Los Fresnos Police Officer Enrique Carrisalez, and his partner turned on their flashing lights and set off in pursuit. They caught the speeding car, which immediately pulled over. Carrisalez got out of the patrol car and approached the other car. The driver opened his door and leaned out to talk to the officer. Suddenly a shot rang out and Carrisalez fell back. He had been shot in the chest. The car shot off into the night.

Carrisalez was brought to hospital where he underwent emergency surgery and was placed in intensive care. His partner was able to give investigators the plate number of the car they had been pursuing, and it was traced to a woman who was the live-in girlfriend of Leonel Torres Herrera. When a photo of Herrera was shown to Carrisalez, he immediately identified it as the man who had shot him. However, he did not pick the photo out of a lineup. He was shown just one photo. Nine days after being shot, Officer Carrisalez succumbed to his injuries.

Within a few days, Herrera was arrested and charged with the murder of both Carrisalez and Rucker. There was a good case against him. Not only had one of the two victims identified him, but it was known by law enforcement that he frequently drove his girlfriend's car. And Carrisalez testified that there had only been one occupant of the car, so there could be no doubt as to who was the shooter. In addition, Herrera's social security card had been found alongside Rucker's patrol car on the night he was killed. And when the shooter's car was examined, splatters of blood consistent with Rucker's (type A) were found on it. Blood was also found on Herrera's pants and wallet. Most damning was that a handwritten letter was found in Herrera's possession when he was arrested, that "strongly implied," according to investigators, that he had killed Rucker.

In January 1982 Rucker went on trial. During the trial, Carrisalez's partner identified Herrera as the shooter. He was convicted and sentenced to death.

So far, nothing out of the ordinary. But during the inevitable appeals process new evidence emerged. Herrera's legal team produced two legal affidavits. One was from Hector Villarreal, who represented Herrera's brother Raul, a convicted felon. The other was from Juan Franco Palacious, a former cell mate of Raul Herrera. Raul had been murdered in 1984, three years after the two cops were shot. The affidavits claimed that Raul Herrera was driving the car on the night in question and had been the shooter. If they were true, Leonel was innocent. As the brothers looked alike, it would explain the evidence of identification.

Herrera claimed that the new evidence of his innocence meant that executing him would violate his Eighth Amendment rights, as executing an innocent man was a "cruel and unusual punishment" outlawed by the amendment.

The case was considered by the Supreme Court in 1993. They had two questions to consider. The first was whether the Eighth and Fourteenth Amendments (guaranteeing due process in a trial) allowed the state to execute someone who was innocent of the crime for which they had been sentenced to death. The second was whether the state should have procedures in place following a conviction to protect against the execution of an innocent person. In other words, did the state have to consider the new evidence or could they ignore it and go ahead with the execution? The court handed down a majority opinion—six to three.

Chief Justice William Rehnquist, delivering the majority verdict, held that a claim of actual innocence based on new evidence was not grounds for the Federal authorities to step in and stop an execution. He said, "Few rulings would be more disruptive of our federal system than to provide for federal habeas review of freestanding claims of actual innocence."

In other words, at a Federal level they were washing their hands when it came to questions of fact.

He did note, however, that if Herrera was innocent the only relief he could expect was that the state of Texas might grant a retrial: "Were the petitioner to satisfy the dissent's 'probable innocence' standard, the District Court would presumably be required to grant a conditional order of relief [stay of execution] which would in effect require the State to retry petitioner ten years after his first trial, not because of any constitutional violation which had occurred at the first trial, but simply because of a belief that in light of petitioner's new-found evidence a jury might find him not guilty at a second trial."

But the Supreme Court and the Federal Authorities did not have an obligation, in this ruling, to order a reexamination of the evidence. Without this pressure the District Court could leave well enough alone and ignore the new evidence.

Which is what Texas did. Rehnquist's opinion held that the Court's refusal to even consider the new evidence did not violate due process. Legally the way was now clear to execute a man even if he was innocent.

Justice Sandra Day O'Connor agreed, but with a reservation, saying, "The execution of a legally and factually innocent person would be a constitutionally intolerable event." She then added that Herrera was not "legally and factually innocent" because he had been convicted fairly by a jury. Never mind that the jury was not in possession of the new evidence.

"Consequently, the issue before us is not whether a State can execute the innocent. It is whether a fairly convicted and therefore legally guilty person is constitutionally entitled to yet another judicial proceeding in which to adjudicate his guilt anew, ten years after conviction, notwithstanding his failure to demonstrate that constitutional error infected his trial."

Stripped of legalese, her opinion was that once convicted, always convicted. New evidence was not grounds for a new appeal. An appeal would only be granted if you could show that the first trial had been conducted improperly.

Justice Harry Blackmun, along with Justices John Paul Stevens and David Souter, dissented from the majority opinion. Blackmun said, "Nothing could be more contrary to contemporary standards of decency or more shocking to the conscience than to execute a person who is actually innocent."

He would have favored a court looking at the new evidence to determine whether a new trial was necessary, and wrote: "We are really being asked to decide whether the Constitution forbids the execution of a person who has been validly convicted and sentenced, but who, nonetheless, can prove his innocence with newly discovered evidence."

Four months after the Supreme Court ruling, Texas had not taken any action on the new evidence. On May 12, 1993, Leonel Torres Herrera was strapped to the gurney for lethal injection. He had refused a last meal. His final words were, "I am innocent, innocent, innocent. Make no mistake about this: I owe society nothing. Continue the struggle for human rights, helping those who are innocent. I am an innocent man, and something very wrong is taking place tonight. May God bless you all. I am ready."

This landmark decision would have widespread implications. With advances in DNA profiling, old cases could be reexamined by eager defense attorneys, but the Supreme Court ruling meant that any new evidence uncovered might be irrelevant; it was not unconstitutional to execute someone who had been fairly convicted, even if they had been convicted in the wrong.

With one in twenty-five on death row innocent, the implications are frightening. So how did states react to the Supreme Court ruling? In theory many proclaim that it is better that the guilty go free than one innocent man be executed, but the practice is different. States tolerate the execution of the innocent so that the guilty also get the chair. Legislators have progressively cut off avenues of appeal, mainly by imposing strict timelines.

The Anti-terrorism and Effective Death Penalty Act, passed in 1996, gives a prisoner just twelve months after his conviction to file a writ of habeas corpus (a request for a Federal Court to review a case for constitutional violations). Most states have their own restrictive deadlines. Some require prisoners to present new evidence within thirty days of conviction, which is clearly impractical in most cases. Often new evidence is uncovered years after conviction. And some states have "closed discovery" rules, which prevent attorneys or journalists from reviewing the evidence after a conviction.

The restrictions can lead to very clear and blatant miscarriages of justice, such as this one from the State of Virginia. Career criminal Joseph O'Dell was convicted of rape and murder in 1986. He was found guilty because tire tracks at the scene of the rape were consistent (not identical) with his truck, and blood stains found on his clothing were found to be "consistent" with the victim's. This meant that they were similar types, not that they had been DNA matched. But O'Dell had been in a bar fight, which would also explain the blood samples.

After the trial, a blood test determined that the blood on his shirt did not belong either to him or to the murder victim. This knocked a vital plank out of the conviction. Within two years of his conviction, O'Dell had asked for DNA testing of semen found in the victim. This could prove conclusively his guilt or innocence, and unless he was certain of his innocence he would not have asked for the testing.

"If I were not innocent of this crime, I would have to be insane to request DNA fingerprinting," is how he put it.

The prosecutor objected to the request and the court denied O'Dell's appeal. In 1997 he was executed by lethal injection. Following the execution, his widow, backed by the Catholic Church and her legal team, asked that the semen sample and O'Dell's jacket be released for DNA testing. The state objected, with an attorney saying, "People will shout from the rooftops that the Commonwealth executed an innocent man."

Rather than have that happen, the judge declined to release the samples and agreed to a prosecution request that the evidence be instead burned. It was a disgraceful decision which demonstrated that saving face is often more important than serving the needs of transparent justice.

If America ever decides to give up on the death penalty, one of the big deciding factors in that decision will be the number of innocent people who face the needle and the chair every year. While the courts might be comfortable with that, many American citizens are clearly not.

18

INTO THE FUTURE

We began this book with the execution of Robert Gleeson in Virginia in January 2013. As he faced the chair, he shouted the Gaelic expression *Póg mo thóin* ("Kiss my ass"). He could have been shouting the epitaph of the electric chair itself. It is very unlikely that we will see another execution in Old Sparky. There are a number of reasons for this, but the chief one is that it is no longer seen as a humane alternative to hanging. Although it was brought in with good intentions, it was as easy to botch as the noose, and over the years has resulted in some horrific death chamber scenes. With a century of advances in technology, the chair has remained a static reminder of a more barbaric past. It has not been modernized at all. The only patent held on any part of the chair was held by Edwin Davis, the original New York State Electrician. The computer age has bypassed the chair.

It is possible that research could have been done to make the chair a guaranteed smooth and painless killing machine, but medical researchers are prevented by ethical considerations from turning their attention to ending life.

Since the lifting of the moratorium in 1976, botched electrocutions have continued to happen, horrifying the observers and officials. This is the chief reason that lethal injection has taken the place of electrocution, after a century, as the method of choice in America. The following ten cases illustrate why the electric chair has to be relegated to the dungeon of the past.

On August 10, 1982, Frank J. Coppola was put to death in Virginia. An attorney who was there said that it took two long jolts of electricity to kill Coppola. The first did not stop his heart. During the second fifty-five-second-long jolt, witnesses could hear the sound of sizzling flesh and Coppola's head and leg both caught fire. Smoke filled the small death chamber, making it difficult to see the writhing victim through the haze.

When John Evans was executed in Alabama on April 22, 1983, sparks and flames flew from his leg, and sparks also came from the hood concealing his head. After the current was switched off, he was found to still have a pulse. The electrode was reattached to his leg and a second jolt was applied, resulting in more smoke and burning flesh, but not in death. A third jolt was required before his heart stopped beating. Evans was left charred and smoking after fourteen minutes.

When George Stephens was executed in Georgia on December 12, 1984, he proved to have a stubborn grip on life. The first two-minute jolt did not kill him, and when he was examined, his body temperature had risen sharply. He was left strapped to the chair, struggling to breath, for a further eight minutes until his flesh had cooled down sufficiently for a second attempt. According to the *New York Times* on the following day, a prison official explained the incident by saying, "Stephens was just not a conductor."

One of the most prolonged and horrific executions took place on October 16, 1985, in Indiana. William Vandiver was still breathing after the first shock of 2,300 volts. Four more jolts had to be applied, over seventeen minutes, to secure his death. The death chamber was filled with smoke and with the odor of burning flesh; Vandiver's attorney Herbert Shaps described the execution as "outrageous." The Department of Corrections admitted that the execution had not gone according to plan.

Horace Dunkins Jr. was mildly retarded. He went to the chair in Alabama on July 14, 1989. It took two jolts, separated by nine minutes, to finish him off. After the first jolt failed to kill him, a guard said to witnesses, "I believe we've got the jacks on wrong." (From the *Birmingham News*). This proved to be the case. The execution took nineteen minutes. Alabama Prison Commissioner Morris Thigpen said, "I regret very much what happened. The cause was human error."

Jesse Joseph Tafero was electrocuted in Florida on May 4, 1990. His was an interesting case. He and his girlfriend Sunny Jacobs and her two children were passengers in a car driven by ex-con Walter Rhodes. They were stopped at a traffic stop and someone in the car shot and killed two police officers. Tafero was convicted. It was his gun, and the driver, Rhodes, testified against him. The gunshot residue evidence was that Rhodes had fired a gun and that Tafero and Jacobs had handled a recently fired gun. But the testimony of Rhodes swung the case against Tafero. Both Tafero and Jacobs were sentenced to death. Jacobs was the registered owner of the gun. She had purchased it for Tafero because he had a prison record and could not buy it himself.

The judge in the case was Daniel Futch Jr., known as "Maximum Dan" because of his harsh sentencing policies. He was a throwback to a less enlightened age. Once, on hearing the case against a man charged with beating a gay man to death he had joked, "That's a crime now, to beat up a homosexual?" He was known to carry a gun under his robes in court and had a battery-powered toy electric chair on his desk. He sentenced Jacobs to death despite a recommendation for leniency from the jury, making her sentence unconstitutional.

After sentencing Tafero and Jacobs to the chair, he gave Rhodes three life sentences for his part in the crimes. Jacobs later had her sentence reduced to second-degree murder. On her release, she moved to Ireland where she married Peter Pringle—a terrorist who had once been sentenced to death in that country for shooting a police officer. The death penalty had not been carried out in Ireland since 1956 and is no longer legal there. Pringle was eventually exonerated of the crime.

Tafero had no such luck. He sat in the chair on May 4, 1990. Prison inmates later claimed that the sponges had been tampered with to make the execution more painful. *Miami Herald* reporter Ellen McGarrahan wrote: "I went to Florida State Prison and watched a man die. The man was Jesse Tafero, and his death was ugly, fire rising from his head as prison officials turned electricity off and on, each jolt setting a sponge on his shaved skull alight. As I watched, I wrote down the time that each bolt hit Tafero, for he was clearly still alive. His death started at 7:06 a.m., and ended at 7:13 a.m., by the clock on the prison wall. Seven minutes is a long time to watch someone burn."

The case became a rallying call for death penalty opponents when Rhodes, the driver of the car, recanted his trial testimony and admitted that he, not Tafero, had shot the two police officers with Jacobs's gun.

The prolonged execution was put down to "inadvertent human error." A synthetic sponge had been used instead of the natural one usually used.

On October 17, 1990, in Virginia, Wilbert Lee Evans went to the chair. As the first burst of electricity coursed through his body, blood spewed from the mask concealing his face. The blood drenched his shirt and caused a sizzling sound as it seeped over his lips. He could be heard to moan when the current was switched off, so a second jolt was administered. The autopsy confirmed that he had suffered a nose bleed when the voltage surge elevated his already high blood pressure.

On August 22, 1991, Derick Lynn Peterson was found to be alive after the administration of the jolt of electricity in Virginia. The doctor confirmed that there was a pulse and then waited a few minutes and checked again, still finding a pulse. Seven and a half minutes after the first shock, a second and fatal one was administered. Virginia officials decided after this execution to routinely administer two shocks before checking for a pulse.

The execution of Pedro Medina in Florida on March 25, 1997, was gruesome. A crown of flames, a foot high, danced over his head during the execution, filling the chamber with acrid smoke and choking the two dozen official witnesses in the next room. A panicked official manually threw the switch to cut off the power early, cutting short the two-minute cycle of 2,000 volts. But the prisoner was still clearly alive, his chest heaving as he struggled to draw in a breath in the smoke filled chamber, according to the *Gainesville Sun*. Medina had a long history of mental illness and there were questions of his innocence. Even the Pope had appealed for clemency, unsuccessfully.

The cause of the flames was either a corroded copper screen on the headpiece of the chair or the improper application of the sponge designed to conduct the electricity to the convict's head.

Allen Lee Davis was a huge man—350 pounds. Florida had to build a new electric chair to accommodate his bulk. He was strapped into it on July 8, 1999. The execution was far from smooth. As the current flowed through him, blood began to pour in a stream from his mouth, dripping onto his shirt. By the end of the execution, the scarlet stain was the size of a dinner plate and had even seeped into the buckles on the leather chest strap holding him to the chair.

Those ten horror stories are symptomatic of why the electric chair has fallen out of favor. When considering a later appeal, Florida Supreme Court Justice Leander Shaw said, "The color photos of Davis depict a man who, for all appearances, was brutally tortured to death by the citizens of Florida."

He added that when taken into account with the executions of Jesse Tafero and Pedro Medina, the executions were "barbaric spectacles more befitting a violent murderer than a civilized state."

Justice Shaw probably reflects the majority view of electrocution now in the United States. But it is not a universal view. Florida State Senator Ginny Brown-Waite witnessed the execution of Davis and saw it in a different light. As the blood flowed down Davis's white shirt, it reached the crease where his chest met his lower abdomen and began to spread outwards, forming the shape of a very crude cross. She took this as a sign that God supported the execution. (Reported in the *St. Petersburg Times*).

The death penalty remains a deeply divisive and controversial topic in America, with as many supporting it as calling for its abolition. So what is the future?

One thing we can be fairly sure of is that we have seen the end of the electric chair. There may be one or two more state electrocutions over the next few years, but these will come to an end. It is possible that Robert Gleeson was the last; although every electrocution over the past few years has been hailed as the last. The only thing that could bring back the chair is a decline in lethal injections.

The current drugs shortage could cause this. In May 2014, the governor of Tennessee, Bill Haslam, approved the reintroduction of the electric chair to that state, but only if the option of lethal injection was not available due to shortage of the drugs used. The electric chair is not an option in Tennessee, but a fallback position, to be used in emergencies. But Richard Dieter, executive director of the Death Penalty Information Center in Washington, said that this could pose a problem.

"There are states that allow inmates to choose [the electric chair] but it is a very different matter for a state to impose a method like electrocution. No other state has gone so far," he told *Associated Press*. He said that legal challenges might arise if the state decided to go through with an electrocution. The state would have to prove that lethal injection drugs were not obtainable and there were concerns about the constitutional protections against cruel and unusual punishments.

One of the main movers of the Tennessee bill was State Senator Ken Yager, who said the move was in response to "a real concern that we could find ourselves in a position that if the chemicals were unavailable to us that we would not be able to carry out the sentence."

Some in Tennessee are uncomfortable with the return to the chair, including attorney David Raybin. His client, child-killer Daryl Holton, was executed on September 12, 2007, the last man in Tennessee to be electrocuted. It took ten minutes to strap the compliant prisoner securely in the chair, which was made from the wood of the old gallows decommissioned in 1916. Then:

Large wet sponges were placed between the metal contacts
and Daryl's skull so as to assure that the electricity had as little
resistance as possible. The guards sopped up the excess salt
water on the floor and put the wet towels into a bucket.

This process was done with absolute precision—not a movement wasted. This, in my view, was the torment. Mr. Holton was certainly not harmed in any way by the endless buckling of belts and the tucking in of moist sponges. I think the sensation of wetness, leather, and a dozen hands about his body must have been maddening. While the guards knew what came next, Daryl had no way of knowing and, I am sure, thought every moment was his last.

When all the water, towels, and buckets had been removed, the guards started leaving the room. I was then asked to go to the witness room. I took one last look at Daryl, since I knew that my next gaze of him would be from behind solid glass. His eyes were still closed, his breathing labored. As I would realize later, Daryl was starting to hyperventilate; he was frightened.

There he was. Daryl Holton was in the electric chair with this helmet on his head and salt water slowly trickling down his cheeks. In my imagination I believed the electric chair was weeping tears for its victim. At this point, Daryl was asked if he wanted a blindfold. He said yes. This was his last audible sound.

Moments later, the execution began:

We heard the whir of the exhaust fan in the death chamber. Five seconds later: BANG! A loud electrical noise. Daryl Holton convulsed and was pinned to the electric chair. A reporter jumped back in his chair as if shocked himself.

The impact of the voltage had to have killed Mr. Holton instantly. We will never know for sure, but it was dramatic. For fifteen seconds the current was applied. Then it was halted and Daryl's body slumped over. Then silence. I looked in vain for any sign of life. Then: BANG! Another shock for some twenty seconds. Holton's body convulsed again.

Mr. Raybin said the execution had not changed his view of capital punishment, which he favors in some extraordinary cases. "That said, what I had just seen was barbaric in the extreme. No medieval torture could be more bizarre. It demeans us as a society to have this electric chair execution on the books, much less to actually use it. The electric chair is a carnival of death which brings no dignity to the victim or our judicial system."

Aside from Tennessee, seven other states still allow electrocution. They are Alabama, Arkansas, Florida, Kentucky, Oklahoma, South Carolina, and Virginia—though in none of these states is it the default method. That remains lethal injection. Eight states allow for other alternatives to lethal injection. Arizona, Missouri, and Wyoming allow the gas chamber, Delaware, New Hampshire, and Washington allow hanging, and Oklahoma and Utah allow the firing squad. But in all those states, lethal injection is the default method.

With lethal injection facing problems, several states have considered what to do next, but none have joined Tennessee in opting for the chair. Wyoming is considering a return to the firing squad. Although limited scientific work has been done on execution methods, in 1938 a prisoner, John Deering, was strapped to a heart monitor during a firing squad execution in Utah. After the four shots entered his chest, his heart went into a spasm for four seconds and then stopped fifteen seconds after the shots. However his breathing continued for nearly a minute more, and he struggled briefly after his heart stopped beating. The experiment proved that firing squad is at least swift.

The unpalatable truth is that ending a life swiftly and painlessly is a medical procedure and doctors are not involved in the execution process. There is no prospect of that changing. In some countries that allow voluntary euthanasia and assisted suicide, doctors have developed protocols for ending life. But these involve a very gentle passage, with the patient slipping into a coma and sometimes dying hours, or even days, later. This is not a solution for executions, which are generally required to be quick and clinical.

Both electrocution and lethal injection can work very well. But they are anything but guaranteed. And when they go wrong, they can go very wrong. The only execution machine ever constructed that guarantees a swift and painless death is the French guillotine. But this looks barbaric, and the end result is a head bouncing off the floor and blood spraying all over the ground. Though it is very humane for the victim, it is considered too gory for the witnesses and officials and was rejected for that reason by the New York Electrical Death Commission in 1888. It would be rejected for the same reasons today. Death must be sanitized. It is in keeping with "evolving standards of decency in society."

America is now severely out of step with the rest of the industrialized world on the issue of capital punishment. The United States is one of only four industrialized democracies that allows capital punishment, the others being Japan, Singapore, and South Korea. But South Korea has a moratorium on them. In 2011, the United States was the only country carrying out executions in the G8 countries or in the Western Hemisphere. Worldwide, forty countries allow capital punishment, though in most, it is a rare punishment. Only China, Iran, Iraq, and Saudi Arabia execute more people than the United States. The worldwide trend is towards the punishment dying out.

But there are countries that buck the trend. In December 2014, Pakistan ended its moratorium on executions, following a terrorist attack on a school in Peshawar. Islamic fundamentalists massacred 149 people, including 133 children, and the government hit back immediately by reintroducing the death penalty for terrorist offenses. Within a week, six men had been hanged, including five convicted of attempting to assassinate the military ruler of the country, Pervez Musharraf, in 2003. Roughly five hundred more were scheduled to hang in the coming months, which would put Pakistan in second place behind China on the number of executions carried out.

Within the United States, attitudes vary from state to state.

Since the moratorium was lifted in 1976, Kansas, New Hampshire, New Jersey, and New York have not performed any executions, and four states (Pennsylvania, Oregon, Connecticut, and New Mexico) only allow executions if the inmate volunteers for that punishment. Only seven have in close to thirty years. Two states (South Dakota and Idaho) ended de facto moratoriums in the past few years, but executions in these states are rare.

Nevada has executed twelve prisoners in the modern era, of whom eleven waived their right to appeal. Both Kentucky and Montana have executed two prisoners each against their will and one each voluntarily. Colorado and Wyoming have only executed one prisoner each in the past thirty years.

Several states have imposed temporary moratoriums, including Maryland, Florida, North Carolina, California, Kentucky, Washington, Oregon, Arkansas, Louisiana, Mississippi, Missouri, Montana, Nevada, Tennessee, and Nebraska. These moratoriums have lasted from months to years. Some have been imposed because of concerns over the death penalty; others because of concerns over a shortage of the drugs required for lethal injection.

On March 15, 2013, Maryland voted to repeal the death penalty, becoming the sixth state in six years to abolish capital punishment.

But there are states where they have embraced the needle with a vengeance. Texas leads the way, executing 517 people (more than a third of the total) since the moratorium was lifted. Strangely, Texas was not a big death penalty state before the moratorium. Virginia and Oklahoma are next, at 110 each, as of October 2014. So three states account for well over half the total. Florida and Missouri fall short of a hundred but are in the high double digits. Of the thirty-eight states that have allowed executions post-Furman, only four have not used the punishment in the past forty years. The Federal Government has executed three people in that time, showing that they are still willing. This will become relevant when the Boston Marathon bombers go to trial—they are facing capital charges in a Federal Court situated in a state that does not allow executions.

Currently thirty-two states have execution on the statutes, and eighteen have removed it permanently as an option. Since the penalty was reinstated in 1976, 1,389 convicted murderers have been executed, of whom fifteen were female. The racial profile of those executed has changed from the days when racial factors crept in to the sentencing process. Now that the penalty comes in for intense scrutiny, more than half those executed are white, while roughly a third are black. The rest are a mix of other ethnic groups. This does not accurately reflect the racial makeup of America, but it comes closer than it did in the pre-moratorium days.

Lethal injection has virtually become the standard method of execution—with 87.3 percent of the total having been by lethal injection, and that has risen as the years have passed. Of the last 758 executions, all but ten were by lethal injection. The electric chair has been the second most popular method, though it accounts for less than 12 percent of the total. The rest have been hanging, gas chamber, and firing squad.

The anti-death penalty movement waxes and wanes in terms of popularity, but is growing. Many influential organizations are behind the movement, including Amnesty International, the American Civil Liberties Union, the National Association for the Advancement of Colored People, and the National Coalition to Abolish the Death Penalty. Changes have happened; juveniles and the mentally ill can no longer be executed. Each case comes under intense scrutiny.

Public opinion is very divided on the topic, with 65 percent of Americans supporting the penalty, and 31 percent who are opposed to it. In fact, half of those in favor of the penalty don't believe it is being applied often enough. Worldwide support for the death penalty (which is not allowed in most countries) runs at about half the population, lower than support in the United States, but not substantially so.

With support quite high in the United States, executions will continue to happen. But the frequency has fallen sharply from the peak days of the late nineties. In 1999, ninety-eight people were executed across the country—two a week. Now it is down to roughly forty a year.

Barring a massive change in public opinion, what will end the death penalty is the cost—both human and financial. Prosecuting a death penalty case costs roughly four times what it costs to prosecute a noncapital murder case. California has spent $4 billion on the death penalty since 1978, a massive drain on a cash-strapped state. In Maryland the average death penalty case costs $3 million. Florida spends more than $50 million a year above what it would cost to replace the death penalty with life imprisonment for first-degree murder. Working the figures, it costs Florida $24 million for each execution, money that could be saved by holding a prisoner for life without parole. In Texas a death penalty case typically costs $2.3 million, about three times the cost of imprisoning someone in a single high security cell for forty years.

Although the financial costs can be worked out, the human cost is not calculable. The cost comes in a number of ways. First, there is the horror of the execution chamber itself. Botched executions repulse even supporters of the death penalty (unless they see the sign of the cross in the blood from burst blood vessels!). The other cost is even harder to bear and harder to justify. It is the certainty that innocent men and women have been, and continue to be, executed. If one in twenty on death row is innocent, and if America really has executed seventy innocent people since 1976, that is a cost that will eventually come to be seen as too high for a civilized society to bear.

Great public tragedies such as school shootings, serial killings, and acts of terrorism, can temporarily increase support for the death penalty, as happened in Pakistan. But the problem of innocence won't go away.

A gambling man would be wise to bet on executions dwindling over the next fifty years and the death penalty being completely removed from the United States some time during the current century.

The odds are less sure on whether we will see Old Sparky switched on for one final encore during that period. Only time will tell if Robert Gleason was the last to sit in the famous hot seat.

SELECTED BIBLIOGRAPHY

Books

Abbott, Geoffrey	Amazing True Stories of Female Executions
Aynesworth, Hugh and Stephen Michaud	Ted Bundy: Conversations with a Killer
Brandon, Craig	The Electric Chair: An Unnatural American History
Cahill Jr., Richard T.	Hauptmann's Ladder: A Step-by-Step Analysis of the Lindbergh Kidnapping
Elliot, Robert and Albert Beatty	Agent of Death: The Memoirs of an Executioner
Essig, Mark	Edison and the Electric Chair—a Story of Light and Death
Mandery, Evan J.	Capital Punishment in America: A Balanced Perspective
Moran, Thomas	The Executioner's Currently – Thomas Edison, George Westinghouse, and the Invention of the Electric Chair
Rule, Ann	The Stranger Beside Me
Turkus, Burton B. and Sid Feder	Murder Inc: The Story of the Syndicate
Wexley, John	The Judgement of Julius and Ethel Rosenberg

Periodicals and Newspapers

Birmingham News
Bombay Gazette
Boston Globe
Buffalo Courier
Cincinnati Enquirer
Commercial Advertiser
The Cork Examiner
Daily Item
Daily Mirror
Daily News
Free Society
Gainesville Sunday
Houston Chronicle
The Lancet
Miami Herald
New York Herald
New York Times
North Carolina Star News
Pittsburgh Post-Gazette
Pittsburgh Press
Proceedings of the National Academy of Sciences of the United States
Southwest Missourian
St Petersburg Times
The Tennessean
Times Manila
Weekly Messenger
The World

Websites

www.murderpedia.com
www.deathpenaltyinfo.org
www.innocenceproject.org

INDEX